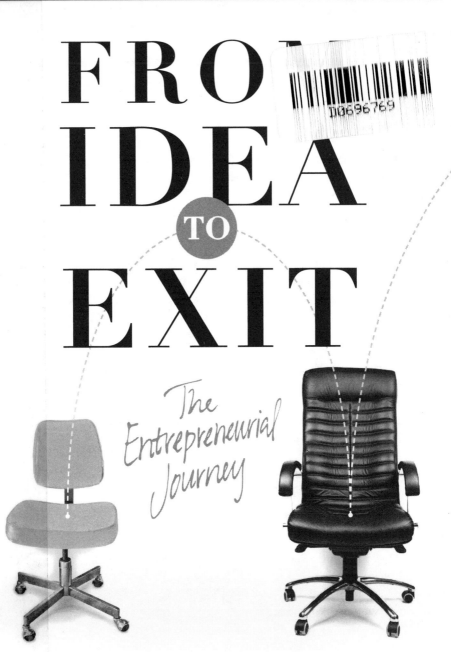

FROM IDEA TO EXIT

The Entrepreneurial Journey

Jeffrey Weber

ALLWORTH PRESS
NEW YORK

Allworth Press books may be purchased in bulk at special discounts for sales promotion, corporate gifts, fund-raising, or educational purposes. Special editions can also be created to specifications. For details, contact the Special Sales Department, Allworth Press, 307 West 36th Street, 11th Floor, New York, NY 10018 or info@skyhorsepublishing.com.

17 16 15 14   5 4 3 2 1

Published by Allworth Press, an imprint of Skyhorse Publishing, Inc.
307 West 36th Street, 11th Floor, New York, NY 10018.

Allworth Press® is a registered trademark of Skyhorse Publishing, Inc.®, a Delaware corporation.

www.allworth.com

Library of Congress Cataloging-in-Publication Data is available on file.

Print ISBN: 978-1-62153-427-3
Ebook ISBN: 978-1-62153-418-1

Printed in the United States of America

Praise for *From Idea to Exit*

"The spirit of adventure permeates this book as Jeff guides us through the entrepreneurial journey. For all of us restless souls eager to take that first big step, this is an invaluable map to guide the way."

—Mark Achler, Senior Vice President, New Business, Strategy & Innovation, Redbox

"There is a certain wisdom about entrepreneurship that only comes from doing it. Jeff Weber has done it, and his reflections on his journey in *From Idea to Exit* are an invaluable resource for anyone setting out on his or her own journey."

—Bo Burlingham, Editor-at-Large, *Inc.* magazine, and Author of *Small Giants: Companies That Choose to Be Great Instead of Big*

"*From Idea to Exit* is an excellent summation of Jeff Weber's entrepreneurial journey that should be a reference guidebook on the bookshelf of all entrepreneurs. It is filled with insights that . . . can be used again and again through all stages of building a startup. Jeff distills his learnings and catalogs them with the precision of a surgeon. As someone who is currently on his seventh startup now, I found myself taking copious notes. I am particularly impressed by how Jeff outlines the process of running and then exiting a business. I can assure you that you'll dog-ear many pages that you are likely to keep returning to."

—Naeem Zafar, Serial Entrepreneur, Author, Speaker, and Faculty Member, Haas School of Business, University of California–Berkeley

"*From Idea to Exit* follows how the entrepreneur and his business evolve from the idea phase through startup, into running, and finally exit. Weber reveals the 'gates' that both the entrepreneur and the business must pass before entering each new phase of growth. Combining research and personal experience, Weber introduces fresh methodologies and theories that are sure to benefit both new and existing entrepreneurs. I get a lot of books every year to review, and this is a really good book!"

—Steve Mariotti, Founder, Network for Teaching Entrepreneurship

"What makes Jeff Weber's book so special is that it addresses the *entire* entrepreneurial process, it's written by someone who *actually* experienced it, and it *integrates* high-level principles and ideas with real stories and practical how-tos. *From Idea to Exit* is required reading for every highly ambitious and driven entrepreneur."

—Raman Chadha, Executive Director and Clinical Professor,
DePaul University, Coleman Entrepreneurship Center

"If you are afraid of venturing out on your own, or wonder if you have what it takes, read this book. Entrepreneurship is scary and thrilling all at the same time. This book will help you think about how to turn your business idea into an avocation that will support you. Jeff Weber understands the path you will need to take and the fears you will need to overcome."

—Jeffrey Carter, Cofounder, Hyde Park Angels

"As a business mentoring expert to entrepreneurs, I often find them searching for the 'how-tos' of becoming successful in business. Jeff Weber shares brilliantly in *From Idea to Exit*, using his own experiences, and delivers the actual framework entrepreneurs can model their business enterprise after. Jeff puts it all out there, sharing his own valuable stories, and then helps evolving entrepreneurs with the skill building they need to thrive in business. His ideas are practical, logical, and at the same time innovative. If you are an entrepreneur or dream of owning your own business, then breathe in every word of this book. It is masterful."

—Terri Levine, PhD, The Business Mentoring Expert,
Bestselling Author of *Coaching Is for Everyone*

"In *From Idea To Exit: The Entrepreneurial Journey*, Jeff Weber provides a tremendous wealth of knowledge of the process by which entrepreneurship evolves. This is a must-read for any young aspiring entrepreneur."

—Jason Baudendistel, CEO, Solutions Consulting Group

"I like this book. A lot. Moreover, I *know* it's a valuable contribution to the development of entrepreneurs everywhere. Nothing could be better than finding out from an expert like Jeff Weber that you really *are* that entrepreneur you dreamed you'd be and then having him help you, step by step, achieve the success you'd always envisioned. Read this book and then . . . Go. Live your dream. Because you can."

—Leslie L. Kossoff, Founder and Principal, The Kossoff Group; Award-Winning
Author of *Executive Thinking: The Dream, the Vision, the Mission Achieved*;
Founder and Editor, ObtuseAngles.net

"Jeffrey Weber elucidates the concept of the Risk Box and provides the means to move the walls by destroying risk, aversion, and fear."

—A. S. Rao, President, Indian Innovators Association

Table of Contents

Introduction

I KNOW WHY THIS BOOK is in your hands: you have that fire within—a compulsory desire to create something new. You want to step over the boundaries that surround your current daily existence, to break away from a career path clogged with people seeking the same predictable, safe, and unremarkable destination. Whether you're a cubicle worker, a small business owner, or a corporate leader, you want to enter new territory—to incubate ideas, break down the walls of risk aversion that surround you, and clear a trail toward something only you can imagine and achieve. I know the journey you're contemplating, because I've taken it, and I remember how little real, practical advice I could find to help me on my way. I didn't read entrepreneurial success stories and wish that I was the guy or gal who'd made it to the top. I wanted to know *how* they got there, so I could do it myself—to start something from nothing and realize success. I think that's what you want, too, and that's why I wrote this book.

A Brief Travel Story

So where did my journey take me?

Its ultimate destination is an attractive multistory office building situated in the very northern tip of the North Shore of Chicago, where I worked as the director of business development for a Fortune 100 company. Every day, after leaving my car in its secure garage, I would enter the cathedral-like granite and chrome foyer of this building and step into an oak-paneled elevator that delivered me to my upper-level floor and expansive office. I often spent the entire day there, making use of the penthouse level's state-of-the-art conference rooms and elegant cafeteria, enjoying its scenic views of the forested suburban landscape that surrounded me. As I gazed out at those views, I often thought of how different this corporate environment was from that of the company I founded, a company acquired by this behemoth back in 2006.

My surroundings there had been far more humble—*far* more humble. But the organizations shared one critical similarity: they both held row upon row of cubicles filled with people dreaming of one day rising to the top of their own organization, where they would enjoy the perks and lofty views of the C-suite class. And, in both organizations, few of those people would ever pursue their dreams. Blocked by fear and uncertainty, they would remain prisoners, unwilling to risk the security they had acquired for the adventure of discovering what they might create.

It's the same story in office buildings all across America, just as it was for me as I put in my time at a different Fortune 100 company back in 1989. It was my first job out of college, and I was working at the headquarters of a nationally known insurance organization—a big, safe company with great benefits and a promise of a long and predictable career. But I was restless. I began going to graduate school at night, and in 1993, with a freshly minted MBA in hand and a young wife and new baby at home, I struck off in a new direction, to become the plant manager of a small textile manufacturer in Chicago, a business that was unlike my previous employment experience in almost every way. I knew nothing about the company's industry, products, or customers, but I jumped in and hoped for the best. My first adventure! After seven weeks of dog-paddling in those foreign waters I was fired, giving me another totally new experience—my first career failure.

As it turned out, that pink slip became my golden ticket. I landed a job with a rapidly growing catalog-based company that provided computer technology products to the primary and secondary education market. Still stinging from my dismissal, I studied hard to learn everything I could about the organization's products, processes, competitors, customers, and marketplace. I rose quickly in a company that was experiencing its own fast-track growth during an unprecedented technology boom.

Eventually, I became one of the organization's top knowledge leaders. I discovered my strength in strategic thinking and innovation at this firm and was able to institute organizational restructuring and corporate partnerships that helped drive my company to the top of its industry. When an idea I had developed for expanding into previously untapped markets was rejected out of hand by the organization's leadership, I decided that I'd do it myself. I used every spare minute to form and launch my own company, initially maintaining my day job while I got my own operation up and running. I incorporated my new business in 1995, while still working both jobs.

I bootstrapped my way through the planning and startup phase, working out of a tiny basement office, writing a business plan, recruiting essential personnel, and pulling together my product line—by the time my first catalog came out, I already had orders waiting. I quit my other job and turned my full attention to the new business. My company grew rapidly, as did my skills as an entrepreneur. I learned what worked to fuel the organization's success and what slowed its growth; when to grab on to the reins tightly and when to let go. By 1998, my startup had grown into a $3 million business. We continued to grow through the storms of the first few years of the new century, reaching sales of $25 million by 2005. But by then, I knew I was ready to move on. That leg of my journey was over.

This time, the company made my exit much easier. During a major round of layoffs in 2009, the home office was trimmed dramatically, and I was given the golden parachute that would mark the end of my adventure—I should say, *that* adventure. As I began mapping out my next entrepreneurial journey, I realized how much better prepared I was for the road ahead. I thought about how much I'd learned, how many other successful entrepreneurs I'd partnered with, and how many tools and techniques I'd mastered over the previous seventeen years. I began writing down my experiences and the insights and ideas they taught me. And that became the first step of my next journey.

Today, I'm an experienced entrepreneurial adventurer. I know the terrain; I know how to anticipate and avoid the pitfalls that can stop entrepreneurs dead in their tracks; I know how to pack for the journey, when to push on, and when to take a moment to re-energize. And because for most entrepreneurs the journey is the thing, I know how to tell when it's time to say good-bye to this destination and begin planning the next. In other words, I've mastered an important set of entrepreneurial skills that serve me well in just about every aspect of my life. I've formed another successful business, speaking in seminars and private consultations, sharing my entrepreneurial processes with individuals, organizational teams, and businesses of every kind. In *From Idea to Exit*, I've collected those ideas, practices, and processes together, to serve as your field guide to the entrepreneurial journey.

The *From Idea to Exit* Framework

We humans are born with the entrepreneurial spirit. By nature, we're curious, innovative, and driven to build and create. Those qualities are essential to our ongoing growth, happiness, and success in every aspect of our lives. Unfortunately, our entrepreneurial nature can become weighed down by other forces: our need for security, our reluctance to take risks, and our dwindling assurance that we can do the things we set out to do.

In *From Idea to Exit* I've drawn upon my own experiences and in-depth research to construct a framework of ideas and practices that will strengthen and sustain the entrepreneurial experience, no matter what shape it might take. In the chapters that follow, I'll outline proven methods for mastering the demands of your evolving enterprise, even as you build the skills of an evolving entrepreneur. I'll show you how, by channeling your innovative drive through the sound practices and logical, planned processes I describe in this book, you can achieve even your most daring goals.

I'll outline the critical ideas and practices that can guide you through the four main phases of the entrepreneurial journey and form a strong framework for its success:

- **Phase I—Idea.** Here, you incubate innovation, determine what form your entrepreneurship will take, and identify what obstacles you must overcome in order to launch your idea. In the chapters that describe this stage, I'll help you clearly face and evaluate the risks that most threaten you as you confront your unique Risk Box and the high-value assets you've locked within it. You'll also learn how to use your own feasibility study and plan to permeate the barriers formed by risk and design a road map that will guide you through the journey ahead, from startup to exit plan.

- **Phase II—Startup.** This is the most exhilarating—and demanding—stage of the entrepreneurial process. Here, you'll be wearing many hats and going all-in with total commitment to launch your innovative idea. Although the work involved in moving from idea to actuality can seem daunting, I'll show you how to break the passage down into logical, manageable steps, from planning (and adjusting) your goals to creating and executing a formal business plan, generating leads, and refining your evolving business priorities. I'll help you harness your urgency to innovate and transform it into an engine that will drive startup success.

- **Phase III—Running.** Now it's time to strip away those many hats you've been wearing and focus on leading your enterprise. In the chapters that describe this stage of the entrepreneurial journey, I'll guide you through the process of pulling together your management team, whether that means an in-house group of experts or an outside crew of trusted mentors and advisors. Here, you'll also learn important practices for building the valuation of your company; scaling its revenue, profitability, and processes; strengthening your organization's ongoing innovative energies; and mastering the demands of fulfillment, cash flow, and an evolving organizational culture and bureaucracy.

- **Phase IV—Exit.** This is perhaps the most critical passage for any entrepreneur, and it is often the most overlooked. Every step you've taken up to this point in the journey has been in preparation for this ultimate destination—your exit plan. In the chapters that describe the Exit stage, I'll coach you through the process of maximizing your organization's value and offer calm, expert guidance through the emotional and financial minefield of finalizing the transaction. If you are leading an entrepreneurial project within a larger organization, I'll show you how to prepare to turn over the reins, so you can devote more of your time to incubating and staging your next idea. You'll learn how to recognize when it's time to go and why, and how to weigh and evaluate your exit options. From maximizing shareholder value to visualizing your "next" life, the chapters in this section of *From Idea to Exit* will give you the survival skills you need to bring this entrepreneurial journey to an end—and to begin planning the next.

Throughout the book, you'll find valuable formulas, checklists, exercises, and planning tools to help guide you through each of the defining moments of your entrepreneurial experience. From understanding your influences and evolution to recognizing and managing risk and assessing your opportunities, the information you gain here will help you apply your entrepreneurial spirit to everything you do—in both your personal and professional life.

So What Can This Book Do for You?

Although the view out my window has changed with each new journey, on one corner of my desk is taped a creased and torn square of paper that I've carried with me for many years—a page from a daily aphorisms calendar I received from my wife while I was still a struggling cubicle worker at my first real job after college. It reads, "If you do what you've always done, you'll get what you've always gotten." These words, which have appeared in many versions and in many places, symbolized my situation at that early point in my professional life. I was working, but it was that job—and the tall, thick walls of risk that surrounded it—that kept holding me back from my true passion. As I looked at this page back then, when it was crisp and new, I realized that I could continue to work for someone else and get what that effort could provide: a predictable salary, benefits, and a long, preordained trudge through regular, stepped promotions and advancement. I also knew that would never be enough. I wanted to control my destiny and have the freedom to create my future.

When I tore off that day's calendar page with its insightful message, I decided to keep it with me through every step of the journey ahead. I taped it on every desk I had throughout my career. It was there on my crowded desktop when I was the president of the company I eventually founded, just as it was on the broad, polished surface of my desktop in that towering building on Chicago's North Shore. It has been my driver, even when I have had no clue as to just where it is that I want to go. I was an entrepreneur-in-waiting back when I first read this calendar page, just as you are now. As you turn these pages, I hope you'll be inspired to carry the stories, tools, and techniques they offer with you on your own journey, and use them as your expert guide to the road ahead.

PHASE I

I GREW UP IN GLENVIEW, Illinois, on the edge of a 123-acre forest preserve called The Grove—a large, unpopulated area of forest and prairie meadow that separated my housing development from its nearest neighbors. Just one block from my front door, where a dead-end street gave way abruptly to grass, stone, and weeds, lay the entrance to The Grove. The path was wide and so well worn that bikes could easily navigate through the arch of branches above it.

I was more interested in the smaller, less visible arterial paths that branched off the central trail and into the core of the forest. They gave me an idea: I would use The Grove to become an explorer. To put my idea into action, I planned journeys down these paths that often occupied entire summer days and took me into territory that seemed totally foreign to the suburban streets and cul-de-sacs nearby. I discovered large meadows where the forest opened up to acres of tall native grasses and prairie flowers. I slogged through swampy areas, turning over the waterlogged limbs of fallen trees to uncover the snakes and salamanders that lived beneath them. I crept silently along thick carpets of dust and pine needles, in areas of the forest so densely wooded that nothing grew beneath the tall trees. I went looking for adventure, and found it down every narrow, twisted path.

After dozens of journeys, I finally discovered the true jewel of The Grove, down a barely visible path that zigzagged around low-standing waters, fallen trees, and other formidable forest hurdles. The path ended at the overgrown but once magnificent backyard of a large two-story, wood-planked house. Neglected and abandoned, every detail of the house had faded into the rain-washed, colorless facade. Just the sight of the place set my mind spinning. How could such a home be abandoned? Was everyone who lived there murdered? Maybe, I desperately hoped, the house was haunted! I never climbed the steps of that house to look in through the dust-filmed windows. It was better not to know what it looked like inside. But I trekked in and around its yard at every opportunity, and considered it my own hidden treasure.

Years later, the home's story became the talk of the entire Glenview community, when the park district took over the property, restored it to its former grandeur, and shared its history with the community. It turns out that the home belonged originally to Dr. John Kennicott, the area's first physician and a noted horticulturist, who built the majestic gothic revival house in 1845 for his growing family and went on to develop the first major nursery in northern Illinois. But I am especially interested in the story of his son, Robert Kennicott, because it captures the spirit of early frontier entrepreneurialism. Robert grew up in the home I stumbled across in The Grove. His fascination with nature led him to explore the wild areas behind his house, just as I would over one hundred years later. In 1853, the 20-year-old Robert began collecting and cataloging snakes for the Smithsonian Institution in Washington, DC. Robert was pursuing his first entrepreneurial idea: he wanted to form a national collection of facts, information, and specimens of his country's natural world. Within just four short years, he helped found the Chicago Academy of Sciences and the Northwestern University natural history museum.

His idea expanded, and his journey continued. In April 1859, he set off on an expedition to collect natural history specimens in the subarctic boreal forests of northwestern Canada and beyond the Arctic tundra. Robert became popular with Hudson's Bay Company fur traders in the area and encouraged them to collect and send natural history specimens and Indian artifacts to the Smithsonian. In 1864, Robert was part of an expedition to Alaska funded by the Western Union Telegraph to find a possible route for a telegraph line between North America and Russia by way of the Bering Sea. When Robert died just two years later, he was buried at a Kennicott family plot in The Grove, which is now a national historic landmark.[1] If the Kennicott house wasn't haunted, as I'd so desperately wished, it certainly was the home of an entrepreneurial spirit.

I greatly envy Robert Kennicott's experiences, while feeling a real kinship with the eco-entrepreneurial curiosity and ideas that drove his adventures.

I would never have discovered the Kennicott house in its wild, abandoned state if I had stayed with the other kids or kept to the sidewalk that ran safely along the outer perimeter of The Grove. I wouldn't have seen the open meadows, explored the dank swamps, or thrilled at the hidden treasure of that "haunted" house hidden deep within the trees. Without the driving idea that *something* worth finding was out there waiting for me, I might not have developed my entrepreneurial spirit—that willingness to step outside the known boundaries to explore what lies beyond them.

CHAPTER ONE

Being an Entrepreneur

THE FIRST STEP IN FOLLOWING your entrepreneurial idea is to understand the Entrepreneurial Idea. In other words, you must gain a clear notion of exactly what it means to be an entrepreneur in any field—business, academia, construction, the arts, government, medicine, public service, you name it. Though entrepreneurs come in every shape and form, they tend to share certain key characteristics, such as a desire to control their own career and destiny, innate creativity and a drive to innovate, a pragmatic approach to risk taking, and a unique way of thinking about their role in the world. One of the most important characteristics of the entrepreneur, however, is a need to find out what lies down the "road less traveled." Whether they've set out to carve a trail as an entrepreneur or simply stumbled upon and seized an opportunity, entrepreneurs rarely find long-term satisfaction in following a formulated path; that's too ordinary and too routine. Entrepreneurship does involve a certain process, but it is one of infinite variety and forms.

Author and professor Dr. Elliot McGucken describes the entrepreneurial process to his art students as similar to the classic "hero" story, in which the hero/entrepreneur "embarks on a quest that requires separation or departure from the familiar world."[1] McGucken hits it right on the head. The entrepreneur moves into the unknown and the unproven, the world that lies beyond the walls of risk. Fear of the unfamiliar stops many from following their ideas and exploring their world. The entrepreneur, however, moves on, passing through a gate represented by the first defining moment of the journey: the discovery of an idea that he or she feels driven to pursue.

The road ahead might take all sorts of unexpected twists and threatening turns as it threads a series of additional gates or milestones that the entrepreneur must pass through in order to achieve success. Those gates are represented by the markers outlined in this book, such as scaling the business or idea, promoting ongoing innovation, building the bureaucracy, and executing a well-planned exit. To prepare to open those gates, we need to better understand the Entrepreneurial Idea, who we are as entrepreneurs, and what role we play in the world we all share. The better you understand the Entrepreneurial Idea, the better prepared you will be for the journey ahead.

Innovating the Future

In order to understand the entrepreneur's role in building the future, let's begin by taking a brief look at the very short history of entrepreneurship studies. As far as we know, the first documented courses taught on entrepreneurism in the United States were at Harvard Business School in 1947. Myles Mace, an economist who earned his MBA there in 1938, continued to work at the school as a research associate up until 1942 when he was called for military duty to serve in World War II. Mace took careful note of the number of fellow servicemen who were sharing hopeful stories of returning home after the war to start businesses for themselves. Accustomed to risk and very much aware of the value of following their dreams, postwar GIs were ready to trade in their traditional industrial jobs for entrepreneurship.

When Mace returned from service in 1946, having earned the Bronze Star, he went back to Harvard Business School and started the first known course on entrepreneurism in higher education. Fifty years later, interest in entrepreneurism surged. By 2009, that lone course had blossomed into a major area of study, with more than 80 percent of the United States' two- and four-year-degree-granting accredited colleges and universities offering courses on entrepreneurism.

There's a reason for all of this focus on entrepreneurship. Simply put, entrepreneurs are the catalyst for all economic creation. Entrepreneurs develop new markets through effective demand; discover new sources of materials; mobilize the resources of land, labor, and capital; introduce new technologies, new industries, and new products; and create employment growth. One of the great societal benefits of entrepreneurialism is in job creation, and that's another important reason that we all owe respect to the men and women who continue to innovate and create businesses.

Many people think that anyone who owns a business is an entrepreneur, but that isn't always the case. There's a real difference between a business proprietor who starts up a business in order to pursue personal lifestyle goals and a true entrepreneur who has the vision and drive to create completely new products, services, or processes that may serve entirely new markets. Because entrepreneurs want to create something, not just manage a business, they have to be innovative and continually generate ideas in order to meet the needs of an opportunity that only they may be able to see. That's not to say that business owners are any less important or worthy than entrepreneurs—both are vital to our economy. The two aren't equal, however, in terms of their contributions to economic growth. Business owners typically serve a product or service need within a community, but if they aren't risking resources on new opportunities, they're doing little to generate wealth and true economic expansion.

One of the earliest researchers in the field of entrepreneurial studies was the Austrian economist Joseph Schumpeter. His theory of economic development gives innovation a critical role, and it will be central to my discussion of the entrepreneur's journey. The theory states the economy should follow a circular flow; that is, firms provide goods and services to households, which in turn pay money for those goods and services. The circular flow of income can increase or decrease, thus providing economic booms or recessions. What can stall the economy are stationary states caused by the lack of innovation. As Professor Sumner H. Slichter of the Harvard Business School once observed, "a community in which everyone attempted to make a living by getting on someone else's payroll would be a community of unemployed." This macroeconomic theory holds true at the individual business level, too. A business that does not innovate will reach a stationary state of nongrowth or, worse, negative growth. That's a recipe for stagnation and, eventually, decay.

These are big-picture considerations for the value of the entrepreneur, but I put them here to help you focus on your role as an individual in invigorating your personal, local, regional, and national economy. Entrepreneurism is seeded in all of us. It drives us to maximize our potential, talents, time, and human contribution, and it's a force that should not be wasted.

I think that maybe the best example of the importance of entrepreneurial innovation is highlighted in the current struggle for global competitiveness. In the United States, for example, we see our educational performance falling behind that of other nations, particularly in mathematics and science, and we have to ask ourselves if we can remain competitive without stopping that decline. These disciplines, like the entrepreneurial journey, require a real investment of effort. Are we growing as out of shape mentally as we are physically? With so many great "things" at our disposal, are we no longer driven to invest in the real effort of innovation and creativity?

The hopeful answer to those questions is that we, like people around the world, are innovative and creative at heart. We're driven to maximize our innovative potential, and that's one of the major reasons that the United States is working hard right now at getting educational reform right. Along with an educational system that increasingly focuses on creativity and thinking skills, the United States government is investing in efforts that invite innovation and research, and the American culture continues to admire and support those engaged in entrepreneurial initiatives. With the failure of many long-standing, high-profile corporations during cyclical economic crises, we in the United States have clearly seen that we need new businesses to drive our economy, and that requires a new generation of entrepreneurs. Fortunately, many Americans want to pursue entrepreneurial dreams, and the country continues to attract foreigners who share that drive. These entrepreneurs will create the new businesses, new industries, and new markets that can once again secure America's global competitiveness.

THE BANK ACCOUNT

Here are some wise words from an unknown source about the value of pursuing your ideas:

Imagine you have a bank account that credits your balance each day with $86,400. Imagine, also, that the account carries over no balance from one day to the next. Every evening it deletes whatever part of the balance you failed to use during the preceding 24 hours. If you were smart, of course, and you had a bank account like this one, you would draw out and use those funds each day. Well, many of us aren't so smart, and we all do have this bank account: it's called time.

Time grants each of us 86,400 seconds each day. We can use these seconds however we wish, but we cannot carry them forward. Any unused time is written off as a loss. There's no going back, no drawing against "tomorrow." I'd like for you to think of this account as you prepare to begin your entrepreneurial journey. Your dreams will always be dreams if you fail to invest the time in making them a reality. And today, you have been given 86,400 seconds to spend.

Everyone has ideas. Some of those ideas are businesses that serve commercial, social, or environmental missions. These ideas are the fuel for job creation, economic growth, and extraordinary lives. What holds us back? Our "time accounts" are limited and reset each day, so let's work to maximize how we use them toward pursuing our ideas—and achieving our dreams.

Destroying the Status Quo and Taking Risks

All of the theories I've talked about in this chapter underscore my firm belief that, as a would-be or existing entrepreneur, *your* role in *your* business is to innovate. And that effort, by nature, must involve some level of risk. We talk about risk assessment in detail in chapter 3, but here, I want to help you understand that taking risk is part of your identity—and your duty— as an entrepreneur.

As we've seen, the entrepreneur harnesses a new idea or invention to create something meaningful and useful with an economic outcome. Trying to capture the essence of what drives and motivates the entrepreneur's desire to do this, Joseph Schumpeter coined the term *entrepreneurial spirit*, which we hear used quite a lot today.[2] He also transformed the term *creative destruction* from Marxist economic theory into today's popular definition, which describes how innovation and creativity destroy complacency and the status quo.

Entrepreneurs convert new ideas into new products, services, and business models that challenge established companies and industries. Their revolutionary approaches catch the established companies off guard and immediately put those firms at a competitive disadvantage. The marketplace rewards the entrepreneurial firm with business, while the old-school firms either adapt or die. The concept of creative destruction says that some businesses will fail due to other firms' innovation, but the benefit of a more dynamic and efficient industry and expanding economic growth outweighs the cost of those losses.

Many popular theories say entrepreneurs respond to opportunities that only they can see. The key word here is *opportunity*. This opportunity might lie in the actual creation of a business or in a new means for harnessing innovation within an existing business. On one hand, the entrepreneur assesses all available information on the opportunity; on the other, he or she assesses the environmental factors that may influence the opportunity's chances for success. Together, these sets of information enable the entrepreneur to make educated decisions on how and if to proceed. And making those educated decisions is the essence of risk assessment.

Both economist Frank H. Knight and management guru Peter Drucker also describe entrepreneurship as being about taking risk.[3] They view entrepreneurs as individuals who make a commitment to follow an idea—a process that might involve risking their finances, career, home, relationships, time, and quality of life on an uncertain and unproven venture. The public's definition of the entrepreneurial experience takes that idea of risk to the next level. I'm sure you've bumped up against the common wisdom that says, if you take the leap into entrepreneurism, you'll either lose everything or win big. This all-or-nothing mythology can add to the allure of being an entrepreneur, but it also contributes to a number of misconceptions. While would-be entrepreneurs rarely have the luxury of waiting for a totally risk-free moment in which to begin pursuing their dreams, they have to be very well prepared to deal with the risks they face.

If you're disturbed by the idea of taking on risk, you might be even more unsettled by Knight's classification of the nature of uncertainty, which he divided into three classifications:

1. *Risk*, which is a type of uncertainty defined by factors that are statistically measurable;

2. *Ambiguity*, which is a type defined by factors that are difficult to measure; and

3. *True uncertainty*, which is uncertainty defined by factors that are impossible to estimate or predict statistically.

As you would guess, Knight classifies the entrepreneur as operating in true uncertainty, and that's a condition that can make risk assessment very difficult. While I don't think that all entrepreneurial types and endeavors operate in true uncertainty, I admit that this is certainly the case for those who engage in new technologies and inventions that create new industries and serve new markets. True uncertainty may even crop up in existing markets where entrepreneurs introduce entirely new variations of established products that are so revolutionary that no one can predict how the market will accept the new player. Think, for example, of the way Groupon revolutionized the age-old process of providing consumer coupons. Not only did the company establish an entirely new method of distributing coupons, it also completely changed the process of using those coupons for both the consumer and the retailer. Groupon founder Andrew Mason had no historic models to refer to when trying to assess the potential risks his organization would face. Mason dealt in true uncertainty in his entrepreneurial experience—but that didn't make his decision to move forward reckless. It just required very careful risk assessment.

It's important to remember that many managers in existing businesses have to assess and take risks, too. We associate the act of risk taking more closely with entrepreneurs because in most cases they approach risk as individuals, rather than as part of a larger organization. Still, smart and successful entrepreneurs aren't freewheeling, risk-loving gamblers as much of our modern business mythology suggests. Instead, they are calculated strategists who are able to assimilate data and apply the results to a vision that they alone can see. In fact, in my research and experience, I have found that talented entrepreneurs have their own form of risk aversion. They won't take a risk unless they know exactly what they stand to lose—*and* gain.

The innovative idea defines the entrepreneur, but it is this calculated approach to risk that actually helps shape the entrepreneurial journey. In this way, entrepreneurs almost become the products of their ideas and innovation. Entrepreneurs become entrepreneurs once they acknowledge their risks and take action to make their idea or invention a reality, not before.

Thinking Like an Entrepreneur

Entrepreneurs scrutinize closely the "what if" scenarios, weigh risks and rewards, and are able to confidently conduct risk assessment better than the traditional worker. Why? Because the entrepreneur is directly accountable to himself or herself. The psychology of subordinate working relationships is gone, and with it all of the "me-centric" questions that can get in the way of sound decision making: What will happen to me if I make this decision? What will my boss think of this decision? Will this decision hurt my career? In the typical subordinate working relationship, the individual thinks first about his or her own best interests before worrying about those of the business. But the entrepreneur *is* his or her business. As the new entrepreneur becomes accustomed to operating in freedom and complete autonomy, his or her thought processes change, eventually forming a level of certitude and confidence that helps the entrepreneur make decisions efficiently and solely in the best interests of the company.

Once an individual takes on the full burden of responsibility for an enterprise, all of his or her senses and cognitive resources become directed toward that entity and its survival. In most cases, only the founder has the intimate knowledge and engagement necessary to instinctively make the right decisions for the business. These gut decisions might seem immediate or off the cuff, but in fact, they are founded on a strong platform of experience and informed instinct. Whenever I've wrestled with a challenging decision, my wife Lisa has asked, "What does your gut say?" After some thought, I would realize that I *did* have an answer that I sensed was right—and, in most cases, my instincts were correct because my gut answers were founded in hard-won knowledge and experience. That's the way most successful entrepreneurs think. The entrepreneur is connected to the business like a spider is connected to its web. Any vibration—in the business, the marketplace, the industry, and so on—elicits an instinctive and well-targeted response.

In fact, adopting the entrepreneur's thought process is really what we're talking about when we say we want to "be our own boss." Being an entrepreneur means having the ability to freely make decisions without scrutiny from higher-ups, to be self-reporting and, therefore, capable of focusing strictly on the business. This ability to take ownership has to come through experience; you can't put someone in a classroom and teach him or her to think like an entrepreneur, you can only prepare that person for the experience. Learning how to truly think like an entrepreneur comes after you've embarked on the entrepreneurial journey, and your success or failure is on the line.

I can't always tell where an individual is from or how old he is, but I can always identify an entrepreneur based on the way he thinks. The vibe I get from entrepreneurs is a combination of confidence, satisfaction, deliberateness, and happiness that, for lack of a better word, emanates from their thinking. Sure, an entrepreneur's life can be extremely challenging. Every day, entrepreneurs might be faced with decisions that could make their idea an explosive success or bring their current entrepreneurial journey to a dead end. But just living in the moment and knowing that you have the opportunity to make those decisions is satisfying and exhilarating. The tough decisions come with the job, and there is no one more equipped to make those decisions than the entrepreneur. Entrepreneurs know how to solve their problems and where to go to get information or guidance. Entrepreneurs are decision makers and wouldn't want it any other way. That way of thinking is what sets an entrepreneur free.

Entrepreneurs rarely stop thinking about their journey—this one or the next. How many times in conversation at a wedding, dinner function, church, or neighborhood barbeque has someone asked that well-worn conversation starter, "Where do you work?" Where others may use the line of questioning to fill time while in line for appetizers, I genuinely like to hear what other people do for a living and to briefly explore their profession for interesting tidbits or connections to my own work. I love it when these conversations reveal a previously unknown territory attached to my entrepreneurial journey or spark a totally new idea. I like finding out whether someone else's expertise can help shed light on a problem I'm having or validate my thoughts on a specific issue. That's me thinking like an entrepreneur.

When I find someone who is pursuing an idea similar to mine or a topic I have an interest in, I first want to mine that person for information and learn from his experience. Second, I want to get his opinion of *my* understanding, approach, and opinion. I'm looking for answers: Am I just crazy, or does this idea have legs? Is the idea feasible, does it have merit, or is it way out there? Are there things I have not considered that will destroy my thesis?

So when I'm asked what I do for a living, I open up my résumé. I give a brief history of where I've been and how it led to where I'm at now. I share my primary objectives in the position I hold, and then I give a glimpse into the future of what I would like to do or what I've been thinking about doing. My hope is that, somewhere on that continuum, I'll find some common ground with my guest, which will contribute to a deeper discussion.

Not only do I believe that entrepreneurs think differently than other people, but I also believe that people think about entrepreneurs as *being* different from everyone else. Consider, for example, that question "What do you do for a living?" When asked, most people who work for a company would normally respond with "I work for XYZ Company" or "I'm a manager for XYZ Company." The one asking the question might then relate to the company, field of work, or some other common thread, and conversation continues down that path.

If, however, as an entrepreneur, I respond with "I own XYZ Company" or "I started XYZ Company," the conversation veers off in an entirely different direction, often with an entirely different level of engagement and responsiveness. It's hard to describe, but I can best say that people immediately seem to develop curiosity and enthusiasm for speaking with me when they learn I'm an entrepreneur. Questions start to fly about what the business does, how long it's been around, and how I started it. I hate to sound like these exchanges are ego strokers, but I guess, in reality, they are. You bust your butt to create a business, and you work harder than you've ever worked and take on risks greater than the average Joe might imagine, so yes, a bit of recognition for that is welcome.

When I get this response from people, I believe it is far less about me than it is about what I've done. Everyone is an entrepreneur at heart, but not that many are entrepreneurs in the flesh. When people encounter one of these elusive beasts in the wild, they want to study it and learn from it. Most people have dreamed the entrepreneurial dream, and many long for an opportunity to make their dream come true. I have the same admiration and drive to learn more when I meet an entrepreneur. Even though I've taken multiple entrepreneurial journeys, I always want to hear another entrepreneur's "travel story" to see what I can learn from it.

Walking the Path of the Revolutionary or the Replicative

We've seen that some common characteristics and ways of thinking link all entrepreneurs, but all entrepreneurs are not alike. The idea that drives your approach to entrepreneurism will determine what type of entrepreneur you become. With all the variety that exists within the world of entrepreneurship, for the purposes of studying the entrepreneurial process, economist William Baumol (with Schumpeter's influence) helped divide all of them into just two groups: *replicative* and *revolutionary* (you might have heard others refer to this latter type as *innovative*, but I don't use that term because I believe that *all* successful entrepreneurs innovate).[4]

The *replicative entrepreneur* is probably the more common type. Replicative entrepreneurs start businesses that are very similar or even directly identical to ones that already exist. Many entrepreneurs gain inspiration from businesses and industries that they know and are familiar with. They learn the business and, more importantly, the industry by working for someone else, and then they decide to go it alone.

To increase the chance of survival and growth, however, the replicative entrepreneur must find a way to differentiate his or her offerings in the marketplace. Simply copying an existing business model rarely is enough to guarantee success, especially when you're targeting the same customer base. Differentiation can come through operational improvements and cost cutting, through new methods to sell or deliver the product, or by incorporating new materials or processes. In the case of my story, which you will learn much more about throughout this book, I replicated my former employer's business model, but I took it to a completely new market. As my company developed and matured, I "microinnovated" to serve our customers in new and unique ways.

JetBlue founder David Neeleman stated in an article for *Fortune* magazine, "I never would have started JetBlue unless I had the experience of starting another airline." Neeleman cites his replicative knowledge from his first airline experience with Morris Air, which he co-founded and later sold to Southwest. Neeleman continued by saying, "I guarantee that I never would have started JetBlue at J.F.K. airport if I had listened to the experts, who said that you can't put a low-fare, customer-centric airline in New York. But I knew we could do it, and I had a wealth of experience behind me that I trusted to make JetBlue a reality."[5]

The replicative entrepreneurs flourish particularly during periods of economic growth by providing needed goods and services to the community or customer base that they serve. Although replicatives are not best known for increasing overall economic productivity or per-worker or even per-capita new wealth creation, they do serve an important function in the economy by creating efficiencies using proven business models and by providing increased employment.

On the surface, you might be tempted to classify most business owners—those who run the dry cleaner, restaurant, gas station, copy center, retail franchise, and so on—as replicative entrepreneurs. They certainly serve a purpose in their community. What earns the title of a true replicative entrepreneur, however, is when individuals innovate and scale their business. Where business owners respond to demand, the replicative entrepreneur creates demand.

Revolutionary entrepreneurs are the ones who grab the headlines by introducing innovative new products and services to market or by creating new markets entirely. They take inventions and make industries out of them. For instance, research and development might yield unique inventions in the form of new technology and substances. Whether created for a single purpose or multiple uses, these new inventions may result in new businesses that take advantage of the discovery. But that only happens at the hands of an entrepreneur. It is up to the revolutionary entrepreneur or entrepreneurial company to turn that new invention into a useful product.

Revolutionary entrepreneurs create wealth by boosting productivity, which in turn establishes a higher standard of living for the economic base touched by that innovator. Nobel Prize–winner Robert Solow, an American economist known for his work on the theory of economic growth, conducted extensive research on innovation and described it as the "cornerstone of economic growth." Revolutionary entrepreneurs lay that cornerstone; they are the elite who fuel progress and spur national growth.

Within the replicative and revolutionary entrepreneurial groups are numerous subgroups that offer a more detailed profile of the entrepreneurs who fit within them. For instance, there are *social entrepreneurs*—those who identify a social problem or issue and create an organization, a fund, an enterprise, or some other entity to address that issue or problem. The measurement of the goals and objectives of the social entrepreneur may not directly align with the traditional financial benchmarks that we use to gauge entrepreneurial success. Success for the social entrepreneur means fixing a social problem or issue. Similarly, another rapidly emerging entrepreneur type, the *green entrepreneur,* is focused on environmentally friendly outcomes with an eye on profits that may take many forms, including those that don't immediately register as dollars and cents.

And then there is the *serial entrepreneur.* This person constantly scans his or her radar for opportunity and can apply innovative ways to exploit it. The deliberate serial entrepreneur launches a business knowing he won't be there long. He wants to grow the business to a sustainable level so that he can then move on to his next idea. Often these individuals create a series of unique businesses, each different from the next. Sometimes, in fact, serial entrepreneurs start multiple ventures simultaneously. Maybe you can identify with the serial entrepreneur's scattered interests in that you may have had dozens of ideas to start a business, all very different from one another.

I believe that these individuals see the world through a completely different lens, one that reveals a clear path toward finding the resources they need to start their next enterprise. Their mindset is completely different from that of the solo entrepreneur, and it's much more difficult to predict where these entrepreneurs will wind up. What drives them is finding ways to predict and meet developing needs and improvements. Perhaps the most famous example of the serial entrepreneur is Sir Richard Branson, who has created many different types of significant businesses in vastly different industries including transportation, music, mobile telephony, travel, financial services, publishing, and retailing. The Virgin Group boasts 300 branded companies worldwide, employing approximately 50,000 people in 30 countries, and appears to be ever-expanding.[6]

The *Internet entrepreneur* is one who creates a business that uses the Internet as a storefront. These innovative businesses have had an increasing role in shaping the direction of global commerce, as they have challenged traditional brick-and-mortar establishments. Larry Page and Sergey Brin of Google aptly fit within this group of entrepreneurs, as does Jeff Bezos of Amazon. This group is responsible for many of the sexy, high-profile companies that grab our attention, and the web represents one of the greatest areas for entrepreneurial growth in upcoming years. Believe it or not, the digital revolution is still in its infancy, and it is exciting to imagine the new resources, services, conveniences, and business models that will emerge from these Internet entrepreneurs.

And finally, I'll mention the *Evangelpreneurs,* a term that I credit to Ron Brumbarger, a replicative social entrepreneur from Carmel, Indiana. By Ron's definition, members of this group follow a faith-based approach to entrepreneurism and entrepreneurial success. Bill Hybels of Willow Creek Community Church in South Barrington, Illinois, for example, could be considered an Evangelpreneur for his creation of one of the nation's largest and most successful megachurches. I suppose many spiritual leaders might think that they're spiritual entrepreneurs, but few have been able to scale and grow their organization like Hybels, whose facility holds the largest theater in the United States and has weekly attendance numbers in excess of 20,00. The Willow Creek Association became a spinoff of the mother church in 1992 and today connects over 11,000 like-minded churches around the world with training and resources. The Global Leadership Summit formed out of Willow Creek serves as an annual training event, with summits in over 70 international sites and over 80,000 attendees.

Entrepreneurs are born from ideas, and their ideas help determine just what type of entrepreneur they become. Just as there is a significant difference between being a business owner and being an entrepreneur, we have seen that there are significant differences between these various types of entrepreneurs. Why should you care about these differences? You may set off on your journey intending to be one thing when in reality you are very much another. You can use your understanding of the types of entrepreneurial approaches and the ideas that mark them as a guide toward appropriate resources and models that help avoid the cost and frustration of figuring things out through trial and error.

The Power of the Entrepreneur

As you can see, there is great variation in the definition and explanation of what an entrepreneur is. Every business owner is not an entrepreneur. The true entrepreneur is someone who takes an idea, innovation, or invention and develops a product, service, or process that fully exploits its potential. In doing so, the entrepreneur develops new industries, creates new supportive businesses, expands job opportunities, grows the economy, and generates wealth.

Entrepreneurs are not merely interesting news stories; they are an integral foundation to any economy and hold the promise of sustaining the nation's standard of living. Harvard Business School professor Arthur Cole put it best: "The entrepreneur provides an economic service" marrying factors of production with economic enterprises. To Cole, nothing in economic life happens without the entrepreneur, who is "the central figure in economic society and whose actions create all economic change."[7]

Entrepreneurs are risk takers, and some of the risk involved in building tomorrow involves the destruction of the world we knew yesterday. But entrepreneurs are masters of risk assessment; they *are* their business, so they don't take the idea of failure lightly. Handling that kind of risk both requires and creates a specific type of thinking. Entrepreneurs are creative, engaged, curious, and determined to forge their own way. Debate has gone on for years as to whether entrepreneurs are made or born, with some claiming that entrepreneurs have a specific personality type, and others leaning in favor of a genetic predisposition to entrepreneurism. My experience and study see entrepreneurism as a combination of both nature and nurture—situation and opportunity combined with a personality disposed to exploration and self-direction. Granted, some people seem more predisposed to the entrepreneurial lifestyle, but I believe that all of us are capable of becoming successful entrepreneurs, if we have what I describe in chapter 2 as an I.D.E.A.—an entrepreneurial concept that is powerful enough to engage our Innovation, Desire, Effort, and Ability.

Entrepreneurs seek the excitement and reward of discovering the unknown. Further, entrepreneurs want to create their future and their destiny—not have it prescribed to them. In order to find their own way, they actively seek opportunities that will allow them to follow their idea and their own direction. If you have this internal gravitational pull that compels you to create your own destiny and manage your own life, and if you are constantly looking out on the horizon for the opportunity to bring you there, then you already are in touch with your entrepreneurial spirit. The next step is to activate the entrepreneur within you—the subject of the next chapter of this book.

CHAPTER TWO

Activating the Entrepreneur

WE'VE SEEN WHAT IT MEANS to be an entrepreneur, but what does it take to *become* an entrepreneur? You need to have a powerful entrepreneurial idea, of course, one with enough potential to fuel your passage through the Startup, Running, and Exit phases of your journey. You also need to be in a position to pursue that idea with all of the passion, commitment, and energy necessary to bring your entrepreneurial vision to life, and to have the opportunity to do so. When all of these factors are in alignment, you are ready to pass through the first gate in your journey and activate the entrepreneur within you. Before we talk about the details of this first defining moment in your entrepreneurial journey, let me tell you a bit more about how I passed through that gate and became an entrepreneur.

As I mentioned in the introduction, I left the first job I had after college with a large, well-established company to embark upon a brief (and quite humbling) stint as a plant manager for a textile manufacturer—a bad career move with a bad outcome. Five months after my lack of background and industry knowledge got me fired from that position, I landed a job as a product manager with Educational Resources, a reseller of computer software to the education market, at precisely the moment when the PC was becoming a mainstream tool. I didn't realize it then, but I was approaching the first gateway into the entrepreneurial experience. That job would help activate the entrepreneur that had been part of my identity from the first time I wandered down those narrow paths in The Grove.

Without any type of technology background, and having just been fired from my last job as the result of a similar lack of preparation, I busted my butt to learn the business. I wolfed down information about my company, its products, and its industry—as much as possible, as fast as possible. I read every industry trade journal from cover to cover as soon as it hit my desk. Knowledge was paramount in that industry and especially in my position. There was no training; things were moving way too fast, and no one had time for it. The '90s were boom times for technology. The people who would make it and do well would be the ones who put in the extra effort and had the desire to be successful. I intended to be one of those people.

My growing command of the business quickly outpaced the company's more seasoned product managers and even some executives. Not only did I master the publishers and products that we represented, but I became an expert in the channel. Even though the technology industry itself was moving at warp speed, I was able to make predictions and bets on new products better than anyone in the company. I had developed not only a passion for the business, but an almost instinctual understanding of the industry. The confidence I built from becoming the knowledge leader made me more competitive and hungry to advance. My ideas were exploding at Educational Resources, and I was determined to use that energy to do something really big and significant. About one year into the job, I found my opportunity when I was able to make a contribution that would become one of the company's greatest tools for achieving success over the next twenty years.

At the time, Educational Resources was primarily a catalog-based company that provided technology products to the primary and secondary education market. We sold software and hardware peripherals to K–12 schools across the country. Microsoft products were, of course, a major component of our sales. Microsoft sold software through two-volume license programs. The first program was called Open, and all authorized Microsoft dealers could sell it. The second was a more flexible and deeper discounted program called Select, which only nineteen dealers in the United States were authorized to participate in. Although Educational Resources was big in the education niche, we were nothing compared to these large account resellers, or LARs, which included Hewlett Packard, CDW, Compaq (pre-HP acquisition), and Dell. I knew that Educational Resources needed to swim with these big fishes if we intended to remain the predominant dealer in education.

With the help of a Microsoft dealer account manager, and over a yearlong process of lobbying and selling, I used my deep knowledge of the software giant's products and our mutual customer, K–12 schools, to convince Microsoft that it should grant LAR status to Educational Resources. I centered my case around the benefits to Microsoft, rather than those Educational Resources would gain through authorization. It was a basic, yet skillfully executed, sales strategy. And it worked. Educational Resources became the first education-only Microsoft LAR and gained a significant competitive advantage over every education dealer in the nation. I was a rock star at the company.

But I couldn't stop there. Although Educational Resources dealt solely in the K–12 market, I began looking into the potential for moving our products, especially Microsoft's, into the higher education market. In fact, productivity titles were more strongly positioned for higher education than they were for K–12. I started to investigate what these schools purchased and how they obtained product, and soon learned that, out of necessity, many publishers established direct relationships with college bookstores and college academic departments. That relationship seemed to be an obstacle to our entry, but I saw it as an opportunity, and set about preparing a plan for entering the higher ed market.

I figured *this* was the next big thing I could bring to my manager and propel my career even further. Here was a great idea for adding incremental growth and revenue to the company while operating from our existing core competency. We had virtually no barriers or cost to enter the market. I felt like I had a leapfrog idea: one that would provide an entirely new market, advance my career, and possibly create a new dedicated division. I could lead this new division! I could run the show and grow this segment and be recognized and rewarded for those efforts.

I wrote up a business plan and presented it to the divisional vice president to whom I reported. The response was swift and devastating: "Thanks, Jeff, for the idea. Good job, but let's get back to what we do best . . . what we have always done."

Man!—did that take the wind out of my sails. How could they not see what a great opportunity I was presenting them? For years, I had wracked my brain to come up with a great business idea, and now I had one. In the past, I had found reasons not to pursue my ideas, to let them die. But as I drove home from work that evening, I realized that this one was different. From that moment on, I was committed to launching my own business to pursue my idea. The entrepreneur within me was ready to go.

Most successful entrepreneurs have experienced the same sort of "this is it" moment, and in that respect, they are a bit like inventors (and, like inventors, they often have to work through a number of failed attempts before they hit on a successful formula). But that moment in time when you commit yourself to an idea and make the decision to move forward is truly miraculous. It's like a shot of adrenaline. The decision to act fosters faith—the faith that leads the entrepreneur through the rough and dark times of developing the business.

As I said earlier, an entrepreneur can't be inspired into being an entrepreneur. You can't bring a person into a seminar and get her so fired up on the virtues and thrill of being an entrepreneur that she then goes out and launches a successful business. First, the individual has to own every element of a compelling entrepreneurial idea, or what I call the I.D.E.A., which is characterized by Innovation, Desire, Effort, and Ability. The idea isn't enough, however. The would-be entrepreneur must be in a personal and professional situation that enables him or her to pursue the idea with all of the intensity and focus necessary to bring it to life. Finally, the opportunity for realizing the idea must be right—the marketplace, the economy, and the industry are just some of the environmental factors that play a role in shaping opportunity. When every element of the equation is in place, the entrepreneur is activated. I call this equation the E-Formula, and here's what it looks like:

I.D.E.A. + Situation + Opportunity = Activation

You can't successfully launch or power the entrepreneurial journey on dreams alone. Every entrepreneur-to-be has to learn to see clearly through the haze of his or her desire to "get started" in order to accurately assess the opportunity at hand. We've all heard the miserable statistics about the likelihood of failure for new endeavors. It's my experience that most of these failures are the result of impatient entrepreneurs who try to pursue an idea without fully evaluating the factors that will impact its success. When you recognize that your formula is complete, you can pursue your idea with the confidence that you're ready for the tough journey ahead. When you hit a sticking point and can't seem to advance forward with your idea, you can use this formula to pinpoint the weaknesses in your entrepreneurial vision that must be either corrected or accepted as a sign that you may have reached a dead end.

In this chapter, we're going to look more closely at each of the elements in this equation. You'll learn how to judge the strength of each element of your entrepreneurial I.D.E.A. And I'll show you how to use this formula to help determine your readiness to begin the entrepreneurial journey or to identify the sometimes invisible obstacles that are holding you back.

Unlocking the I.D.E.A.

The hardest part of being an entrepreneur is starting. To move beyond writing notes on napkins and half-started business plans and make the full commitment to see your idea through takes real strength. Much of my Idea phase was a time of frustration. The years leading up to the launch of my own company were spent conjuring up idea after idea for new business ventures that never materialized. I felt like I was in the grip of a powerful curse, longing to start a business but unable to find an idea explosive enough to trigger that first step, let alone power me through the long and demanding entrepreneurial journey. Author Wilfred Peterson once said, "Big thinking precedes great achievement." I recommend that you remember those words when you're slogging through a lengthy period of brainstorming in the process of finding an idea that clicks. Your efforts to open the gate and begin your entrepreneurial journey will be less painful and more productive if you can focus on the lessons failed ideas can teach you, rather than the frustrations they bring with them.

Eventually, every successful entrepreneur begins by making the decision that not following his or her dream is worse than all of the potential negative outcomes of trying. Belief in our dreams gives us the courage to act on them. When it came to realizing my first entrepreneurial vision, I can truthfully say, "I wouldn't have seen it if I hadn't believed it." As I've said, however, dreams alone won't unlock your idea. The E-Formula is your key, and that formula begins with a strong I.D.E.A. that encompasses the characteristics of Innovation, Desire, Effort, and Ability. Let's take a closer look at the four critical elements that must support any successful entrepreneurial idea:

- **Innovation.** Innovation starts the entrepreneur's journey and is the dominant characteristic of the Idea phase. Your innovation must be the core deliverable of your venture and the specific tool for differentiating your offering within the marketplace. The primary difference between the manager, the business owner, and the entrepreneur is that the entrepreneur seeks and uses innovation to break into unchartered areas of the market or to create a market that didn't previously exist. Is your idea innovative enough to meet that goal?

- **Desire.** Desire compels and drives the entrepreneur through the process of accomplishing his or her vision. Without that overwhelming desire, you're likely to fail in bringing your idea to life; with it, you can overcome many of the obstacles that would otherwise halt the entrepreneurial journey. As the philosopher Eric Hoffer once said, "It sometimes seems that intense desire creates not only its own opportunities, but its own talents." Your desire to bring your idea to life must be strong enough to drive you through the tough work involved in that process.

- **Effort.** Effort is the physical, mental, and emotional work necessary for achieving an entrepreneurial vision. The Startup phase of the entrepreneurial journey will require the most intensive investment of effort you may ever be asked to make. Typically, entrepreneurs have to create a business (*every detail* of that business) from scratch, in relatively little time, and then grow it into a sustainable venture. This process leaves very little time for rest. Sweat equity and the long hours and sacrifices that accompany it are the hallmarks of the effort required of an entrepreneur. Your idea must be strong enough to sustain you in these efforts.

- **Ability.** Entrepreneurs learn how to maximize the abilities they have, find outside resources to supply those they lack, and then manage all of the abilities they've brought to the table. Everyone has certain skills and talents, but yours must be suited to pursuing this specific idea if you are to successfully launch the entrepreneurial process. Although your talents and skills will be drawn upon through every stage of the journey ahead, they will be most critical during the Running phase of the business. Your abilities must help you manage your business, once the effort and desire you poured into the Startup phase have made your idea viable.

THE BIG I.D.E.A.

Ideas strong enough to support an entrepreneurial endeavor must be incredibly solid. Remember to consider these four building blocks as you assess the strength of your entrepreneurial idea:

1. **Innovation.** Your idea should be truly innovative, in that it either opens up new areas of an existing market, finds a revolutionary new way to serve that market, or creates a new market altogether.

2. **Desire.** Your desire to launch this idea must be strong enough to carry you through the difficulties of the process that lies ahead.

3. **Effort.** Make sure you understand and have fully considered the effort that you'll need to invest in bringing this idea to life, and that you are willing (and able) to throw everything you have into that effort.

4. **Ability.** Finally, your abilities must be suitable to accomplishing this idea, and you have to be capable of finding the outside resources you'll need in that process.

If, after carefully evaluating your idea, you feel confident that it rests firmly on a foundation built of these four attributes, then bam!—you've made a strong first step toward activating your entrepreneurial experience. If the idea feels shaky on any of these four elements, you need to either find a way to shore up those weak areas or find another idea. Remember, entrepreneurial success doesn't have to be measured in dollars, but it does have to represent a viable and sustainable venture. Ideas that meet the I.D.E.A. profile are successful components of the E-Formula. That's the kind of idea you need to be shooting for.

Assessing Your Situation

Even the most exciting and solid idea must be planted in fertile ground before it can grow. In other words, the situation must be right in order for you to successfully pursue your entrepreneurial idea. Situation is the second element in the E-Formula.

When I use the term *situation*, I'm referring to a particular condition or set of circumstances that are present in your personal and professional life and environment. Personal factors that shape your situation include, for example, your marital status, children and other family responsibilities, health, economics, location and ability to relocate, education, hobbies, and so on. Professional factors might include your current employment status and all of the circumstances surrounding it, such as benefits, vacation, salary, location, prestige, title, tenure, relationships, future outlook, and level of satisfaction. Environmental factors that have an impact on your situation can vary dramatically, and they include things such as war, recession, inflation, taxes, global events, legal factors, resource availability—even the weather.

When the personal, professional, and environmental factors in your situation are in a neutral state, they have little impact—negative or positive—on your efforts to move forward with a new venture. When those factors are in a disruptive state, however, they can throw some serious roadblocks in your path, and they can magnify the negative outcomes should the venture falter. Positive situational factors, on the other hand, will increase the potential upside of your entrepreneurial efforts. Few of us have the luxury of being in a perfect situation for launching an entrepreneurial venture, but all of us have to very carefully assess our situation and all of the potential benefits and pitfalls it brings to the process.

Consider this example: let's say a would-be entrepreneur has a child who suffers from a long-term illness, which contributes to a disruptive or

negative personal situation. Her professional situation is positive and provides her with health insurance, as well as having helped her hone some
of the most critical skills necessary to succeed in her entrepreneurial venture. She has good, solid contacts and a strong professional network that
will remain with her should she start off on her own. Her environmental
factors are neutral—the economy is down, but the potential market for her
idea remains strong, and her research has revealed little on the horizon that
will alter those factors.

This individual may have a tremendous idea that she knows will be successful, but if she moves forward, she will lose her much-needed health
insurance coverage. That's a huge negative factor in her situation—certainly,
it offers more risk than it would for a young, single person with no family
commitments or health issues that make insurance a financial necessity.
In determining whether her situation is right, this individual must determine how she would meet the financial obligations of supporting her child's
healthcare as she got her entrepreneurial idea up and running. That challenge may or may not be an impassable obstacle, but it's a situational factor
that this woman must assess when determining whether or not to move
forward with her entrepreneurial idea.

For this individual, and any person contemplating the entrepreneurial
journey, the combined impact of *all* situational factors must be weighed
and balanced before that journey begins. As I said, few would-be entrepreneurs are lucky enough to be operating from an ideal situation, so you
don't need to consider that as the make-it-or-break-it condition. You can
probably move forward, for example, if one of your situational factors is in
a disruptive state. But if multiple factors combine to create a negative situation, you are beginning your journey weighed down with an overriding
potential for failure. If you stumble, you're likely to hit the ground hard.
Risk is inherent in entrepreneurism. But you must assess your situational
factors to be certain that none of them presents you with unsustainable risk
that can doom your journey before you've even begun it.

Weighing Your Opportunity

Arthur Cole, a mid-twentieth-century economic historian who organized
the Center for Research on Entrepreneurial History, divided entrepreneurs
into four types: the Innovator, the Calculating Inventor, the Over-Optimis-
tic Promoter, and the Organization Builder.[1] Cole didn't divvy up entrepreneurs based on their personality traits; instead, he classified entrepreneurs
according to the types of opportunities they faced. There may be some

truth in Cole's premise, but I would add that many would-be entrepreneurs don't *know* what types of opportunities they face, because they can't (or won't) see them.

Of course, that's what makes opportunities valuable: not everyone can see them. Opportunities are sitting there waiting to be picked off the vine, but only by those who are acutely aware of where to find them. The collapse of the US auto industry in 2008–2010 shuttered hundreds of dealerships and sent General Motors, Chrysler, and various suppliers into bankruptcy. Most budding entrepreneurs would have seen this as an industry they should avoid like the plague. For those with the right I.D.E.A. and situation, however, this dramatic event presented just the right opportunity to get in the game. Shortly after the drumbeats of auto-industry bankruptcy began, entrepreneurs began springing forward with ventures aimed at everything from revolutionary fuel injection models from startup Transonic Combustion, to recharging stations for electric cars from PEP Stations (PEP stands for plug-in electric power), to modular manufactured cars from WIKISPEED.

I'm not trying to present entrepreneurs as superheroes who can turn every obstacle into an opportunity, but successful entrepreneurs can remove or reduce obstacles through careful planning and a thorough grounding in their idea. At the same time, they can't take a leisurely approach to the process. The entrepreneurial idea is closely aligned to opportunity, and both are perishable. Your opportunity will be born when favorable circumstances align at a suitable time for pursuing your idea. If you don't start taking action on your idea at that time, you can expect that opportunity to fade or to be co-opted by someone else.

Five years prior to writing this book, I had an idea that triggered my deep and immediate entrepreneurial desire; I wanted to start a company that created digital medical record-management software. The idea was born from a problem—the lack of an easy, reliable, and safe medium for storing and transporting individual patient health records. I wanted to find a way to speed up the process of transferring medical records when people change jobs, insurance carriers, and healthcare providers. I also thought that individuals should be in possession and control of their own health records, rather than having them held hostage by the healthcare system.

As I researched my idea, I encountered plenty of obstacles. Proprietary software publisher systems that didn't communicate with rival systems, HIPAA compliancy and concerns over patient privacy, doctors' resistance to change, and related costs to upgrade were just a few examples. For these reasons the problem seemed insoluble (we'll talk more about the role of problems in the entrepreneurial process in the next chapter of this book). Over the next few years, I occasionally revisited the idea, always bumping into the same problems and accepting the same negative feedback from industry experts before returning the idea to the back burner. I had other things occupying my mind, and I didn't have the will to focus my efforts on pursuing my idea.

Then, one day something reignited that initial desire. I knew that the naysayers were dead wrong, and that this problem was one that needed to be solved. I started designing my blueprints for a cloud-based application of personal healthcare records—an application that anyone with an Internet connection could access. The application would include a feature that would enable doctors' offices without a constant online connection to download and upload data when appropriate. An elaborate patient-driven methodology of permissions-based management would enable or block outside access to the database, and the entire system would be protected by the latest in security software and firewalls. The potential to streamline, share, and view medical information offered by this system had staggering possibilities and enormous potential for good. The only thing left to do was to launch the business.

But my window of opportunity had fallen shut. Just as I was wrapping up my work on the project, I stumbled across beta versions of Google Health and Microsoft Health Vault. The beta screen shots had been leaked to the Internet, and they seemed to be identical in function to my own designs. It was amazing to see my concepts and visions right there before me. No, these organizational behemoths hadn't stolen my idea. As is so often the case with innovation, I wasn't the only one working to bring this brilliant idea to life.

Seeing the advancements made by these two digital media superpowers and knowing the resources behind them, I walked away from my project, and for days recited the mantra of missed opportunity: I was too late. I lacked the resources. I lacked the knowledge of the industry. The competition was too big. These reasons were all substantial, but I knew that if I had urgently pursued my idea five years earlier, when I first saw the opportunity before me, the story may have been different. Opportunity wouldn't wait for me, just as it won't wait long for you—although, as we'll see later, opportunities sometimes change, rather than disappear entirely.

Your ability to see opportunities as (or even before) they arise and to create opportunities through your own innovation will, in large part, hinge on your immersion in the industry and marketplace in which your entrepreneurial idea will "play." By educating yourself about developments, trends, and even the history of markets similar to those you'll be creating or competing in, you'll be better able to assess the opportunities available to your venture.

Jumping In

I've always compared the process of starting a business to the act of jumping into a pool of cold water. I'm drawn to this analogy by my memories of taking swimming lessons at the YMCA when I was in kindergarten. I still remember the fear that gripped me as I stood at the end of the low diving board that stretched over the Y's Olympic-size pool. I don't know if I was afraid to swim or if the water was cold—probably both—but my apprehension, anxiety, and even a tiny bit of excitement built rapidly as I crouched and prepared to dive. Those feelings didn't let up until I hit the water. Then, a rush of adrenaline washed away everything but determination from my mind, as I splashed frantically to the edge of the pool. And I knew nothing but relief, exhilaration, and pride as I reached the exit ladder.

I think most entrepreneurs experience that same evolving rush of feelings as they leap through the gate and begin their entrepreneurial experience. The exhilaration of setting out to create your own future, based on your own innovations, desire, effort, and ability is a feeling that can't be explained, only experienced. The E-Formula can give you the security you need to launch this bold adventure with courage and determination.

LEAPING FORWARD WITH THE E-FORMULA

That rush you feel when preparing to launch a new venture can be frightening if you don't feel safely tethered to reality. The E-Formula is your tool for making sure that your leap into entrepreneurism is based on solid ground. As you weigh the potential benefits and risks of moving forward, remember to carefully test each element of the equation:

$$I.D.E.A. + Situation + Opportunity = Activation$$

Notice that the formula does not include factors specifically dedicated to money, time, talent, or resources. Those factors play a role in each of the E-Formula elements, but you will deal with them individually and specifically in your business plan. Don't use the formula to try to solve all of the important issues you'll need to resolve in order to grow your idea into a successful venture. Instead, use the formula as a safety measure, to avoid leaping into opportunities too soon without proper readiness and a sound idea. After all, if you aren't careful, you can drown.

You can use the formula to help ease the indecision you might feel during the process of developing the right opportunities and arriving at the right situation. By recognizing the strength of all of the equation's elements, you can avoid wasting a wealth of time, effort, expense, and energy by following an idea that isn't yet viable or worth your commitment. Walk yourself through each component of the formula and determine if, at this point in time, *this* is the right opportunity and situation to explore *this* idea. If you find yourself hesitating to take that first step, you can be relatively certain that some element of your E-Formula isn't working. Return to the formula again, and study each element in detail to find weaknesses that might be holding you back. Only by honestly facing those weaknesses can you determine whether they are fixable or fatal flaws that threaten your success.

In the time leading up to my own first entrepreneurial experience, my E-Formula was solid. I had developed an idea that I knew would succeed. I had created a situation in which I had developed the necessary in-depth knowledge of my marketplace, products, processes, customers, and so on. In addition to my own expertise, I had numerous industry contacts and resources that I could draw on. I'd even written a business plan. The opportunity was ripe; I would be tapping into a largely neglected but growing market that I understood intimately. I just had to jump into the pool. And then, my company gave me the final push I needed.

Just a couple of months after that disheartening meeting when I'd pitched my idea to the company's leadership, my boss quit. Educational Resources needed a replacement to fill his role as Vice President of Marketing, and my hard work, knowledge, and innovative ideas made me the logical candidate. Finally, I was able to advance my career—at least, that's what I thought. Instead, the company hired an outside candidate with a portfolio of marketing experience unrelated to our industry.

Was I disappointed? You can't imagine. I had put a great deal of time and effort into this company, had tremendous results, created new programs, and established numerous cost-saving efficiencies. Their decision felt like a slap in the face. With my career path blocked, my professional situation changed abruptly; and almost instantaneously, everything clicked into place.

I had a great idea just waiting to be developed. I had a creative vision for serving a totally new market that was just beginning to develop and whose needs would certainly grow at a rapid rate for at least the next 10 years. I knew the products, the manufacturers, the method of distribution, costing, and marketing, and I had relationships that would help me. I could do this! For years, I had dreamed of starting my own business. Now, I was ready. I would sell software to the higher education market, and my business would be one of the first to do it. Any anger over the rejection of the VP position was gone. I was ready to make the leap into the hard work that lay ahead of me.

Of course, I didn't have any guarantees of success, just as the strength and alignment of your I.D.E.A., situation, and opportunity aren't any guarantee that your venture will succeed. These elements are the essential foundation from which you begin preparing for the entrepreneurial process, but each of these elements harbors its own set of risks. As I said in chapter 1, it is the entrepreneur's *duty* to deal in risk. That means acknowledging risk, rooting it out wherever it hides, and determining how best to avoid it, conquer it, or accept it and move on. Risk will be your ongoing companion during the entrepreneurial journey, and so, in the next chapter, I'll give you the information and tools you need in order to understand and manage it.

CHAPTER THREE

Mastering the Risk Box

*Often the difference between a successful person and
a failure is not one has better abilities or ideas, but
the courage that one has to bet on one's ideas, to take
a calculated risk—and to act.*

—Andre Malraux, author

MANY PEOPLE STANDING ON THE threshold of their entrepreneurial dreams
will say they are unable to commit out of fear and doubt. We've learned
about one technique for confronting the doubts you might have when contemplating an entrepreneurial venture. As you've seen, the E-Formula offers
a powerful tool for gauging the strength of your idea (and its components
of innovation, desire, effort, and ability), the soundness of your personal
and professional situation, and the richness of the opportunities available
to support your entrepreneurial vision. Getting this equation right is your
first defining moment of the Idea phase of the entrepreneurial process, and
the first step toward activating the entrepreneur within you.

But you can't stop there. To fully move through the Idea phase and into
Startup, you first must come to terms with your fears—and the walls of risk
in which those fears can imprison you. Taking control of your relationship
with risk is the second defining moment of your entrepreneurial journey,
and the subject of this chapter. Here, we'll talk about the nature of fear, the
link between entrepreneurism and risk, and the role your attitude toward
risk can play in the success or failure of any entrepreneurial effort. I'll
introduce you to the Risk Box—the four-walled enclosure of possessions,
age, health, and position that can grow so thick and high that it blocks you
from pursuing your idea, even when every element of the E-Formula is in

alignment. By learning to separate your notions of fear and risk, and by understanding how to work with risk, rather than running away from it, you'll be better able to break down the artificial barriers that can stand in the way of your progress as an entrepreneur. Mastering risk is an essential threshold you must cross in order to begin the process of launching your business. Consider this chapter the key to the next phase of your journey.

Facing Your Fears

Fear and doubt are two of the strongest enemies you'll face as you pre-pare to launch your business. While the E-Formula can help you erase the doubts you may have about the viability of your idea and the likelihood that you can see it through, no formula can help you eliminate your fears. Why is that? Well, let me begin to answer that question by asking you to con-sider another one: what is fear? Fear is an idea; a feeling; the anticipation of something that is yet to happen or that may not happen at all. Fear isn't a living thing or an object; it exists only in our mind. It's that very intangibility and those deep psychological roots that make fear such a daunting enemy.

Being scared is an outcome of fear, but there's a difference between the two emotional states. In most cases, we become scared because something very real has happened to us. You might be afraid that the icy roads will cause you to have an accident, but when your car starts skidding out of control, you become scared. It's scary when you lose your job. It's scary when you lose your house because it was collateral on a business loan. Those are real outcomes, negative events that actually have occurred to entrepreneurs. When the conditions that scared you are dealt with or pass—you find a new job, you move into another home, you reach your destination and stop driving on the icy road—you no longer are scared. Fear, on the other hand, has no end point. It plants the seeds of danger and failure in your mind, and those seeds don't rely on hard evidence. Feeding on nothing more than vague ideas and speculation, fear can quickly overwhelm your thinking, choking out your ability to see any outcome other than doom and disaster.

We can allow our fears to become very powerful. In fact, our fears can drown our hopes, even when the outcomes we hope for are much more likely to occur than are the outcomes we fear. Fear can trump logic, because the two don't play by the same rules. You can quantify the strength of your idea; you can evaluate how well your situation positions you to pursue your idea; you can logically assess the opportunities available for marketing your idea within the prevailing economy, industry, and marketplace. But facts don't always smack down fear, because fear isn't always about facts—or logic, or reason, or reality.

For all of these reasons (and many more), fear can have no place in your decision-making process. Business continuity managers earn their living developing recovery plans to help organizations make a speedy bounce-back after *real* disasters (either natural or manmade). These experts recognize fear as an emotional albatross that can have a paralyzing impact on even the most well-informed and educated judgments, and they make it their job to eliminate fear from their clients' planning processes wherever possible. You, too, must banish fear from the decision-making table, as you evaluate when and where to fully activate your entrepreneurial venture.

HOW FEAR CONTROLS BULLS AND BEARS

It has been said that Wall Street traders are guided by only two things—greed and fear. Studies seem to indicate that of these two emotional influences, fear plays the stronger role. Psychologists who have studied traders and investors have discovered that, although everyone who participates in investing is in it to see a profit, fear of losing money can be nearly twice as influential in traders' decision-making process as the desire to make a profit. In bull markets, when prices are rising, traders are less likely to take an aggressive approach to their deal making than during a bear market, when prices are dropping. During a bear market, traders should expect to lose on new investments, and therefore be less prone to making them. Instead, it seems that the traders' fears of losing capital actually grow stronger as stock prices begin to rise.[1]

With all of their training, experience, and finely tuned formulas, many Wall Street traders still can fall victim to decision making guided by fear, not facts. You can't afford that kind of weakness. Fear will drive your entrepreneurial enterprise into the ditch if you let it take the reins. One of the most important tasks you can accomplish as you prepare to activate as an entrepreneur is to stop listening to fear and, instead, focus on true risk assessment and planning.

Fear is personal, and it typically stems from personal values that have no relevance to the business decision. The fear of loss is deeply ingrained in most humans, and it is a powerful, innate characteristic that will skew and cloud decisions. As you think about all of the personal things in your life that might be put at risk if you walk the path of the entrepreneur, fear takes control, enabling you to focus only on the negative potential outcomes. "I may lose money." "I may lose all of the progress I've made in my career." "I may lose possessions or any number of other valuable items." But those fears don't really offer any answers for moving forward; they can only hold you back. That power to keep you from taking on challenges that involve some element of risk is fear's one great trick. So, yes, it's true that if you never step forward, you can never be shoved back. But you can never advance, either.

Don't get me wrong; fear can be a valuable emotion. Fear truly can help keep us safe from danger, even disappointment. We learn fear through life experiences, and that's why it can become a larger presence in our decision-making process as we grow older. An element of fear surrounds every decision that we make, and it sometimes helps us avoid injury, pain, expense, sadness, regret, and embarrassment. But fear is a double-edged sword. If we allow fear to guide our behavior, we will also miss many of life's most rewarding experiences—some of which will *require* that we experience pain, or injury, or regret. As an entrepreneur-in-waiting, you need to examine your fears carefully, following both their roots and their branches to reveal what, if any, reality is feeding them. Then, you can choose to eliminate, avoid, or accept any true risks you uncover.

Eleanor Roosevelt once said, "You gain strength, courage, and confidence by every experience in which you stop to look fear in the face."[2] In fact, that's how you can use fear as a tool for growth. Your challenge is to recognize when you are making decisions based on fear, and then to analyze those fears carefully and weed out anything that doesn't represent a true risk. The understanding you gain about risk in this chapter, along with the exercises you learn in chapter 4, will help you with that process.

We look at those who have accomplished great things, and all we see is their success. We rarely see or hear what they did to get there: what they sacrificed, how they failed, how they feared the process and questioned success. As you prepare yourself for the demanding process of entering the Startup phase of your entrepreneurial experience, you can expect to be afraid. That's only natural. But if you want to arm yourself to successfully finish the journey that lies ahead, you will need to face your fears and eliminate their influence on your risk-assessment and decision-making processes.

Risk Breaking Versus Risk Taking

As I mentioned earlier, the term *entrepreneur* seems to be synonymous with *risk taker* in much of the prevailing mythology that surrounds the world of business, so it's important that we understand what constitutes a true risk. Most of the fear that you'll face as an entrepreneur will be associated with risk. For most entrepreneurs, that fear tends to be greatest as they enter the Startup phase and actually decreases significantly once their business is launched. Risk involves putting something of value at stake. In launching a new business, your risks might include an existing job, savings, a home, possessions, time, and even relationships. The prospect of failing in an entrepreneurial venture may not seem like an impassible barrier, but you may be stopped cold by the fear of losing what you must put at risk. Activating as an entrepreneur involves some risk taking, it's true. More importantly, though, it requires risk breaking—destroying the powerful grip of risk-aversion-based fear that can hold you back from pursuing your idea.

Achieving nearly anything worthwhile requires some form of risk. In that regard, life is like poker. You have to ante up something of value in order to play the game—or, at least, in order to enjoy the experience. If there's no money on the table, poker feels pretty pointless. At the same time, I've seen people have as much fun at penny ante as the big dudes seem to be having at those $1,000-minimum-bet tables in Vegas. The amount of pleasure we get from playing poker isn't directly linked to the amount of money we have staked on the game; instead, it comes from the direct connection between our mental life and our learned affiliation to money.

The close relationship between money and mind forms a roadblock that has stopped many would-be entrepreneurs from pursuing their dreams, so don't be surprised if it shows up on your own path. In fact, perhaps the *biggest* obstacle you will have to overcome in order to start a business is your mind, not your money (or lack thereof). I've often heard people claim that they simply don't have the money to pursue their entrepreneurial idea, but when we dig deeper into the obstacle before them, we most often find that they're butting up against mental barriers that they themselves have erected.

Why is that? Why do some people start businesses while others watch from the sidelines, wishing they could be in the entrepreneur's shoes? Why do we hear so often about immigrants who come to this country with nothing and then go on to become multimillionaires, while others around them still struggle in nine-to-five jobs they hate? Or how about the story of the twenty-something billionaire genius who starts a multinational business in his parents' basement—don't you ever wonder how those people can do it, if you can't?

The simple answer is that you are holding yourself back from being that person who succeeds, and the reason has everything to do with what's in your head and your learned fear of risk. According to statistics from the Kauffman Foundation, in the United States, immigrants continue to have a substantially higher rate of entrepreneurial activity than native-born citizens, and that's because they accepted risk as a partner when they stepped

foot on that plane or boat to come to America.[3] Once they decide that the
potential for success on the road ahead is greater than the potential regrets
they might have for the things they're leaving behind, the sky is the limit
for what these folks can achieve. They've already faced their fears and come
to grips with the nature of the risks they're taking; with that ante on the
table, they have to throw every ounce of their focus, time, and effort into
winning the game.

Many of the rest of us, however, have an oddly contradictory relationship
with the idea of risk. When we consider investing our time, money, and
other resources in an entrepreneurial venture, we fear the worst-case scenario of losing it all, even if we have a very good shot at gaining it all back
at a later date. At the same time, that fear of losing doesn't keep us from
engaging in other, even riskier behavior. We take risks every day that can be
much more real and immediate than those we face when starting a business.

We risk our retirement savings by contributing to 401(K) plans that are
invested in the stock market, and then just stand back and let others take
control of our financial future. We watch with joy as the principal goes up
and cringe with disgust as it goes down. In fact, month after month, some
of us throw money on the 401(K) roller coaster and don't even bother following its ups and downs, figuring we'll just wait and see what happens
when the ride is over. Seriously, how closely do you read the prospectus
on the mutual funds in your 401(K) or for your kids' 525 college savings?
But we ante up those dollars with none of the fear about the stock market's
unpredictable swings that we feel when considering the business cycles our
startup venture might face.

And then there's our comfort with the risk of personal debt. Many of us
have put our financial security at tremendous risk by taking on an over-
sized debt burden, using credit cards and home equity to buy more and
more stuff, even when it threatens our ability to put the kids through college or retire in any kind of security or comfort. It's easy to become more
concerned about visible signs of wealth (concerns based in fear) than about
the dismal view of a future with no means of financial support (which represents a true risk). Some of the same people who are willing to risk all they
have in a gamble with personal bankruptcy, a risk that offers no real payoff,
would never consider taking on the risks involved in starting a new business. You have to have a much healthier understanding of risk than any of
the people I've just described if you want to survive and thrive as an entrepreneur. And the first step toward improving your risk-breaking capabilities is to become very familiar with the risks that most frighten you.

Deconstructing Your Risk Box

As you saw in the E-Formula, your personal and professional situation is one of the critical elements in your readiness to embark on an entrepreneurial journey. The components that define our situation vary, but, in just about every case, they come from the same four categories: possessions, age, position, and health. These categories represent the high-value assets and liabilities that weigh most heavily in our decision-making process. Together, they form the four walls of what I call the Risk Box (figure 3.1), a psychological enclosure that you will need to break through in order to move forward with your entrepreneurial idea. Understanding what's contained in your Risk Box is an essential step toward becoming an entrepreneur.

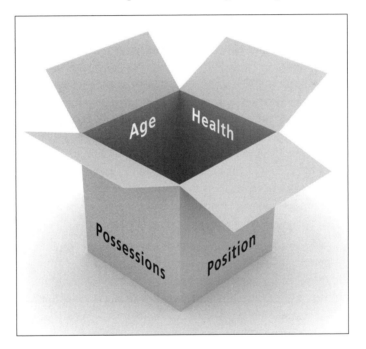

Figure 3.1: The Risk Box

We all reside within a Risk Box, and for good reasons. All decisions have a degree of risk associated with them, and every risk has a cause and, in many cases, a consequence. We start building our Risk Box at birth. We learn to approach certain people, places, and things cautiously, and to completely avoid others. As we collect a broader and deeper idea of the risks life has to offer, those ideas form psychic walls within which we retreat in order to protect ourselves from disappointment or danger. Gradually, over time, we begin putting things we value in the Risk Box for protection; the more we put in the Risk Box, the thicker and stronger its walls become, as we place more importance on keeping everything inside "safe."

The purpose of the Risk Box is to protect, and that can be a very valid and noble function. But just like an older home that's subjected to ongoing remodeling and additions, over the years, our Risk Box can become clunky, outdated, and less effective in meeting its true purpose. You're going to need to be able to move freely outside the walls of your Risk Box, so let's take a closer look to see just what those walls are made of.

Wall #1: Possessions

Face it, we Westerners are a materialistic bunch. We highly value our possessions, and many of us have a sense of entitlement so great that we don't let our ability to pay get in the way of acquiring new things. Thanks to creative financing, we don't have to. Lots of people are able to get their hands on bigger homes and fancier cars than they truly can afford. Our possessions include everything involved in our lifestyle, including our clothes, memberships, service plans, and savings. Possessions not only pacify our desires for pleasure, convenience, and so on, but they also provide a sense of security—even identity. Our home provides shelter; our car gets us to and from the places we need (or want) to be; our savings help to keep us afloat during the times when we're not working, whether that means our "golden years" or simply a lengthy period of unemployment.

Okay, so we all understand the concept of possessions. But how can our attitude toward possessions skew our ability to activate as an entrepreneur? Think for a moment what would it be like to have everything you want in terms of possessions: what would ever draw you outside your comfort zone and into new experiences? The more possessions you have, the more you must protect, and the thicker the possessions wall of your Risk Box becomes.

Possessions offer security, but they also bring with them their own hidden pitfalls. As a new entrepreneur, you cannot allow yourself to become focused on the protective power of your possessions. Rather than allowing your possessions to form an impenetrable barrier between you and your entrepreneurial aspirations, you must find ways to use the security of your possessions as a platform for exploring new territories, new ideas, and new elements of success. By separating your sense of identity and security from your possessions, you're better able to focus on the things you *really* cannot afford to risk. Your character, capabilities, intellect, and ideas are your most valuable possessions because those are the qualities that helped you accumulate the rest of the stuff you have now, as well as all of the new possessions you'll acquire in the future.

WEALTH AND THE WOULD-BE ENTREPRENEUR

Wealth is probably the curse of the entrepreneur, in that it can extinguish desire. Where wealth should be the greatest catalyst to fund an entrepreneurial dream, far too often it just fuels complacency. The wealthy have much less motivation to go through the effort of building something new. They might have a notion of a new business or process that might interest them for a while. But because they have little riding on the success of their efforts, it can be easy to just walk away from them when the going becomes difficult (as it always does, at some point in every entrepreneurial experience).

I think children born into wealth are the best example of this innovation-killing disease. They are born into a Risk Box with thick, prefabricated walls formed by inherited possessions, and those walls only grow stronger over time. Often, they don't feel the need to be challenged, and they don't want to be challenged. Billionaire investor and philanthropist Warren Buffett has referred to children of wealth as being "members of the lucky sperm club," and he's been quoted as stating, "I don't believe in dynastic wealth." Buffett plans to donate over 85 percent of his fortune to charity and once commented, "I want to give my kids just enough so that they would feel that they could do anything, but not so much that they would feel like doing nothing."[4] Buffett, one of the wealthiest people on earth, practices what he preaches. He still lives in the same house he bought in 1958. A Reuters article in 2010 noted that his total compensation package had risen that year to just under $520,000. According to the article, his salary at Berkshire Hathaway remained at $100,000 (which it had been for the previous 25 years or so), but his compensation package also included $344,490 for "personal and home security services."[5] This is just more evidence of the great cost of guarding our possessions and our health (which form just two walls of the Risk Box).

Wall #2: Position

Our position in life is defined by the personal and professional attributes that we have accumulated over the years. We constantly invest in our position with what is perhaps the greatest and most limited resource any of us will ever have—time.

Your personal position might consist of a variety of factors, such as marital status, children, or a caregiver role. It can also represent your economic status or your involvement in groups, clubs, school, local government, charities, or religious organizations. Personal position extends to your interests, such as gardening, travel, sports, and so on—activities that you like to invest your time in. And all of these factors will be affected by your decision to start a business.

Your professional position is what you do for a living, and you may have, like most of us, worked very long and hard at building a professional position. We invest heavily in maximizing our professional goals, through education, relocation, working time, and sacrifices of personal pleasure. The career ladder we hear so much about is nothing more than the passageway to a professional position and significant achievement; wealth and respect are granted to those who climb the highest. Position feeds the ego. That benefit alone may prove too powerful for some to concede in pursuit of new endeavors.

Position is an investment that we hate to risk; it may be the most heavily fortified wall of our Risk Box because its investments are so tightly linked with those we make in our possessions and wealth, and even our age. When you give up a position at the top of an existing business or organization, you give up more than income. You may forego stock options, bonuses, hefty vacation accrual, and allowances, not to mention the special treatment, respect, and other perks you might command in an executive-level position. Leaving a position to follow entrepreneurial endeavors can knock you off the career ladder indefinitely in your industry, making it very difficult to restart where you left off if your endeavor goes belly up. Breaking through this wall of the Risk Box requires a willingness to take on new challenges and to define yourself by where you're going, not by where you've been.

Wall #3: Age

Entrepreneurism has no age limits. According to the *Kauffman Index of Entrepreneurial Activity, 1996–2006*, the highest rate of entrepreneurial growth during those years came from individuals aged 55–64. The average age for entrepreneurs who founded technology-oriented startups during that time was 39.[6] Nevertheless, many of us believe that entrepreneurism is for the young—depending on your definition of young. The reason is simple: younger people, say those under 30, have fewer possessions, have had fewer experiences, and, typically, are more willing than their older counterparts to take risks and accept their results. As you age, the walls of your Risk Box grow thicker and calcify. You gain more possessions, and your personal and professional position takes on more meaning and importance. People changing careers late in life might be putting a lot at stake in making such a change, and thus must rely on the clarity of their longer vantage point to see through the walls of risk that surround them.

The Risk Box walls are designed to protect *our* assets and *our* relationships so *we* can live a safe life. At the same time, the Risk Box walls often are shaped by society at large, not by our own ideas and desires. Popular wisdom and our own personal experiences show us how horribly wrong things can go in any new enterprise, and that knowledge teaches us to be careful and protect what we have. The older we get, the more desperately we may cling to the things we've stashed in our Risk Box. When that happens, our assessments of opportunities tend to be influenced more heavily by the need to protect, rather than to pursue new possessions or positions in life.

While some folks may choose to sit safely within the walls of their Risk Box, true entrepreneurs are more likely to charge on through life, always expanding their world rather than finding a way to be content within artificial limits. And age is one of the most common of these perceived limitations, whether it manifests itself as "I'm too young to take on this much responsibility" or "I'm too old to start over." Breaking through the age wall of your Risk Box will require that you use your age as an entrepreneurial tool, whether that means drawing upon the endless energy and optimism of your youth or the accumulated wisdom and experience of a long working life.

Wall #4: Health

Your own personal health plays a very important role in determining your ability and desire to start a business. It's vitally important to be both physically and mentally prepared to take on the work of launching a new business or enterprise. Any startup is extremely demanding and requires stamina, endurance, patience, and the ability to deal with stress. Long, fast-paced hours will press the capabilities of any new entrepreneur. Being in poor health could compromise success. More importantly, the demands of startup could take a real toll on your physical and emotional health.

But protecting your own health isn't the only form of concern that can add to the bulk of this wall of your Risk Box. Your concerns also include the health of close family members and friends, all of which can greatly influence your performance and resulting entrepreneurial success. Caring for elderly parents, a sick spouse, or children will take priority over any other activities. Balancing a new business with long-term care needs of loved ones can take its toll on any new entrepreneur. These are situational factors that you have to carefully consider when determining whether or not you are ready to pursue your entrepreneurial idea. Remember that breaking through any wall of your Risk Box isn't a one-shot deal, and that truth applies particularly here. As you move into the Running phase, health risks might take on new dimensions. Should health issues develop unexpectedly during your entrepreneurial journey, you may have to find supporters or new partners to keep the business going.

Seeing the Opportunity in Risk

The possessions, age, position, and health that thicken and strengthen your Risk Box walls are independent variables in determining the outcome of a business venture. Being able to break through the walls of your Risk Box won't guarantee the success of your new venture; that rests in the strength of your idea, the thoroughness of your planning, and the depth of your commitment to see it through. But your ability to break through the barriers of risk that surround you does determine whether you will become an entrepreneur.

While the Risk Box is most closely associated with the situation factor within your E-Formula (I.D.E.A. + Situation + Opportunity = Activation), it can also dramatically shape your perception of opportunity. Not only can the Risk Box prevent you from moving forward to pursue opportunity, it can block your ability to even see the opportunities that are available to you as an entrepreneur.

The Risk Box isn't the reason you can't start a business; it's an excuse to avoid trying. The contents of the box have come to us through a lifetime of experiences, and we don't want to part with any of those "valuables" even for a short period of time. The truth is, however, that by risking some portion of our security, we might be repaid many times over in new possessions, a new position, more security at any age, and a healthier physical and emotional environment. If we can't see that those opportunities exist, however, we aren't likely to pursue them. In fact, the Program Management Institute (PMI), the world's leading not-for-profit association for professionals who study risk, actually views risk as an "opportunity." Taking on risk equals taking on opportunity, which means growing rather than maintaining the status quo.

Remember the immigrant entrepreneur I mentioned earlier? The immigrant I described has a Risk Box with very thin walls. His mind does not block the path with fears of losing wealth, possessions, or position in life because he is starting with basically nothing—a clean slate. It's less about entrepreneurialism than it is about survival. I'm not saying that the less you have, the greater your chances of being an entrepreneur. Look at T. Boone Pickens, who has accumulated much and, at age eighty-one, was still pursuing new entrepreneurial opportunities.[7] Yes, he's a unique individual, and his story is truly remarkable. But it's also true that his willingness to take on risk in the pursuit of an idea that he believes in is something that any of us can cultivate. It's this quality, as much as the money in his bank account, that enables Pickens to operate without a net, and as a result he achieves remarkable success.

So remember: it's not the quantity or monetary value of our deposits within the Risk Box but the *value we place upon them* that determines the thickness and strength of the walls of risk we must push through in order to become an entrepreneur. Your entrepreneurial activation occurs when your commitment to pursuing your idea is stronger than the walls of your Risk Box. As an entrepreneur, you will mitigate the risk of loss by careful planning, research, and effort in launching the idea.

Moving Out of the Risk Box and into Your Future

Today, everyone needs to be an entrepreneur. Corporations increasingly expect their employees to develop a feeling of ownership about the organization and to approach their work with an entrepreneurial spirit. The economy doesn't run on predictability these days; it demands flexibility and a willingness to innovate and change on a dime. And the age of the good old reliable lifetime employer is over. As safe and untouchable as we might like to feel tucked away inside the walls of our employer's business, our cubicle, our Risk Box, our situation can change in an instant.

In reality, the protective value of the Risk Box is nothing but an illusion. Your finances and savings can be wiped out by a swindler or through powerful market forces in seconds. Over 80 percent of equity trading is done by hedge-fund dealers and other institutional investors, so the individual solo investor doesn't stand a chance in today's equity markets. Your job can be eliminated due to downsizing; you can be diagnosed with a life-threatening illness without warning. These threats can break through the walls of your Risk Box in an instant. The more you allow yourself to entrench in the status quo, the greater the impact unstoppable events will have on you. The Risk Box won't protect you from risk, but it can make you less innovative and therefore less capable of dealing with the events of life as they unfold.

In 2006 Daniel H. Pink wrote *A Whole New Mind: Why Right-Brainers Will Rule the Future*, which formulated a hypothesis that global demand for analytical, process-oriented left-brain thinkers is diminishing as the demand for creative right-brain thinkers—such as successful entrepreneurs—grows rapidly. To quote Pink, "The last few decades have belonged to a certain kind of person with a certain kind of mind—computer programmers who could crack code, lawyers who could craft contracts, and MBAs who could crunch numbers. But the keys to the kingdom are changing hands. The future belongs to a very different kind of person with a very different kind of mind—creators and empathizers, pattern recognizers and meaning makers. These people—artists, inventors, designers, storytellers, caregivers, consolers, big-picture thinkers—will now reap society's richest rewards and share its greatest joys."[8]

Our society too often trains us to be good workers rather than creative thinkers and problem solvers, and that makes entrepreneurial thinking a highly sought-after skill. The one talent I look for most when I'm hiring new employees is an ability to think creatively. The left-brain programmers, accountants, and such have become commoditized, so their skill can be shopped for the lowest price. Those exercising entrepreneurial gifts such as bold approaches to risk taking, problem solving, creativity, and innovation will be most sought after in this new era, which Pink has called "The Conceptual Age."

You become a prisoner of the Risk Box by submitting to "the system" and turning your destiny over to others. Careers and money can be replaced, but when you allow your identity to become so tightly wound up in those things and society's rigid benchmarks for success, the outcome can become deadly. We've all heard the stories of how people snapped during the Great Depression—and even the Great Recession—as the walls of their Risk Box closed in around them. But what we hear less about is how deadly the Risk Box can be for dreams and opportunities. We'll never know how many businesses, ideas, and inventions have been blocked by Risk Box walls.

Living in the Risk Box is a highly addictive habit, but it's one you can break. Understanding and managing the enslaving properties of the Risk Box will help you move closer to living an entrepreneurial life, in everything you do. By developing the dexterity and innovative energy of entrepreneurism, you're doing something *real* to arm yourself against the negative impact of personal, professional, or economic change.

We humans have an instinctual drive engrained in us over generations. That drive is to live within the orderly structure of the society created around us. It tells us to get an education; find a job; work to support ourselves, our family, and our home; and prepare for retirement. Stay on the sidewalk, don't walk into The Grove, and don't take the path less traveled. Entrepreneurism is a competing drive, one that challenges society's narrow direction. By following our own ideas and abilities, we can break through to find the more fulfilling life that waits for us just beyond the Risk Box walls.

I'd like to end this chapter with a story about my father, who I think truly illustrates how even the most cautious people—people with no desire or intention to pursue the life of an entrepreneur—have to embrace risk in some fashion in order to build a fulfilling life of personal and professional success. His story also illustrates that only *you* can determine if the entrepreneurial experience is compelling enough to draw you through the walls of your Risk Box.

My father was no swashbuckling risk lover. In fact, he was a risk mitigator—someone I would describe as an old school conservative product of the '40s. He was extremely hardworking and reliable. He supported his family and planned for his future, and he used stability, consistency, and predictability as the platform for that plan. He also worked in a 100-percent-commission-based sales business, with no guaranteed income above the $30 per week stipend (generously negotiated by his union) he received for collecting insurance premiums from his clients. My father understood the nature of the risk involved in commission-only work, but he felt up to the challenge of avoiding the negative outcomes those risks might entail. He was right; he retired from Prudential after thirty-five years of successful service and received a well-earned pension.

Sometime during his fifteenth year in business, my dad was presented with an opportunity by State Farm Insurance. That company was growing under a different model than Prudential, in that independent agents owned and ran their own State Farm office. Much like a franchise, the agencies were similar to running your own business. State Farm wanted to add offices in the area, and in particular the company wanted certified life underwriters (CLU) to expand the State Farm product portfolio to life insurance from what had traditionally been home and auto coverage. A few agents in my dad's office made the switch as the commissions were greater and the prospect of ownership was appealing. The downside was the lack of benefits and retirement guarantees that my dad valued so much at Prudential, not to mention the risk of starting a new office.

State Farm approached my dad and wanted him because of his CLU certification and years of experience. He would have to start from scratch or convince his customers to switch to State Farm upon their renewals, but there was tremendous upside potential for his efforts. The only problem was that my dad was not cut out for ownership. His personality needed the structure and guarantees of an employer. I'm sure a great point of consideration for not moving ahead with State Farm was stability and our family health insurance. My brother had developed diabetes when he was four years old. That existing condition would make it difficult and extremely costly to change to another carrier upon becoming an independent agent. My dad turned the opportunity down. There were significant risks involved, but those risks weren't the overriding reason for his decision. The idea of ownership didn't appeal to him at all; he chose his current lifestyle over that of the entrepreneur.

My dad was a tremendous success in his career and life. He was able to provide very well for his family. He put me and my brother through college loan free; he paid cash for his house, paid cash for his cars, bought me a car for college graduation, established a reliable pension, took wonderful family vacations, and built an incredible nest egg to retire comfortably on and provide a legacy for future Weber generations. He had a solid plan that went far into the future, much like the products he sold. A neighbor of my parents did start a State Farm office, and by all indications it was very successful. I hope my dad never regretted not making the change. I hope he never looked back.

I've added this story to assure you that I'm not advocating that entrepreneurism is the single pathway to a happy, successful life. Our lifestyles, like our attitudes toward risk, fulfillment, and success, are formed from very personal ideas. But you cannot let other people's notions shape those ideas for you. You have to take control of your approach to risk, rather than letting the fear of risk control your approach to life. In fact, throughout your entrepreneurial journey, you'll have to supply the will and drive that keep you moving forward. No matter how much encouragement and assistance you gain from family, friends, partners, and advisors, your progress will be determined by your own strength, stamina, and determination. Building that kind of entrepreneurial "muscle" takes careful planning and preparation. The Entrepreneurial Exercises you'll work through in the next chapter of this book will help you in this process by positioning you to take on the demanding work that lies ahead in the Startup phase of your journey.

CHAPTER FOUR

Entrepreneurial Exercises

WHEN YOU MOVE OUT OF the Idea phase and into Phase II, Startup, your hard work will begin. You will have invested a lot of time in mental preparation, and soon, your business will be born. For me, the end of my Idea phase marked the close of a long period of frustration, of wanting to become an entrepreneur but not having an idea—I should say an I.D.E.A.—strong enough to act upon. Once my E-Formula had all the right elements, I was anxious to be on my way. I had much to do to establish my business plan and gather all of the critical information I needed in order to incorporate. I was impatient to begin, but I still had to understand the legal and administrative aspects of setting up a company before I began actually working on my entrepreneurial idea. The planning and preparation I was about to undertake would have been much easier if I had put myself through some Entrepreneurial Exercises ahead of time. The information in the next chapter of this book will take you through your first steps in the planning and preparation necessary to launch your own startup. The exercises in this chapter help you get ready for that process.

These exercises won't be of much use to the accidental entrepreneur who has a great opportunity fall into his or her lap, but they will help those who know in their heart that entrepreneurship is their desire and who are committed to finding (or creating) their opportunity. Entrepreneurial Exercises can help you prepare for the work ahead, before the opportunity even presents itself. By working through them, you'll shorten the time between the Idea and Startup phases and eliminate some of the difficulties involved in launching your business. These exercises require no financial expenditure and are centered on the types of pre-startup research applicable to any business or service. With a deep understanding of the industry you are targeting, you can adapt the exercises to make them more specific to your needs.

WARM-UP: DEDICATING SPACE

The research you're about to conduct will lay a strong foundation for entering into the hard work of the Startup phase. You may be tempted to rush out and begin searching for office space and equipment or designing a logo, but please don't—not yet. Start with these exercises, then move on to the preparatory work I outline in the next few chapters of this book.

You do need to arrange some dedicated space to conduct the research involved in these exercises, and you'll also need a system and some space for organizing and storing the results of your research. You will gather a lot of material related to your idea, and you need to be organized for future reference. You will forget why you tore out that newspaper article or copied that URL months later, so you need to be sure that you're collecting and labeling all of the information you gather according to its type and topic. When you are ready to act on your idea, you'll realize that the time you spent organizing your storage of entrepreneurial ideas and material was a great investment.

Even though we live in a digital age, you'll still be collecting some print materials—articles, newsletters, and so on. I prefer to use a physical file cabinet with hanging folders to hold printed matter, but you might prefer to use a simple multifolder portfolio. If you don't want to collect any printed material, you can electronically scan the printed information you're gathering and organize a series of folders on a portable drive or desktop. The exercises that follow will help you set up and organize the folder and file topics for containing all of the ideas, examples, news clippings, industry data, experts, resources, and potential competitor profiles that will help you get ready to enter your Startup phase.

Legal Exercises

Before becoming an entrepreneur, you need to conduct lengthy administrative research into the legal aspects of activating your idea. Establishing a business is a multistep task that can feel like a dive into unchartered water for the new entrepreneur. Researching this information in advance and filing it in an organized fashion will pay big dividends for you down the road.

Here's a checklist of legal research items and activities you can conduct before Startup:

- ☐ Research the types of ownership structure and the implications of each specifically on tax, liability, and ownership transfer.

☐ Using the Internet, library, or local Small Business Association (SBA) office, learn what is involved in incorporating a business in your desired location and what laws and practices dictate the acquisition and use of these legal items:

    ☐ Articles of incorporation (the governing management rules you create and file within the state you incorporate)

    ☐ Federal Employer Identification Number (FEIN) (necessary to pay withholding taxes on employees)

    ☐ Certificates (if there is great certainty as to what industry you may enter, explore what certifications or permits may be required, their benefits, and how to obtain them)

☐ Start seeking recommendations for a law firm that can guide you on your startup requirements and advisory needs. Typically, friends and family can direct you to a trusted source, as can the local chamber of commerce.

Resource Exercises

There are several resources you will need to draw upon in your Startup and Running phases, regardless of the type of business you start. For instance, most likely you will need a website, and you'll need a developer, hosting service, and source to buy a domain name. So much information is free on the Internet today that a bit of time invested in online research should yield answers to your most basic resource questions. Documenting information online and identifying experts you will want to involve in your Startup will take a lot of pressure off of you as you activate your idea.

Here is a checklist of research activities you should complete as you gather resource information in advance of your Startup phase:

☐ Obtain and review business plan templates.

☐ Develop social networks now to expand your reach to resources and to communicate awareness of your company when ready (LinkedIn, Plaxo, Facebook, Twitter, and so on are excellent sites for establishing your presence).

☐ Seek out experts, coaches, and mentors who own businesses or are in your desired field.

☐ Read actively and retain anything you feel is relevant for your journey.

☐ Seek out information on best practices and global business topics such as search engine optimization, social networking, technology, cloud technologies, mobile applications, and communication tools that you feel may be relevant down the road. Consider subscribing to magazines like *Fast Company, Entrepreneur, Forbes*, the *Wall Street Journal, Businessweek, Harvard Business Review*, or *Inc.* (some of my favorites).

☐ Subscribe to Internet-based news services, groups, societies, clubs, and so on that are relevant to your idea, market, industry, and competition. And remember, the most powerful competition arises from unexpected places, so be as broad as possible in your research and activities.

Understand your own knowledge gaps. Most entrepreneurs are not accountants, for example, so taking a basic course in understanding financial statements at a community college may be a good investment. Even though you'll have to invest some time and money into this type of research, furthering your education is always a good investment. You also need to identify and evaluate these resources prior to launching your business:

- Accountant or accounting firm
- Website developers, domain registration, and website hosting
- Graphic artist
- Information technology specialist (voice/data, networking, backup, mobility, email)
- Lawyer (generalist, patent, contractual, intellectual property, and so on)
- Tax attorney who can explain implications based on type of incorporation, location of incorporation, desired funding sources, and estimated exit strategy
- Software tools (accounting packages, CRM, web conferencing, and so on)
- Insurance assistance (life, business, workman's compensation, and so on)
- Payroll service or a professional employer organization (PEO)
- Employee benefits and human resource intelligence (401[K], federal and state employment law, and so on)

Financial and Funding Exercises

Most startup businesses are self-funded—otherwise known as "bootstrap" ventures. You also may plan to obtain loans from banks, family, or friends. Start to investigate and understand the financing methods, limitations, and conditions you'll be working with, as well as their resulting obligations and requirements.

Here's a checklist of activities that will help prepare you in advance for financing and funding your new business:

- ☐ Talk to a banker to understand the business loan process and requirements.
- ☐ Make sure you understand business bank/checking account fees, services, and so on.
- ☐ Start building personal savings, and establish your current personal living expense budget.
- ☐ Reduce or eliminate your personal debt.
- ☐ Investigate credit union and "micro loan" establishments, along with their fees and requirements.
- ☐ Determine how to structure your personal assets from the business entity to protect yourself. Look into the benefits of creating a will and personal trusts.
- ☐ Understand what is involved in declaring—and emerging from— personal bankruptcy, as well as its implications.
- ☐ Examine pro forma financial statements from sample business plans (found abundantly on the Internet), and learn their components.

Few startup businesses will attract or require sophisticated funding; however, if you think yours will, then start now to investigate the pros and cons of funding via angel, venture capital (VC), or private equity. An increasing number of entrepreneurial funding events are taking place, especially in major metro areas. You can subscribe to an angel or VC user group via LinkedIn or similar sites to find sources for learning more about these events and opportunities.

Operational Exercises

The actual running and administration of a business will involve a number of operational aspects. Researching these aspects of your future business can be a somewhat more specialized process than the other Entrepreneurial

Exercises in this chapter. The information you gather here, however, will prove to be highly beneficial to you during startup, even if you ultimately adopt alternative operational tools and processes.

Here's a checklist of the operational services, suppliers, and information you should look into in advance of the Startup phase:

- ☐ Communications (phone systems, cell, virtual capabilities)
- ☐ Office space and rents (location, county tax differences, lease terms)
- ☐ Support capabilities of available business services, such as FedEx Kinko's, temp staffing, US Postal Service, UPS, and so on
- ☐ Cost-saving/efficiency tools and processes used by other business owners
- ☐ Offshore development, services, and manufacturing knowledge (if applicable)
- ☐ Sources for new and used office furniture, copy machines, or computing equipment
- ☐ Merchant banking for e-commerce
- ☐ Outsourcing opportunities and how to leverage them during startup
- ☐ Internet marketing techniques, including search engine optimization (SEO), social media, cloud applications, and mobile technologies

Feasibility Analyses Exercises

Your faith in yourself and in your idea moved you through the Idea phase, but now you need to visualize a business model with a means to monetize your idea and to prove that you can make it happen. The most comprehensive method to position yourself for planning and preparing to launch your idea is to conduct a three-pronged feasibility analysis. Let's take a look at the activities involved in this critical Entrepreneurial Exercise.

Financial Feasibility Analysis

This exercise might seem like it came straight from a textbook, but financial feasibility is the area where most entrepreneurs get hung up. As a result, they use it as an excuse not to move forward if they can't (or choose not to) use bootstrap financing. I've found the vast majority of business ideas can be launched without professional funding if the entrepreneur is willing to put some skin in the game. Here are some questions you can ask yourself *in advance* to be prepared for the detailed financial work involved in preparing the financial sections of your full business plan (which you'll learn more about in chapter 6):

- What capital and resources will you need to get the idea launched?
- How much capital will you require to sustain the Startup phase until revenue is reliable and consistent?
- What financial resources will you need in order to scale the business?
- What will be the estimated earnings from the effort and subsequently the bottom-line return on the initial investment?
- What unavoidable costs will you incur in the first year that will require cash?
- What costs can be diverted by virtue of barter, granting equity, deferring payments, obtaining loans, hiring 1099 workers rather than employees, and so on?

Product/Service Feasibility Analysis

If you didn't have the greatest confidence in your product or service idea, you wouldn't have made it to the end of the Idea phase. But a feasibility test can help you be certain that you actually can produce your idea and that there is a customer demand for it. Ultimately, you'll have to identify your target market and its specific need for your product or service. You can prepare for this analysis by creating prototypes, conducting focus groups and surveys, gathering demographic data, and even doing in-person sampling.

Industry/Market Feasibility Analysis

Often the most difficult analysis you'll have to perform is on the industry in which your new product/service will reside. That analysis is difficult because the kind of information you'll be looking for tends to be well guarded and especially difficult to access by anyone who isn't already in the industry. Here are the types of questions you'll need to ask:

- Is the industry in decline, growth, or a static condition?
- Who are the industry leaders, and why and how have they earned that title?
- What niche can you carve out in this industry?
- What is the resulting addressable market within that niche?
- What forces (external and internal) influence the industry?

To create a fuller and more detailed set of questions for exploring this area of your feasibility analysis, you can use an analysis tool developed by Michael Porter of the Harvard Business School called the five forces model. In essence, the five forces model states that the following elements influence any particular industry to greater or lesser extents:

- The power of suppliers
- The threat of new entrants
- The threat of substitutes
- The power of the buyer (customer)
- The competitive rivalry within the industry

Competition thrives within and between these forces as firms find innovative ways to differentiate themselves based on one or more of the elements in the model. Consciously or not, many entrepreneurs abandon their ideas because they lack knowledge about the influences outlined in the five forces model, and many companies that fail can trace their demise back to those knowledge gaps and deficiencies. The better you know and understand how your entrepreneurial idea addresses or dramatically impacts these forces in its own industry, the better able you will be to fund, launch, sustain, and scale your new venture.

Back in chapter 1, I mentioned that the disruptive entrepreneur introduces technology, processes, or models that literally destroy the old way of doing things in an industry. In doing so, the entrepreneur reinvents how the game is played in one or more of the elements within the five forces model. Investors love to back new business models that enter industries with a large number of homogenous firms where no one competitor has dominance. That chemistry creates an industry ripe for an innovative business model to enter and disrupt the status quo. In fact, that's the same disruptive formula that Circuit City followed to create CarMax in 1993.

Seeking diversified opportunities outside its core business, executives at Circuit City were attracted to the vulnerable elements of the five forces model in the used-car market. At the time, that market had no dominant leaders; it was made up of many small players, all following the same business model. Circuit City launched CarMax to leverage the ease of entry into that market, and to take advantage of the lack of buyer strength and confidence in existing players, the abundance of supply, and the long history of an unchallenged business model. Your idea may not have the same opportunities before it that Circuit City enjoyed with its launch of CarMax, but familiarizing yourself with the model as it applies to the industry you'll be entering gives you a powerful knowledge base from which to begin planning your strategy.

Passing through the Gate

This is the last gate you'll pass through in the Idea phase of your entrepreneurial journey. In reaching this gate, you've learned what it means to be an entrepreneur in the way you think, innovate, and look at the world. You've learned how to master risk by recognizing the walls of fear and doubt that surround you, and by understanding how to limit the strength of your Risk Box, rather than letting it limit your effectiveness as an entrepreneur. The Entrepreneurial Exercises you've worked through in this chapter will help prepare you for the challenges of managing risk and laying the strong foundation of information and preparation on which you'll form your new organization.

In Phase II, Startup, you'll begin the actual work of bringing your idea to life. Emotion and the passion to create have powered you through this phase. You'll need all of that energy, in addition to commitment, determination, and physical and emotional stamina, to complete the demanding tasks that lie ahead. But the ideas, techniques, and exercises you've gained and practiced in becoming an entrepreneur will help keep you on track as you continue your journey.

PHASE II

Startup

As you reach the end of the Idea phase of your entrepreneurial journey, you will have already accomplished some major goals: your E-Formula looks good; you have an innovative, compelling idea, and you are ready to pour all of your desire, effort, and abilities into launching it; your situation is right, and you are ready to seize the opportunity before you; you've moved past your fear of failure and scaled the walls of your Risk Box. Now, you're ready to begin the next leg of your journey, the Startup phase.

Get ready, because this will be one of the greatest periods you'll experience while owning your business—far better even than hitting your first-million-in-sales mark. In the Startup phase, you turn your attention away from the fears that may have held you back in the past in order to focus all of your energy and attention on following your passion in pursuit of what you want in life. Whether your venture succeeds or fails, you're already a winner; you went for it, and that in itself is a tremendous life accomplishment that few experience. How cool is that?

For all of its glory, the Startup phase is also the most demanding of the entire entrepreneurial experience. In the months ahead, you'll take on several critically important tasks, and both you and your new business will pass through a series of defining moments as your idea evolves into a functioning business. Your first job is to position your startup for success, by preparing to avoid the common pitfalls that so often trap first-time entrepreneurs. Next comes the detailed planning; in this stage, you'll be creating a mission statement, writing a business plan, generating leads, and refining your business processes as you gear up for the long haul of running your new operation.

As part of this preparation, you'll have to address what is perhaps the most important, and frequently overlooked, aspect of long-range planning for the entrepreneur, your exit strategy. As you'll learn in this part of the book, planning how you'll *leave* your new business or venture is as important as planning how you'll get it up and running. Without a clear idea of your ultimate destination in this journey, you run the risk of becoming sidetracked—or maybe even hopelessly lost. The Startup phase also involves finding the funding you'll need to launch and sustain your entrepreneurial endeavor, and choosing the partners, advisors, and other human resources who will help you in your work.

As I told you at this book's opening, one of the things I really enjoy in life and that I hold a personal passion for is the outdoors and nature. I am especially fascinated with the behavior of sea turtles. I mention them here because, in many ways, their determination to survive reminds me of the entrepreneurial struggle to bring an idea through the Startup phase, despite all odds and obstacles.

Consider the Kemp's Ridley sea turtle, for example, which is known to nest on one single beach in the world. Regardless of what humans or other animals are on the beach at the time, and no matter how far development has encroached upon the shore, these turtles rise up from the sea and move forward, in the darkness of night, to deposit their eggs. The turtles bury up to 200 eggs in one night, in order to get them under cover before predators discover their location. Those eggs that escape predators' attention incubate under the sand for 45–70 days. Then, the newly hatched turtles spend several days digging their way to the surface. Most emerge at night (again, an instinctive timing to avoid predators), then struggle to make their way across the beach, enter the ocean, and feverishly swim for an estimated 24–48 hours to move into safer waters. About 10 percent of the original egg cache will survive through this stage, and go on to grow into mature animals, measuring four to six feet in length and weighing almost 200 pounds. At that point, their survival rate improves dramatically.

Both turtles and entrepreneurs have to be tough in order to make it to maturity. Entrepreneurs who hatch new business ventures follow a grueling journey as they struggle to survive. Many "predators" can take down an entrepreneurial idea. Whether due to a lack of funding, resources, confidence, or any other number of factors, a high percentage of businesses don't make it through year five. Even though the reasons vary greatly, the odds against a new business reaching safe waters are daunting. But like the sea turtle, given the right balance of determination, skill, planning, effort, and good fortune, the strongest entrepreneurs will make it through the treacherous waters of their early days and on to safer shores. In these chapters, you'll find the tools and advice you need to guide your own fledgling business through the Startup phase of your entrepreneurial journey, with its positioning, planning, and resource management challenges, so you can take it successfully on to become a mature and thriving organization.

CHAPTER FIVE

Positioning Your Startup for Success

PEOPLE ALWAYS ASK ME HOW I did it—how did I start my company? It's easy for me to explain how I generated my initial idea and how I made my successful exit from the business, but all of the details in between can be too involved for casual conversation. No one at a cocktail party wants to spend the evening listening to me outline the details of my business Startup phase. But with a captive audience (that's you), I'm ready to revisit each step of that experience. And the first of these was really more of a sidestep, a detour designed to avoid the pitfalls that slow—and often derail completely—new entrepreneurial enterprises.

My first task involved gathering information and putting ideas into my virtual parking lot. I needed to find information that would help me flesh out my entrepreneurial idea and give me some insights into the nuances of my marketplace. I had a head start, in some ways, because I was a replicative entrepreneur. The services I planned to offer with my new business were based on those of my (then) current employer, Educational Resources, but targeted toward the untapped market of higher education.

I knew this new market would be different from that of K–12, but I had no idea to what degree. Sure, I had done all of the research and planning necessary to take Educational Resources into this market, but now it was going to be my dime on the line. I reached out to publishers and distributors who could provide details on higher education customers and what products they bought. I struggled to find publications focused on technology and higher education and found little aside from newsletters put out by a technology-focused higher education think tank named EduCause, which would ultimately yield substantial insights.

In other words, I set out to explore every avenue that might help my new business to succeed and every misstep that could doom it to failure. I had good reasons to fear failure, and the first among these centered on the common assumption that 90 percent of all new ventures fail. If you're entering the Startup phase of your own entrepreneurial experience, you'll have to prepare to beat these awful statistical odds, just as I did. But first you should know the truth behind these statistics. Understanding why new businesses fail is critical to any new entrepreneur. As you prepare to define your own entrepreneurial idea through a mission statement, a business plan, staffing, and so on, you need to be fully aware of the challenges you'll face in Startup. When you understand the types of problems that can swallow new businesses whole, you don't have to be afraid of falling into them. Instead, you can use this information to navigate around the potholes and pitfalls that lie ahead.

Seeing through the Statistical Gloom

Depending on what you read, the percentage of new business failures is high—very high. An online search will turn up claims that somewhere between 80 and 90 percent of all ventures fail in their first 10 years.[1] That percentage is staggering, but it grows even higher for specific businesses, such as restaurants; I've seen them pegged at a 90 to 95 percent failure rate within their first few years. With those odds, it's a wonder that *anyone* would open a new business.

Bankruptcy is, perhaps, the ultimate badge of business failure. In 2005, there was an average of 169,903 bankruptcy filings *per month* in the United States, which had seen substantial year-over-year percentage growth. In 2006, the average dropped dramatically, but that undoubtedly was the result, in part, of the Bankruptcy Abuse Prevention and Consumer Protection Act of 2005 that made it harder to declare bankruptcy.[2] While business failures aren't the source of all bankruptcies, without question, bankruptcy plays a primary role in the entrepreneurial journey—just as predators play a role in the baby sea turtle's mad scramble across the sand. Fear of bankruptcy prevents many entrepreneurs from ever starting down the path, and drives others to feverishly throw every ounce of their resources into succeeding.

We all have to be concerned about these statistics, because entrepreneurs aren't the only ones who lose when their new business goes under. Consider, for example, the U.S. Small Business Administration's claim that our nation's small businesses employ about half of all private sector employees and represent almost 45 percent of the nation's payrolls. Small businesses created between 60 and 80 percent of the total "net new jobs" over the last ten years, so, in the United States, employment growth rates since 2001 would actually be negative without the hiring from new startups and small businesses. We don't want these businesses to fail! But before you slam this book shut in frustration or fear, let's peel back the layers of our common mythology about business failure to find what truth lies within it.

First, the numbers we typically see don't necessarily reflect all the data and circumstances surrounding business failures. In other words, sometimes business closings represent success, not failure. Successful money-making businesses close every year, and yet they are incorporated into these "failure" statistics. By these definitions, my own story would be deemed a failure, but I can tell you that when I sold my idea to a new owner and dismantled my business, the closing was by no means a failure. In fact, as you will learn in later chapters, that closing was a nearly perfect realization of my exit plan. My outcome was unusual, but not unique.

Years of labor studies of small businesses by author David Birch dissected the reasons for business closures, in an effort to learn more about those pessimistically high failure rates cited by the U.S. Bureau of the Census. After examining and categorizing all available data on the causes of business closings, Birch determined that, in fact, 85 percent of businesses included in the surveys survived their first year, 70 percent the second, and 62 percent the third. And once a business hit its fifth year, the odds of its survival went up substantially.

Advanced study into the rate of restaurant failures gives us a far more encouraging look at that industry, too. From Ohio State University, Professor H.G. Parsa conducted a study of Columbus, Ohio, area restaurants from 1996 to 1999. He found that the failure rate of the restaurants included in his study closely mimicked that of traditional business, as reported by sources such as Birch, with 26 percent of new restaurants closing in their first year, 19 percent in their second, and 14 percent in their third. And, as in Birch's findings, Parsa's study found that the survival rate increased greatly for restaurants after their fifth year in business.[3]

Statistics do a poor job of differentiating the reasons why a business no longer exists; they simply record its closure. Many businesses that get lumped into the failure bucket have, like mine, been sold. Sure, some businesses get sold when they fall upon duress or other factors that necessitate the owner to bail, but many others sell at a profit and provide newfound wealth for the founder. Other businesses have a "statistical failure" when the owner decides to incorporate or change to a different type of incorporation, thus killing one business by name or tax identification and generating life into a new company.

Entrepreneurs are a wily bunch, and some just switch gears and decide to do something new. They may close or transfer ownership of a perfectly good business simply to explore new interests. They may have entered a business late in life and have now reached retirement. Personal circumstances such as divorce, health, death, or other life-altering events take place that contribute to the closure of a business, but have nothing to do with the failure of the entrepreneur or the entrepreneurial idea. So, yes, statistics show that sustaining a business for the long term is challenging, but those statistics aren't as daunting as some popular reports would suggest.

Navigating around the Top Four Startup Pitfalls

I did some of my own investigation into the entrenched myth that says nine out of ten businesses will fail within a relatively short life span. As a result, I discovered that many business "failures" are, as we've just seen, simply the result of the business—and the business owner—evolving over time. Of those closings that actually *do* count as failures, I determined that the reasons for most come from just a few categories. The better you understand these common pitfalls, the better able you'll be to dodge them in your own business startup. Let's map them out.

Startup Pitfall #1: Inadequate Education and Training

A great deal of study has gone into the correlation between years of accomplished education and the rate of startup success. It may not surprise you to learn that education really does make a difference in predicting whether an entrepreneur is likely to succeed in a new business venture. A study conducted by Mohammad Al-Zubeidi, for example, in the course of completing his doctoral dissertation at the University of North Texas, found a statistical link between the success of businesses and the owners' college education.[4]

In his study, Al-Zubeidi found that business founders with minimal education whose business had failed tended to have an "inability to recognize their own strengths and weaknesses and act accordingly." He also noted that "incompetence, mismanagement and lack of experienced employees," the curses of any small new business, can be directly correlated to insufficient education.

Many first-time entrepreneurs make the management mistake of hiring people they know or like instead of hiring the well-trained and educated talent they need. Regardless of the type of business you have, there will always be a line of friends and relatives waiting for employment. Avoid the easy path, and make your hiring decisions based on education, ability, training, and talent. That can be a difficult decision to make, but if you give in to sentiment and staff your startup with unqualified workers, you're crippling its chances for success. And if you think it's difficult to refuse a friend or family member a job, try firing one of them who has proven to be disastrous to your fragile new operation.

In today's complex global marketplace, a good education is critical in preparing you and your team to succeed. Advanced education and training enable you to be more adaptable to changing conditions and, therefore, better able to see and leverage new opportunities as they arise; to predict and outpace your competitors' advances; and to foresee and avoid developing problems. In other words, an advanced education prepares you to make better decisions and manage your business more effectively. The advice here is clear: get the education and training you need to make your business succeed, and pay attention to the education and skills of the partners and other human resources you bring into your new venture. Don't let a lack of formal or on-the-job education drag your startup into failure.

Startup Pitfall #2: Poor Preparation and Planning

Education and training aren't the only types of preparation required to launch and sustain a successful business. Poor planning can doom even the most promising entrepreneurial venture. One of the most common planning deficiencies among new entrepreneurs is inadequate (or even nonexistent) goal setting. Many failed businesses have just one goal: opening for business. Without a vision of how the business should operate, the entrepreneur is on a one-way road to irrelevance. Entrepreneurs who fail to set revenue, profit, and operational goals have no milestones to help guide their progress throughout the life of the company. Here is a message you cannot afford to forget: planning for any new business or operation must include some visualization of the venture's endgame on all levels. What will marketing, accounting, and customer service look like on day one? In six months? One year? Five years?

In your rush to bring your brilliant idea to life, don't make the mistake of shortchanging the planning process. Inadequate planning accounts for plenty of business failures. At a minimum, you can count on wasting money and other resources in costly attempts to get a poorly planned business on track. I know, I know; we are an impatient people who want immediate results. But if you want your entrepreneurial idea to survive and thrive, you can't afford to dupe yourself into believing your enthusiasm alone is going to provide enough momentum to keep it going for any length of time.

Don't mistake my message here; I don't mean to contradict my earlier advice about pressing forward even though all of your ducks aren't lined up in a neat row. A business can survive if less critical aspects of the operation aren't completely ironed out. When I started my business, for example, I knew we would be ordering product from distributors and shipping product to customers. I didn't take time to document the processes required for those tasks, because I knew I would work out those details later. As Roy Ash, cofounder of Litton Industries, has said, "an entrepreneur tends to bite off a little more than he can chew, hoping he'll quickly learn how to chew it." You need to be able to make solid decisions in real time, in order to succeed as an entrepreneur, and that includes filling in any blanks that might have been neglected in some of the finer details of your startup.

But mission-critical and core-competency aspects of your operation need to be as solid as possible, right from the beginning. Founders who prepare poorly may not establish the proper legal structure for their business, for example. That can be a truly disastrous planning oversight that is highly likely to result in a business failure. Establishing as a sole proprietorship, as most small businesses do because it is easy and inexpensive, shares the business's legal exposure to debt and liability with the individual founder. That means your personal property and income are on the line, right up there with your business assets, should the business go under. Incorporating a business, on the other hand, establishes the business and the founder as separate legal entities.

Each corporate structure has its own pros and cons, so you should seek professional guidance in making these decisions. In chapter 6, you'll learn more about these and other types of planning and preparation activities you need to cover in your startup process. As much as you may want to skip ahead to the "real" work, you can't afford to fall into the fatal trap of poor planning that stops so many new entrepreneurs from succeeding.

Startup Pitfall #3: Inadequate Management Skills

Poor financial and operational management have been the death of businesses, big and small, throughout history. The types of money problems entrepreneurs encounter are so numerous I could write an entire book just on that topic, so let me begin talking about the pitfalls of bad management by addressing this gaping trap into which so many entrepreneurial startups have stumbled.

Some of the best examples of poor—no, dreadful—financial governance occurred during the dot-com era of the 1990s. In those days, you weren't a sophisticated entrepreneur unless you could boast the biggest cash burn rate, with the least amount of earnings. Honestly, that's what founders talked about with pride—the rate at which they were burning through their startup capital. Investors shoved money down the throat of these typically inexperienced entrepreneurs, novices who had no clue they were merely part of a numbers game run by the venture capital firms that controlled them. And that game was pretty simple: throw a bunch of money at ten prospective companies, and hope that one of them hits a home run that brings in a payoff far greater than the total amount of money "invested" in all ten candidates. If the other nine weren't producing, they lost their funding and died on the vine.

I'm not faulting the venture capitalists in this simplified scenario. By the very nature of their business, they take calculated risks. Many of the business founders who received venture capital money spent it on image instead of focusing their resources on their customers and their product. Elaborate office furniture, inflated head count, and well-stocked kitchens were common amenities for dot-com entrepreneurs. The initial web development firm for my company fit this profile to a tee. It was out of business in a year—never showing a profit for the untold sum that was poured into it. The company almost certainly would still be around today if it hadn't burdened itself with nonessential, up-front expenses that rapidly eroded its equity and killed any chances it had of ever going into the black. To quote the title of an article written by Simon London for the *Financial Times*, "A surplus of cash invariably leads to a shortage of sense."

Taking on debt to establish a business is another way to get your entrepreneurial idea off the ground or to the next level, but you have to be extremely conservative in projecting your future cash flow to determine just how much debt you can take on. When a venture capitalist throws money at you, that investor is taking ownership in the company. When you borrow money from the bank, that bank is taking claim to your business, and maybe your personal, assets. Not properly factoring in expenses or being overly optimistic in your future sales prospects leaves you vulnerable to failure. Covering your debt obligations can be a very tricky business, and rushing forward with unrealistically favorable projections can spell disaster for your startup. Have patience and be willing to grow into your business; that experience truly is half of the fun and reward of bringing your idea to life. As a society, we may want what we want now, but when it comes to starting a business, patience must prevail.

THE BENEFITS OF BOOTSTRAPPING

Jerry R. Mitchell, president of the Midwest Entrepreneurs' Forum and advisory board member of DePaul University's Coleman Entrepreneurship Center, regularly addresses the virtues of bootstrapping to start a business. In his *Bootstrapping* newsletter, Mitchell challenges the prevailing wisdom that in order to launch a successful high-tech business you need to secure substantial funding and bring in lots of high-powered talent. Instead, Mitchell encourages entrepreneurs to provide the majority of resources and wear multiple hats, as necessary, to get their new enterprise off the ground and running. Mitchell says, "Bootstrapping ensures that you build your business on a legitimate, real-world value proposition. When you're bootstrapping, you're forced to deal with customers and to fulfill their needs from day one."[5] External funding can distract the entrepreneur from the real point of focus (the customer) and the real job of entrepreneurship (selling).

Nothing drives entrepreneurial urgency more than time and the need to make money. Funding, especially generous funding, reduces that urgency and can lull you into thinking that you don't need to get out and sell—and, for that matter, to develop a selling process. As an entrepreneur, selling is one of your most important and ongoing opportunities to establish and improve your operation. Many of your most important lessons about improving products, delivering services, and running the business will come to you through the selling process. The bootstrapper has to start selling immediately, in order to get to market quickly. You'll gain a great advantage with your focus and attention on making your new operation a success, delivering the best possible product, and making sure that you exceed your customers' expectations. That's how you survive and succeed as an entrepreneur.

Lack of a fat bank account spurs creativity in all aspects of the business and, as Mitchell says, "forces unconventional thinking." When problems need to be solved, and you don't have the option of writing a check to make them go away, those issues can spur creative thinking and drive out-of-the-box solutions that stretch your problem-solving capabilities and strengthen your understanding of your business. In that sense, bootstrapping offers advantages to the entrepreneur that aren't available to a more well-financed counterpart. Managing through tight financial times puts your critical thinking skills on the front line and requires you to constantly assess all aspects of the business. Hiring other people to solve problems and fill roles can really dilute your intimacy with your product, company, and customer—and it can kill much of the incentive for innovation that drives truly successful organizations. Most importantly, bootstrapping develops the greatest ownership skill of all—managing your organization's resources and respecting the value of money.

I went to a seminar where the keynote speaker discussed his boom-to-bust venture capital startup story. What struck me was that he didn't sound like an entrepreneur; he sounded like a manager or a corporate MBA. He didn't relate any of the struggles and tribulations of startup because he never experienced them from his vantage point behind a protective layer of cash. He did remorsefully acknowledge his disregard for cash management by citing how his fledgling company would call on $300-an-hour network technicians, knowing that they were absurdly overpriced, simply because they were convenient. He focused the financial metrics of his company on its estimated (and inflated) valuation, which is rather meaningless to a startup. Who cares what the company is worth at this point, unless you intend to sell it today?

That speaker made the same management mistake made by many entrepreneurs; he focused the organization's finances and concerns on internal issues, rather than on the organization's products and services, its customers, and its marketplace. The vision or purpose of your business needs to be, as author Michael Gerber has said, impersonal.[6] A personal purpose, one that serves you and your desires, is destined to fail. The business has to address your customer's needs and desires foremost. If you go into business to make a bunch of money, have flexible hours, and enjoy all the perks of being "the boss," then you aren't really an entrepreneur. And you certainly aren't a skillful organizational manager.

Don't misunderstand me: I'm not advocating that you try to launch your startup with too little funding or "on the cheap." In fact, entering a startup that you don't have the funds to support (and sustain) is probably a more certain road to failure than starting out laden with debt or with compromised ownership. This issue goes back to planning and preparation. Launching a business only to run out of cash with no reserves or sources to tap for bridge financing simply reflects poor planning, improper preparation, and inadequate forecasting. Insufficient funding can quickly kill a company that could otherwise grow to become sustainable.

Finally, don't allow greed to motivate you into a startup. A keen desire for fast cash isn't part of the E-Formula; money is a result of the E-Formula executed properly. Virtually all of the successful entrepreneurs I've known or studied were led into their business as a result of an innovative idea that intersected with the right situation and the right opportunity. The "get rich quick" plans either never launch or close in a very short time frame. Your business needs a mission and purpose, but if they're merely restatements of your desire to make money, you'll find little room for customers in your value proposition.

Failing to share your success when the company is doing well is just another form of greed, and one that can hamstring growth. Down the road, you may need to offer key employees extra incentive in order to keep them working to grow the business to its next level or eventual exit strategy. Founders can get stingy with retained earnings and equity. I heard Silicon Valley serial entrepreneur Jerry Kaplan say, "Don't hoard the equity," because doing so creates a fundamental mistake in growing your startup. According to Kaplan, "Equity is like shit. If you pile it up, it just smells bad. If you spread it around, lots of wonderful things grow."

Fundamentally, running a business requires exceptional skills involving management of all aspects of the enterprise. Researchers blame most startup failures on the founders' "managerial incompetence." Embedded into mismanagement comes poor decision making and an inability to lead. As you prepare for the Startup phase, be sure you've assessed your own management abilities and identified any weaknesses that might jeopardize your success. Then, you can get the training or advice you need to improve those weaknesses or find appropriate talent to offset them.

Startup Pitfall #4: Imbalances in Personal and Professional Priorities

Most of us acknowledge that family should come first on our list of personal priorities. As an entrepreneur, however, you often may have no choice but to place the needs of your business first, at least in its earliest days. This is the reality of the Startup phase. Launching your business is going to take a significant time commitment, and it will pull you away from family and friends—all the more reason to pursue an entrepreneurial idea that you love, instead of just chasing after money. You and those you love must understand that this initial all-in commitment of time and attention will be temporary, and won't (indeed, should not) last through the duration of the business. The most successful entrepreneurs never lose sight of their personal priorities and commitments.

Your absence during Startup can and will be hard on you, and on your family and friends. Many entrepreneurs become fully immersed in the startup process and, as a result, neglect other aspects of their lives. Even when that level of focus is essential, you need to remain aware of its costs and avoid indulging in it for too long. It's easy to develop a self-centered mindset that says, "Everyone just needs to understand the importance of what I'm doing." That attitude can cause discord at home, which can complicate an already stressful time.

The entrepreneur who has yet to activate is struggling to emerge. Those living with that person also have to endure the struggle, and—honestly—it can drive them absolutely nuts. The would-be entrepreneur is always coming up with ideas, then dismissing them, and then complaining about the frustration involved in the whole process. Living with a new entrepreneur isn't any better. I would compare it to living with a madman (or madwoman). The new entrepreneur will experience mood swings, bursts of enlightenment, and sudden lows, often accompanied by crazy talk of far-fetched ideas and late-night sessions spent scribbling down yet another "master plan." You should almost prescreen a spouse for these entrepreneurial desires, so you can fully understand what you might be in for. I was blessed to have a very supportive and understanding spouse, in-laws, parents, and children who seemed to know that life couldn't be any other way for (or with) me.

Your family will be continually tested as you dedicate yourself to your entrepreneurial startup, and its patience will continue to be tested even as your business matures. Ideally, your family will adapt to your life as an entrepreneur, and your business will almost become a part of the family. In fact, you may draft your family members into some form of support, and they'll quickly come to realize that the business is their sustaining economic structure. When that happens, everyone in the family develops a sense of responsibility toward the business.

But you can't count on all of your friends and family immediately accepting your entrepreneurial preoccupation. With such a high rate of divorce in our country, you need to fully acknowledge and be aware of the impact your entrepreneurial decision will have on those you love the most, and understand that life is not all about you. To avoid adding the stress of decaying personal relationships to the pressures you'll encounter during Startup, you need to incorporate your personal life into your business plan. Here are three ways you can do that:

1. **Get their buy-in and support.** Discuss your business plans and anticipated time commitments with your family and/or closest friends. Let them know why you are doing this, and what it means for you and your family. Explain what sacrifices you (and they) may need to make, and why you think those sacrifices are worthwhile. Give an estimate of when you think you'll be able to establish a more favorable work/life balance. Talk about conflicts that might develop and how you all might deal with them; discuss hypothetical situations, such as missing or being late for events, working late, passing up on vacations or outings, and so on. Ask your family and others with whom you have a personal commitment if they agree to endure the sacrifices of this period, or have alternative suggestions.

2. **Set personal life goals and a time table.** Establish a goal and
    related time table for when you will restore work/life balance, and
    describe what that balance should look like. Perhaps it is a gradual
    increase in nonwork activities, or maybe bringing certain activi-
    ties back on line faster than others. Your vision of restored balance
    may be entirely different from your loved ones'. Eliminate sur-
    prises and disappointment by discussing your goals and estimated
    time frames before you get too far down the startup trail. Keep in
    mind that your personal life goals are important for you, too. You
    should have a life outside of work, and a new business can become
    all too encompassing, swallowing the person you used to be. Don't
    entirely abandon your hobbies, interests, and activities, even
    during Startup. Nonwork-related interests and activities help keep
    you well, which, in return, contributes to the health of your enter-
    prise. Every successful business needs a founder who is mentally
    and physically prepared to face the challenges of the endeavor.

3. **Incorporate your personal life goals into the written business
    plan.** Your personal life is intertwined with your business life, and
    that intermingling should be reflected in your goals. Develop a
    "personal business plan" to parallel your formal business plan, to
    help you keep both aspects of your life in focus. A personal busi-
    ness plan encompasses the personal goals and targets that you
    have outlined—activities such as coaching a child's sports team,
    involvement in the community, volunteering, running a mara-
    thon, vacation time, personal growth and development, taking an
    art class, family succession plans, or other personal milestones.
    The goals and time frame you establish to rebalance your work
    and personal life need to be written down in your personal busi-
    ness plan and interlaced with the goals and timelines of your regu-
    lar business plan.

Entrepreneurs are fiercely independent, a characteristic that allows them
to go off on their own and take the risks associated with starting a business. But taking on those risks all on your own can inadvertently establish
barriers that prevent those you care about most from participating in your
world, where they could be helping to alleviate the strain you'll be under
as an entrepreneur. That kind of alienation creates unnecessary stress that
trips up many new entrepreneurs as they launch their initiatives. Active
family engagement in the endeavor takes a tremendous amount of pressure

off of the entrepreneur, spreads understanding, deepens commitment, and creates a sense of unique family pride.

Still Want to Do It? I Thought So

The statistics may scare some off the entrepreneurial trail, but once all of the E-Formula ingredients are aligned, most are still ready to jump in the pool. The E-Formula is what compels you to start your business. The only real barrier preventing your activation is fear. Fear no longer becomes a dominant topic during the Running phase of the business because in most cases the fear is gone or greatly subdued. Confidence conquers fear once you initiate Startup.

In my own case, I came to realize that if I were never to have the experience of starting my own business, I would have robbed myself of an important part of what I wanted out of life. Writer Fulton Oursler eloquently states this thought in his book *The Greatest Book Ever Written: The Old Testament Story*: "Many of us crucify ourselves between two thieves—regret for the past and fear of the future."[7] Avoiding the pitfalls that threaten the success of a new startup isn't an easy task. But for me, it was much easier than living with the regret of never attempting the entrepreneurial journey. I could always recover from even the most damaging bankruptcy, but I'm not sure I could have ever been at peace with myself if I failed to pursue my dream.

As you move forward with your business launch, you'll find that most of your fears are no more than shallow barriers, a façade of sorts, held up by flimsy props, rather than the daunting fortress you might have anticipated. We build up in our minds the cataclysmic outcomes of failed startup attempts and sadly attribute very little to the cost of not attempting. As you've seen in this chapter, well-planned and managed risk taking gives a business startup a much lower price than has been popularly advertised. The pitfalls are very real, but research, education, training, financial and organizational preparation, and planning for both professional and personal goals are strong navigational tools for making your way through the Startup phase of your entrepreneurial journey.

My own Startup phase required lots of planning. After the lengthy period of research I described at the opening of this chapter, I had to get my business plan under my belt. My intention from the beginning was to be the biggest provider of software to the higher education market. As I mentioned earlier, I planned to take a replicative approach; just as we did at Educational Resources, I wanted to produce a quality catalog manned by a skilled inside sales force. With that goal in mind, I had to create a business plan that would give my company a strong presence, out of the gate, and that included lining up my finances and bringing on essential staff. With that, I knew I could quickly establish a customer perception that I was well beyond startup and running a successful business. I was confident enough to move forward with my idea, but I hadn't totally eliminated my fear of failure. Instead, I used that fear to fuel my effort.

My Startup also required a lot of work. Yours will, too. In the next few chapters of this book, I'll walk you through the planning and preparation activities that you'll need to accomplish in your own Startup phase. With that information, and the ideas you've gained in this chapter, you'll be well positioned to avoid the pitfalls, beat the odds, and move successfully onward.

CHAPTER SIX

Planning for Success

THE STARTUP PHASE IS ALL about launching your business, something you may have been itching to do since the first glimmer of your great idea began to take shape. Before your launch can occur, however, you have to work through the critical step of planning. Planning represents the first gate that both you and your business will move through in the Startup phase of your entrepreneurial journey.

In the last chapter, we talked about the variety of planning and preparation tasks you need to perform in this stage, including beefing up your training, education, and management skills, preparing yourself for the personal and professional sacrifices you'll be making, and getting the buy-in and support of those closest to you. At the top of your list of essential planning activities, however, is writing a business plan.

Your business plan is your blueprint for building a successful business. In pulling that plan together, you create a clear and comprehensive picture of what your business will be, how it will operate, what markets it will play in, what early, midterm, and exit goals will drive it, and how it will be funded. Focusing on planning, when the only thing you want to do is get your business up and running, takes a lot of patience. That makes the planning stage one of the most difficult stretches of your entrepreneurial journey; it's also one of the most critical. As you saw in the last chapter, without proper planning, you can expect your venture to run up against a number of obstacles, including failure. I'm not going to walk you through the detailed steps of writing a formal business plan; there are hundreds—no, thousands—of sources out there to guide you through that process. Instead, in this chapter, we're going to look closely at the details of the entire planning process and the activities you'll need to accomplish in order to create and execute your business plan.

You can make the planning process easier and more successful by using your best organizational skills and a few basic planning tools. For example, I began with a simple software package that led me through the process of writing a formal business plan. Although I was impatient to hang an OPEN sign on the door, I also was smart enough to know that I had to go through this exercise if I wanted to have a fighting chance of turning my idea into a successful operation. The software package I used helped make the process more bearable—and effective. Writing the business plan forced me to think about all aspects of the business before I invested a dime. It gave me a road map, along with every critical milestone I would have to meet in order to make this thing happen. The plan helped convert my idea into fully functional business processes so I could see, for example, how lead-generation efforts would turn into sales. Later in this chapter, you'll learn about other planning tools and techniques that can help you get more benefit from your work during the planning stage. Find an online resource, software package, or other tool to help you write your business plan, but don't neglect this important element of your planning and preparation activities.

Another critical part of your planning process is the search for funding, and your business plan will play a major role in that task. You'll need a business plan in order to obtain funding, whether it is as simple as a bank loan or as elaborate as venture capital or private equity. Most entrepreneurs start their businesses with borrowed money, and just about any reputable source that loans you money will require that you have a complete and thorough business plan. The type of funding you seek will dictate the format of your business plan, as each funding source uses its own template for determining eligibility. Even if your "bank" of choice is family and friends, have your business plan together before you broach the subject of a loan. Think about it: you don't want to ask your family and friends to sink money into your entrepreneurial effort if you can't show them a strong, well-thought-out business plan charting the way toward your venture's success.

Your business plan will communicate your understanding of the business to any investor or lender, and it will help establish the mental buy-in and commitment of these partners. The more your key partners believe in your vision and idea, the more committed they will be, and the less you will have to answer to them through every step of your progress through Startup. Further, should the venture not succeed, there is less chance of hard feelings, broken relationships, or future credit problems if everyone who invests in your startup is equally committed to and supportive of the concept. We talk in detail about funding your startup in the next chapter of this book, but for now, just be aware that the strength of your business plan will play a major role in securing the funding you need during the Startup phase.

THE PLAIN TRUTH ABOUT SHARED SACRIFICES

You have to assume the worst when starting a business, and part of that assumption must be that your business startup might fail. You'll need to consider the ramifications for family and friends, whether they are involved in the business through money, through labor, or simply as a support line. When you go through the process of starting a business, all those around you—particularly your spouse and children—go through it as well, whether they want to or not. Your time will represent your largest contribution to the Startup phase. Your planning needs to take that into consideration, along with everything else you can expect to sacrifice in the process of getting your business on its feet.

In my planning process, I committed myself to at least a solid year of 14- to 16-hour days, six or seven days a week, and no vacations. I didn't expect my hours to return to normal until year three, because I was going to bootstrap my business myself, with no outside funding. I had to carefully weigh what this would cost my relationships. It meant I would spend less time with my wife and my brand-new daughter. Further, it would cut into time with my parents, brother, friends, neighbors, and in-laws. I deeply treasure all of these relationships, so this sacrifice didn't sit lightly with me.

I understood that everything had to come second to the business—but only for a while. You need to understand that as well. Your all-in, second-to-none commitment to your business cannot stretch on indefinitely. At some point, the demands of your business have to level off so you can balance your work and personal commitments. If your plan doesn't accommodate this eventual reduction in your professional commitments, both your personal relationships and the success of your business are in jeopardy. Running a business is difficult under the best of circumstances, but it's nearly impossible while having personal relationships crumble around you. Shared sacrifice can help strengthen relationships, but not when it cuts too deeply. Make sure you plan for easing the pain of that sacrifice, before it does permanent damage.

Launches always require extra effort. When you watch a goose take off in flight, notice that all of the hard work is at the beginning as the bird tries to gain momentum. Its long neck is strained forward, and its wings and legs pump to lift the bird's large torso into the air. Once the goose is in flight, its progress looks effortless. Much is the same for the entrepreneur starting a business. All of the hard work and effort is needed in the beginning just to get the enterprise off the ground. Once the processes of the business are working, the entrepreneur can begin to ease up and focus on guiding the company toward its destination.

Taking a Deep Breath before You Begin

While "winging it" might be a great way to get around Europe with a backpack, it's not so great an approach to creating a business plan. The temptation to just walk away from the planning table and open for business is tremendous, but resist—resist! I don't know the statistics on the percentage of businesses that succeed without a strong business plan, but I'm pretty sure it's right up there with the Chicago Cubs' percentage of World Series wins. The important thing for you to remember as you prepare the formal planning process is that you can't get bogged down in an ongoing search for perfection in every stage of the Startup phase. Actively seek out the help you need, do the best you can, and keep moving.

Bear in mind that your business plan does not have to be a static document. You can begin by just throwing all of your thoughts and research into the main categories of the plan (Marketing, Sales, Finance, and so on). Don't worry about editing or fine-tuning the grammar; just get your information and ideas collected and categorized. This will help you immediately identify the areas where you need more preparation. When you reach this point, the Entrepreneurial Exercises you learned about in chapter 4 become really valuable.

Entrepreneurs are a bit like men not pulling over to ask for directions when lost; they always like to feel that they can work through their problems on their own. Don't waste time with that kind of DIY stubbornness. In any phase of a business, and especially during the planning stage, you should actively seek advice from everyone who will listen. It is ideal if you can establish mentors and other people who will take an active role in your development and provide guidance and direction. People who have been through a startup themselves can be great sources of relevant advice, knowledge, and experience. Even if you don't find the perfect mentor, you should be able to find people with whom you can bounce around questions and ideas.

As you study your business plan, you will find areas that require expert knowledge. You may have legal, banking, real estate, or lease questions, for example. If your circle of friends and advisors doesn't include people that you can tap into for advice on these topics, go out and find them. Use your networking skills to find people who know people that you can reach out to. Make sure everyone in your circle knows that you need help with XYZ; inevitably, someone will know someone to refer you to for information. And thanks to the advent of social networking tools, your six degrees of separation will be a lot easier to navigate than they would have been a few years ago.

Get to know your local banker early on. You may be asking for money one day! Plus, bankers know every business person in their region. Odds are if you are seeking a specific talent, your banker can introduce the right match—and will be happy to do so. Most bankers are in the relationship business. Since you're starting a business, you are now in the relationship business too. Just remember to pay it back and help the next budding entrepreneur when you get on your feet.

Finally, remember that the business-planning stage isn't about polishing every facet of your idea to perfection. In fact, that's probably not possible. In the Startup phase, you can expect to be understaffed, underfunded, and short on time. When you're wearing all of the hats, you can't expect them all to fit perfectly, and that's okay. I'm not encouraging you to produce a shoddy product or service—very much the opposite. Your product or service is the reflection of the company you're founding, and so it should be your best work. But some of the ancillary tasks and processes and equipment that you need to get your company completely up to speed can wait. You almost have to adopt a "get by" mentality in the beginning, just to keep moving forward.

I'm speaking to the perfectionist in you, because I'm one myself. When it comes to my business, I want every facet of it to be rock solid. However, I'm also a realist. If I spent too much of my time in the Startup phase on the minor details and nuances of the business, I would never have gotten my product on the shelves. You can expect to walk a fine line, at times, in choosing what must be taken care of now versus what can wait until later. As your Startup phase progresses, however, making those choices becomes easier, simply because time in the day runs out or important deadlines approach, and something has to be dropped, sidelined, or put on hold. Your goal is to eventually circle back, clean things up, and improve on items that have been neglected or patched over with a Band-Aid solution. That's prioritization and continual improvement at the Startup level.

Recognizing up-front this need for balance within the business planning process is critical, especially for the perfectionist. The guy who won't raise the curtain until every piece of the set is perfectly positioned is likely to never see opening night.

Pulling Together the Plan

There are seven components in planning and preparation that directly support your idea, and they are absolutely critical in every aspect of your business's future success. You can consider each of these elements as a planning tool that can make your startup activities more efficient and effective. They include:

1. Your mission statement
2. Your SWOT (strengths, weaknesses, opportunities, and threats)
3. Your written business plan
4. Your goals
5. Your key performance indicators
6. Your startup's GAP analysis
7. Your exit strategy

Although each of these components represents an age-old principle of business planning, they can be easily overlooked by anxious entrepreneurs in the Startup phase. Many sources have written about these planning elements, but I want to take a moment here to look at their most critical aspects, in order to give you a useful road map for your own planning activities. Let's step through them in the order in which you should address them.

1. Mission Statement

Although a mission statement may not seem necessary for launching your business, it is a basic starting point. An effective mission statement must objectively describe your business's purpose and guide its actions. Your mission statement doesn't have to be set in stone; you can refine it as your company grows. It must, however, address how your organization will be responsible to its primary stakeholders, customers, and stockholders. The statement may include products and services your company will offer. It also must define what the company aspires to become, and how it differs from its competition.

A well-crafted mission statement will act as a guiding force as it reminds you, your employees, and your customers why your company exists. The mission statement will be your answer to strategic questions when crafting marketing material, deciding on new markets, and determining where and how to allocate resources. My company's original mission statement was "to become the largest supplier of technology to the higher education market." As the marketplace and other environmental factors shift, your mission statement may need to evolve as well. As my business matured and its organizational focus changed to meet an evolving marketplace, we adapted our mission statement, which then became "to be the most recognized provider of enterprise software to the education market."

Simple questions you must answer when creating your mission statement include:

- What is the purpose of my company?
- What are the goals of my company?
- Why does my company exist?
- What are my customers' pain points, and how does my product or service address them?

If your mission statement answers these questions, it will provide you with the kind of guidance you need as you formulate your organization's strategies and tactics.

2. SWOT (Strengths, Weaknesses, Opportunities, and Threats)

A SWOT analysis is a strategic planning method attributed to the work of Albert Humphrey of Stanford University. You can use this technique to evaluate the strengths and weaknesses of your new venture, as well as the opportunities and threats it faces. Conducting a SWOT analysis is a vital part of your Startup planning cycle, but you also should repeat the analysis throughout the life of your business (at least once a year). A SWOT analysis can evaluate the entire company, or it can focus on a single department, product, or marketing initiative. The goal of the analysis is to get on the table the internal and external factors that are favorable and unfavorable to achieving the business's expected objectives. You will roll the results of your initial SWOT analysis into your business plan.

When conducting this analysis, you'll evaluate the strengths of your management team and experience, technology, intellectual property, brand, niche capabilities, location, funding, relationships, knowledge, and so on. Your evaluation may show that your weaknesses fall within some of those same categories, and you also may uncover talent gaps, lack of supply channel relationships, inadequate credit capacity, geographic limitations, or other organizational shortcomings. Your organization's opportunities will, most likely, include those that first encouraged you to move forward with your entrepreneurial idea, while its threats may result from changes in the marketplace or competitor responses to your organization's successes. An initial and ongoing analysis of these factors will help you in planning and executing every facet of your operation.

3. The Business Plan

The core of your planning efforts is the formal business plan, which encompasses all facets of the business or operation you are about to create. The plan forces you to dissect your dream and lay out its every aspect on paper. Many entrepreneurs, especially those not seeking capital outside of their own self-funding sources, feel they don't need to put the time and effort into a formal plan. Many are too anxious to get started, and claim they're too creative to deal with such a rigorous process, but these would-be entrepreneurs often simply lack the discipline necessary to think through all necessary Startup phase details. You can't afford to be one of those people.

As I noted earlier, the plan is mandatory for investors; the more detailed your plan, the better your chances for securing funding. Some will say a business plan can be a "build as you go" exercise, and I agree that your plan can be tweaked and changed once the business is launched. But you need to build a plan to get the Startup phase rolling.

Every business plan is unique, but any plan should include these elements:

- A general company description and definition of purpose
- An explanation of the problem the business solves and how it offers that solution
- A description of the product or service the business offers
- An explanation of why this is the right time for this business to emerge
- A clear identification of the target market, the size of that market, and the business's plan for reaching it
- An outline of existing competition and (likely) future competition
- The business model you plan to use
- A detailed description of the marketing and sales efforts you'll use to attract customers
- A description of your management team and an explanation of its strengths
- An estimate of expected startup expenses
- A three-year pro forma financial projection
- A one- or two-page executive summary

There are dozens of resources for business plan templates, and many are on the Internet. If you are seeking external funding (from an angel investor, a venture capitalist, a bank, or another source), look for a plan template most likely to trigger the positive response of your funding source. For example, venture capitalists and angel networks have preferred business plan formats for technology, consumer products, and medical device and other niche startups that they may supply to entrepreneurs who seek their funding. If you intend to self-fund your startup, you still need a business plan. In that situation, however, the plan is strictly for you, and it should include the components most applicable to your entrepreneurial venture.

Most business plan templates are thorough, but be sure that your business plan includes information that answers these critical questions:

- Who will be your mentors or serve on a board of advisors?
- What has failed in this market in the past and why?
- What intellectual property will your business create or own?
- How will you differentiate yourself from competitors and defend your position?
- What resources can you obtain through bootstrapping versus funding or financing?
- What milestones will your business need to reach across all facets of the company?
- What metrics will you use to monitor performance, quality, and goal obtainment?
- Will your business address a customer pain point or meet customer desires?
- How will this market change five years down the road?
- How can your idea disrupt this industry or market?
- What is the exit strategy for investors, for the business, and for yourself?

4. Goal Setting

Too many business owners put all their startup efforts into establishing the physical attributes of their business to meet their "opening" date and don't make time to establish basic goals. Goals provide a completion target for all the strategic initiatives you are about to undertake. The goals aren't exclusive to sales activities; they should represent all major milestones for moving the company forward. Make sure, therefore, that your goals cover every operational aspect of the business you are planning to launch. During the Startup phase, your goals must include creating demand for your product or service and branding. To meet those goals, your sales and marketing strategies must create a sustainable and reliable funnel of customer demand. Your goals will eventually shift to demand fulfillment, once your business reaches the Running phase.

5. Key Performance Indicators

Key performance indicators (KPIs) are financial and nonfinancial measures to help evaluate how well your company is progressing toward its long-term organizational goals. KPIs serve as a dashboard to the company's current health and performance. KPIs are predetermined metrics that, as part of your overall business plan, you will monitor throughout the Startup and Running phases of your business. Consider establishing internal KPIs that provide information on profit, customer satisfaction, customer acquisition and retention, human and systematic productivity, equipment utilization, and waste, as well as external KPIs that measure market share and related competitive efforts. E-commerce KPI metrics might measure average order value/quantity and revenue generated versus dollars spent to acquire the lead, or customer service metrics such as those used to measure visitor duration or website ability to deflect inbound service calls. Finally, regardless of site purpose, most will measure percent of unique visitors, number of page views, form completion, and quantity of lead generation.

In order to establish KPIs, you need to develop business processes and define their required outcomes. You can then periodically use your KPIs to assess the progress of your business toward the performance goals you have set for it. Your KPI measurements will help you determine when you need to adjust your processes and where you may need to apply more or fewer resources to keep your business's performance on track.

6. GAP Analysis

After your startup has been operational for a period of time, you will need to conduct a GAP analysis to determine whether or not your company is following its plan. Be sure to include a timetable and plan for this analysis as part of your initial preparation and business plan. The GAP analysis can be a very simple or elaborate procedure, depending on your style and needs. At the heart of the GAP analysis are two questions that you must answer: "Where are we?" and "Where do we want to be?"

The acronym GAP stands for *good, average, poor.* Using data generated from KPIs, financial reports, and other resources, your management team will give one of these ratings within each metric to rate your organization's current performance and to identify areas where its performance must change in order to meet the standards you've set for it. By reviewing the outcomes of the GAP analysis, you also can tweak existing goals and objectives, or create new ones.

You and your management team will determine how frequently you need to conduct GAP analyses based on your organization's ability to adjust the metrics, your available resources, and the impact of the GAP analysis results on the overall health of your company. This analysis can take place daily, weekly, monthly, quarterly, or even yearly, depending upon the relevance of GAP findings to your organization. But for every organization, the GAP analysis is a strong tool for comparing actual performance to the potential or planned performance of the business.

7. Exit Strategy

Every successful beginning includes a plan for the end. Before taking off on a flight, for example, you always want to know where the plane will be landing. Every savvy entrepreneur who is contemplating a new business needs to create a sound exit strategy as part of the overall business plan. Your exit strategy—a firm vision of how, why, and maybe even when you will leave, sell, or close your business—is for you, not just your company; it's part of the "endgame" for your vision, and it will be very personal to you. When you have a vision and goals for how you want to end your active involvement with the company you're launching, every subsequent decision you make will be determined by those outcomes. Your job will be to guide your journey toward the exit plan you've envisioned. The specific time frame for your exit may be unpredictable or even irrelevant. In general, your exit strategy reflects both your ultimate goals and objectives for the company and your own personal ambitions.

We talk more about planning your exit strategy later in this chapter, and about executing your Exit phase later in this book; but for now, be aware that your exit strategy should be incorporated in your overall business plan. The strategy may change during the course of the business, and that is perfectly acceptable. After all, conditions change. It's important to understand, however, that you must formulate, right up-front, how you intend to exit the business you're starting so you can manage your efforts to achieve that goal.

Planning for the Long Haul

The entrepreneurial journey is daunting, and many won't make it to a successful exit. My exit was relatively unusual; less than 1 percent of businesses end up being acquired (profitably) by a Fortune 100 company, as was mine. That's not to say that my outcome represents the ideal for every entrepreneur and business, but I think it's worth exploring why so many entrepreneurs are unable to successfully orchestrate their (or their organization's) endgame. Sadly, I've come to believe a failure in planning is the cause of many less-than-successful endings to the entrepreneurial journey.

You may not have given much thought to how you'll leave the business you're so totally involved in at the moment, but you should. You're a human being, not an entity, and you won't physically be able to manage forever the business you have founded. An exit plan is forced upon all of us whether we like it or not. Too often entrepreneurs fail to consider their exit from the business until they start thinking of retirement, and that's too late.

An exit strategy and retirement aren't the same thing, and, in fact, you should view them as being irrelevant to one another. Establishing retirement as a reason to leave your business can greatly diminish the valuation of your business. In many cases, the founder *is* the business. All of the "tribal knowledge" that both grounds your business and propels it forward may be stored in your head. Potential buyers who recognize this fact will want you to stay on after the acquisition, in order to ensure a successful transition. If your plan is to sell the business and run out the door with a check in your hand, you may lower the value of your company or even sink the deal.

Even if you do plan to retire from your business, you should manage your venture with an eye toward the succession planning or sale of the company. If retirement is your ultimate entrepreneurial goal, your business will never be positioned to succeed, and you will never be able to maximize the personal wealth you achieve from your entrepreneurial efforts. Starting a business with the idea of riding it to retirement can be as damaging as starting a business with the sole goal of making a fortune by selling your company to the highest bidder. You can't start a business whose primary purpose is to make money for you or give you a job for life. For your business or operation to succeed, it must address your customers' needs, and doing so should be part of the reward you're planning for from the beginning.

So much of starting a business is about attitude and developing a positive mindset. I know you've heard this before and more than a fair share of "motivational" speakers have preached this message, but having the desire to complete your vision is undeniably a prerequisite for starting a business. You have to believe in and visualize yourself moving successfully from the Idea phase through the Startup and Running phases of your business, and meeting your goals along the way. And those goals should include your final stage of involvement with the business.

The "New Thought Principle" (with eighteenth-century roots) produced the phrase "energy flows where the focus goes," meaning things will happen and results will materialize where you focus your energy. As we saw in chapter 3, you can't afford to focus your energy and thoughts on the negative predictions of doomsayers. If you do, the fear of those negative outcomes, rather than your determination to achieve the positive outcomes you've imagined for your entrepreneurial venture, will drive your decision making. This is one of the critical reasons that you must create a positive and clear vision of how you want your involvement with the business you are launching to end. That final vision will guide every step you take during the remainder of your entrepreneurial journey.

Not only do I think it's essential to include an exit strategy in your Startup plans, I also think it's important to let others know about that strategy. By definition, a self-fulfilling prophecy can only be realized when the public prediction is made true. The power of this strategy lies in the mindset that it engages in you. I had spent two years writing "around" this book, and then completed it in just six months. What happened to spur me on? It was only in those last six months that I began publicly telling people that I was going to write a book. With that public affirmation of my intentions, I had to put forth the effort and time commitment to make it true. I could have stopped at any time—and believe me, there were times I wanted to. But my public statement to family and friends kept me going. The same will be true of all of the goals and strategies you create for your organization, including your exit strategy. By clearly expressing your vision of how you will finish the work you are beginning here in the Startup phase, you can build a self-fulfilling prophecy that will go beyond a personal goal to become a public commitment that you will feel driven to make a reality.

Drawing on Your Desire, Effort, and Ability— At Work and at Home

You may remember that I outlined the major components of any successful entrepreneurial I.D.E.A.: innovation, desire, effort, and ability. At no stage in your entrepreneurial journey will you be more dependent upon those qualities than during the Startup phase.

You'll draw upon all of your abilities as you work to create all of the necessary preparations, or battle plans as I like to call them. You will build your plans around the innovative niche that you have identified in your market, and that is central to your entrepreneurial idea. But ability alone won't convert these planning documents into the physical reality of a business. There may be many times during the Startup phase that you will want to give up. Meeting the demands this phase places on your time and your consciousness will possibly be one of the greatest professional challenges you will ever face. You will need to draw upon your overwhelming desire to be an entrepreneur and your unstinting effort to move successfully through the planning stage of the Startup phase. In fact, desire and effort will help you achieve what those with greater talent, intelligence, and money could not.

When I talk about entrepreneurial desire, I am referring to passion. Desire unleashes passion, an emotion that creates a sense of longing or hope focused squarely on a specific area of interest. Desire also funnels that passion into motivation, which, in turn, leads to action. Your desire and passion will spur your efforts to act and create. Desire provides that extra effort that pushes you to work a seventy-plus-hour workweek. Desire triggers your decision to skip your weekend plans or turn off the television to work on fulfilling your passion. I didn't know what prime-time television was while I was getting my company off the ground. My priorities—and my passions—were my family and our business. I didn't have much desire to focus on anything else.

As you use the tools you've learned about in this chapter to pull together your business plans, remember that your relationships also require careful planning and preparation. In fact, I encourage you to consider writing a mission statement, a SWOT analysis, a GAP analysis, and established goals for your relationships as you work through the Startup phase of your business—and beyond. Think about it. If you don't take time to plan how you want your relationships to grow, then how will they evolve along with you and your business? If you're planning to keep your key relationships and your business separate, well . . . good luck with that. In my experience, you can't have two passions fighting equally for your time and attention without introducing them to each other.

The key to channeling your desire and effort to successfully attend to *all* of your passions is to establish a balance—a balance measured not in time but in focus. I'm returning to this subject here to reiterate what I said earlier: you need to incorporate the time and effort necessary to maintain your personal relationships into your business plan—seriously. If you don't take into consideration your primary relationships and how they will be impacted by your decision to work on this business, you will be putting at risk the most valuable aspects of your life. And these risks, like many of the others we've discussed in this chapter, will be the direct result of your lack of planning.

In my case, I involved my wife, Lisa, directly in the first stages of my planning process. My Startup phase was going to be particularly challenging, because I planned to remain working at Educational Resources until I got my own business off to a strong start. Yep, that was me: fully committed to taking off, yet still keeping one foot on home base. My planning process, therefore, had to take into account three overriding desires: to get my new business off the ground; to maintain strong and reliable performance with my current employer; and to remain engaged and involved with my wife and children.

Complicating my process even further, I had determined that I would self-fund my business. That decision made my wife and family even more active "partners" in my entrepreneurial journey. As I mentioned earlier, the search for funding goes hand in hand with the process of crafting a business plan. As you can imagine, the tools and techniques I've outlined in this chapter played a critical role in pulling together this complex battle plan for my future.

In the next chapter, we'll take a closer look at the steps involved in securing any type of funding source for launching your entrepreneurial idea. But remember: launching a new business or organization demands that you step outside the walls of your Risk Box to realize the possibilities of your idea. In the process of taking that step, however, you may well be pulling others outside their Risk Box, too. There are no guarantees for success in any entrepreneurial journey. But it's your responsibility to do everything in your power to avoid putting yourself, your colleagues, and those you love in harm's way by making sure that you adequately plan each step along the path you've chosen.

CHAPTER SEVEN

Mastering Your Money

As I moved through the planning stage of my new business startup, I had a long and growing list of needs to consider. First, I needed an above-entry-level phone system; the system would be one of my closest links to customers, so it had to be high quality. Next, I wanted to enter the marketplace with the perception that my business was bigger and more established than it really was, so I was going to need to pull together a big four-color catalog. What I really needed was an extra pair of hands—actually several extra pairs of hands. At minimum, I'd need a graphic designer, a sales director, a marketing manager, and someone to work full-time during the week while I was still working at Educational Resources. I also needed a home base of operations where someone who knew the business could take calls during the day. My house wasn't suitable for housing the business, and while Lisa was on board, she wasn't going to answer customer calls regarding technology she knew nothing about. As I considered the list, I realized that every item on it was actually just part of the one large, looming need shared by all new entrepreneurs: money.

As you wade into the first stages of your own Startup phase, money will play a central role in your plans, too. You have several options open to you for funding your new venture, and we'll talk about many of them in this chapter. But remember that, as an entrepreneur, you are the ultimate source of all of your organization's funding, wherever the money comes from. That's because funding your startup will be your job, and it all begins with selling—your idea, your plan, and your ability to make it all happen. Whether you're pitching your idea to a potential investor or to a potential employee, your ability to translate your passion into an articulate, compelling, and clearly outlined plan for success will determine your ability to gather the resources you need.

When you've chosen a funding source, all of your subsequent planning (and much of your selling) will be targeted toward gaining the source's buy-in. In this chapter, I'll talk about determining which type of funding source is most likely to respond to your business idea so you can customize your funding search to appeal to that source. And because landing your startup funds isn't an end goal, this chapter also offers ideas for creating a strong, workable plan for managing the funds you acquire. Money management, during the Startup phase and beyond, will draw heavily on your skills in both frugality and innovation. I've capped this chapter with a short history of my early experiences as a "frugal-preneur." As you'll see, I'm a big believer in frugality, but not just because it saves you money. Yes, money matters; as an entrepreneur, however, frugality—not money—can provide the most fertile ground for growing your creative skills and energy. The lessons you learn in money management and frugality during the Startup phase can continue to spur success as you move through the Running phase of your business and on to a profitable Exit phase.

Of course, money is just one of the resources you'll need to gather during Startup. In the next chapter, we talk about bringing in partners and human resources, and there, we'll talk more about the first partners who joined me in the early days of planning and launching my company. But I want to begin this chapter by telling you about a few who *didn't* join me, because that story is all about money—and the choices we make in using it to launch a new business.

Weighing the Costs and Benefits of Debt

When I first began approaching people about joining my new company, I had nothing to show or offer other than a dream. What I shared was an idea for a business along with a rather extravagant exit plan with no specific time frame. I felt strongly that our early entry into the college market would result in rapid growth and, eventually, attract the attention of Fortune 500 suitors to purchase our company. I provided realistic scenarios as to how my vision would unfold, and I did so with a level of compelling and captivating exuberance that came straight from my heart. I was painting a scenario that had less than a 1 percent chance of becoming a reality. My passionate message was fueled, however, by the power of the entrepreneur. I believed in my idea, and I wanted to share it with others who could join me in bringing it to life. I was being genuine and nonmanipulative, but my entrepreneurial pitch was powerful.

That power and passion had helped gain the buy-in of the first two people I had approached about joining my business. But I still needed to fill two vital roles: I needed a marketing manager and a sales manager. There were two people at Educational Resources that I knew would be excellent candidates to fill these positions. I decided to take a risk, confide my plans to them, and ask them to come on board.

My biggest concern was the sales manager position. During my time at Educational Resources, I hadn't had much real exposure to selling, even though my efforts helped drive sales. I had never worked in sales, and I was a bit intimidated by that whole area of business. Setting sales quotas, creating commission plans and sales strategies, managing the reps—every aspect of sales seemed to be part of a closed universe in which I had no expertise or talent.

To fill that critical role, I turned to one of my former product managers, Dan Figurski, who had moved into an inside sales manager position at Educational Resources (and would eventually become its president). Dan is a character: an extremely personable guy with a great sense of humor, the kind of guy everyone enjoys being around and who can talk forever about nothing. While we often jokingly called Dan a "classic bullshit artist," he was a good communicator and formed strong connections with ER's customers. If Dan went out on a golf outing, he'd come back with a sale.

For the marketing position, I was hoping to recruit another ER product manager, Nancy Ragont. Nancy is a very talented and confident professional with an incredible drive for success. I knew that Nancy wanted to advance. She was looking for more responsibility and greater challenges than she had in her current position. Nancy was a master at the marketing game; she knew products, she had the contacts, and she could put it all together.

As I said, I was taking a chance by disclosing my idea for forming a new company to Nancy and Dan, but I approached them with confidence. All of us had talked together in the past about our dreams of becoming entrepreneurs, and we had developed a close and trusting relationship in our work together at ER. I explained to them that I intended to bootstrap my business, using my own funds to launch the business, rather than taking on debt. We discussed the roles I wanted them to fill and, as a result of my limited funds, the offer of equity in the business rather than a guaranteed salary during startup. I was excited at the prospect of working with these two friends and colleagues, and felt almost certain that they'd be equally excited to join me in my new venture. But I was wrong; both turned me down.

The problem wasn't that they doubted the strength of my idea. In fact, they were very engaged and receptive to the proposal. Their main concern was that I had no startup funding for the business. They weren't comfortable with foregoing a salary for an undetermined period of time while the business ramped up. In other words, they doubted my potential for success based on the bootstrap financing approach I had presented. I understood their reluctance to join me in my new venture, but the loss of my potential sales and marketing partners brought home a painful reality to me: I was going to have to wear both of those demanding hats during the critical Startup phase of my business.

I suppose I was pushing my luck in thinking I could convince these two very talented individuals with very secure, well-paying jobs to come work for nothing but a dream and a promise. Their decisions to pass on my offer made me question whether I wasn't as daring an entrepreneur as I had thought. Was I conservative to a fault? I could never afford paying salaries for these individuals right out of the gate with no immediate revenue stream, but having them on board would certainly propel the business forward. I could have investigated a bank loan to secure funding, or I could have dug deeper into my personal savings to offer them a salary. Did the fact that I hadn't done that indicate that I was less than fully committed to my dream? Was I jeopardizing my future success simply because I had an ingrained (and maybe unwarranted) resistance to taking on debt?

You'll have to answer some of those same questions during your Startup phase as you weigh the options for funding your new business. Maybe, like my father, your parents hammered into you the idea that debt is a bad thing, to be avoided at all costs. I hate to argue with my elders, but that idea isn't always accurate when it comes to business. Well-managed debt can sometimes be the best investment you can make in launching an entrepreneurial venture or even during some stages of running a business. Think about it: no garden will grow without some kind of investment. Sure, planting the seeds may not cost much, but getting those seeds to grow requires a sizeable outlay of time, labor, water, fertilizer, weeding, adequate sunlight, and protection from outside forces (you know, those nibbling bunnies). Launching your business will require an incredible investment of time and money—and, as the saying goes, time *is* money, especially when you're in the early stages of growing a new venture. It would be a shame to allow your new business to die on the vine because you're philosophically opposed to debt.

By not taking on debt, you might be doing your seedling operation more harm than good. Inadequate funds can restrict your organization's development, just as a failure to fertilize your garden can stunt its growth. I made the very personal choice that sweat equity was the wisest funding choice for my new business, as opposed to taking on debt. I have always been a hard and independent worker, and I felt relatively certain that, no matter how grueling or difficult the work might be, I could "do it all" in the beginning; my choice to self-fund meant that I had to.

In the end, I stuck with my original self-funding plan, I made it through the period of wearing too many hats, and my business went on to be a success. But that doesn't necessarily mean that I made the right choice. That's why I want to emphasize to you that you need to carefully weigh the costs and benefits—both short term and long term—of whatever type of funding you are considering (we talk more about that later in this chapter). Money has power, it's true; but to be a successful entrepreneur, you have to learn to take charge of your money and control it, rather than letting it rule your every decision.

Selling the Idea: It's Up to You

Many people think money, or rather the lack of it, is the greatest obstacle to launching a business—and it is a big one. As I said earlier, though, the most important element in funding your business will be you and your ability to sell your idea.

The vast majority of startup businesses, like mine, will be self-funded by the founder or from a small pool of relatives or close friends who dip into their personal savings. If you aren't going to foot the bill for your startup yourself, you are going to have to solicit funding. That means you are going to be selling (in some cases, to strangers), and the primary "product" you'll be selling is you. Your idea has to be solid, but the idea exists only in your head at this point. Only your passion and confidence in that idea can convince someone to entrust their money or time or other resources with you. Successful deal making is nothing more than the transfer of enthusiasm and emotion. And remember: everything we humans do is driven in some part by emotion.

People want to be a part of passionate undertakings. If you can convey your passion effectively to others, they'll find themselves naturally drawn to your ideas. Many entrepreneurs don't realize the kinetic power they command until later in their entrepreneurial career, but it's there from the beginning. For investors, passion conveys confidence and dedication, essential qualities for launching a new venture. Many entrepreneurs exude strength, determination, and commitment to making their ideas a reality. This is the almost pheromone-like lure that attracts investors to the entrepreneur.

Don't misunderstand me: charisma alone won't be enough to obtain funding. This is when all of your careful planning and preparation comes into play. Any logical investor is going to want to see your idea on paper, and this is where your business plan, SWOT, mission statement, and other planning documents we discussed in chapter 6 will be scrutinized. As you learned in that chapter, however, the strength of those planning and funding tools will lie in how well you adapt them to the specific source you've chosen to tap into.

Targeting a Funding Source

Acquiring startup funding can be a complex process, but you can streamline it considerably by targeting your efforts toward the type of funding source most likely to invest in your type of business. Although many entrepreneurial ventures are self-funded, the remainder receive funding from a few of the most common investor types: venture capitalists (VCs); private equity firms; banks or other lending institutions; and angel investors. Let's take a brief look at what types of businesses and ventures these sources traditionally fund.

Popular wisdom seems to be that the first door an entrepreneur should knock on in the search for funding is that of a venture capitalist or VC. After all, an estimated $26.2 billion went into startup firms in 2010 from this source alone, according to VentureSource (a Dow Jones company). Unfortunately (or fortunately, depending on your experience), a very small number of startups (2,799 in 2010), most coming from just a few industries, will be funded by venture capitalists.[1] Typically, VCs invest in early-stage, high-potential growth companies in the information or scientific technology sectors that retain innovative intellectual property. For all practical purposes, the minimum venture capitalist funding level is $1 million–$2 million. Venture capitalists plan to realize returns on their investment through an IPO (independent public offering), or sale of the company, and so they are particularly interested in entrepreneurs who come to the table with a definitive exit strategy in mind.

Most entrepreneurs can save themselves the trouble of seeking funding from a private equity firm. Increasingly, these firms are putting their investments into existing businesses rather than new ventures. Private equity firm investment methods may involve leveraged buyouts, mezzanine funding (debt or preferred equity), or straight capital funding. Private equity firms are far more selective than other sources in their investments, and typically fund businesses that are more mature (that is, generating revenue) than most startups.

FUNDING SOURCES: A QUICK GUIDE

Your research into funding sources will give you a good overall education in the various forms those sources take. But here's an at-a-glance guide to the most common external funding sources:

- **Angel investors** typically are affluent individuals who invest their personal capital into an early stage company—usually one that operates in an industry that's familiar to the investor. These investments might range from a few thousand dollars to hundreds of thousands of dollars or more. Angel investors may structure their investments as debt; more often, they require equity in return for their risk.

- **Venture capital (VC)** is a type of private equity funding geared toward high-growth, early stage companies. The VC investor is typically a company that invests a pool of money into firms that meet very strict criteria, with an intended exit outcome of a third-party sale or IPO.

- **Private equity** investments come from firms that typically invest in established private companies where opportunity to the investor is seen through a leveraged buyout, a sale to a third party, an IPO, a debt offering, or some other profit-seeking tactic.

A much more likely source of funding for your new business may be a loan from a community bank or possibly the Small Business Administration. Securing a loan may not be as sexy as landing private equity funding, but it does allow you to retain ownership and control of your venture. Many entrepreneurs require more startup capital than they can obtain from a single bank loan, however, and so they turn to an angel investor. The typical angel investor is a wealthy individual or small investment fund looking to invest amounts smaller than the $1 million–$2 million minimum VC threshold. It is estimated that in 2007, angels invested $26 billion in 57,000 companies, as compared to the nearly $31 billion that VCs invested in just over 3,900 companies. Out of the more than five million businesses that start up each year, just over 1 percent will obtain VC or angel funding.

Understanding the investment choices of these funding sources can help you determine which is most likely to be interested in your entrepreneurial venture. Don't waste time trying to chase dollars that only have a 1 percent chance of coming in, unless you truly have an innovative product or service that meets the stringent investment criteria of these funding sources. At the same time, you need to be resourceful about tracking down and appealing to sources that may be willing to stake you. A simple Internet search for angel and venture capital firms in your area can disclose a number of potential funding and support resources that may align with your business model. If you believe in your idea enough to have reached the Startup phase, you can't allow your progress to be halted because you don't have the money to fund a new business. Over 440,000 people every month figure out how to do it, and so can you.

Creating a Money Management Plan

Acquiring the money to fund your startup is an important step, but it's even more critical to your success as an entrepreneur that you understand how you are going to manage those funds. Managing your money is the only way you can maintain control of your business.

Notice that I'm talking here not about *spending* money, but about *managing* it. You have to have a strong money management plan if you want to limit the amount of money you have to seek from outside sources. The more you have to borrow or take from investors, the more equity and control you give up. When venture capitalists or private investors invest in your company, they gain ownership. When a bank loans you money, it has access to your financial performance data, and it gains the right to question your decisions. Money comes at a price, and if your ongoing need for external cash infusions erodes your ownership to less than 51 percent, you no longer control your company. In fact, at that point you're no longer an entrepreneur; you are a manager with an investment in the company you work for.

It is your job to act as a proper steward of the funds you receive, and believe it or not, bare-bones finances can help make you better at that job. In some ways, having more money than you need can be almost as damaging to your potential success as having no funding at all. Excess money can lead to wasteful and unnecessary spending. As difficult as your struggle to make ends meet may be in the early stages of the Startup phase, you may find it much more difficult to raise additional money after burning through your startup funds. And remember: venture capitalists who eagerly offer to front you additional rounds of capital as the Startup phase progresses aren't doing it just to help you; they know you have a good business cooking, and they want to own more of it. Your job is to keep all of those other chefs out of your kitchen.

If you are the source of your funding, determine—up-front, during your planning stage—how much you want to invest in the Startup phase of your business. As difficult as it may be, you will have to separate your dual roles of founder and financier. Your emotional passion for the business as founder can inappropriately influence your personal fiscal responsibilities. Far too many entrepreneurs have excavated their own personal money pit by shoveling too many dollars into the pursuit of their dream. If you do that, you're jeopardizing your personal financial stability. As founder *and* financier of your business, you can't afford to weaken your position in that way.

If you find that, in spite of careful management and planning, you're going to burn through the original startup investment, take time to adequately calculate and reflect on what additional funds you need to get the business into a sustainable condition. Then, you can determine if it makes sense for you to reinvest. Navigating this situation successfully takes considerable discipline; you may need to consider selling your equity as the next best option at this point.

THE DOWNFALLS OF FALSE PRIDE

Here's a piece of advice I hope you'll take to heart: one of the strongest tools you can bring to the table when it comes to successful funding and money management planning is a sense of humility. Resisting the urge to step out of the starting gate looking like a well-established company will go a long way toward cash preservation. Yes, I know that a certain image requirement may be necessary; I've already confessed that I was determined to present my company as a stable and established business when it first left the gate. But I knew, and you must remember, that no startup can afford to sink too much of its precious funds in creating a façade. My company's "image" investment was limited to its catalog and phone system, two critical core components that directly touched our customers. Behind the phones we scrimped and got by on bare necessities.

Pride has no place in a startup, and you can't drop your vigilant money management after you move into the Running phase of your business, either. Success has a way of eating into your ability to remain humble and thrifty; the more successful your business becomes, the more you will be tempted to invest your valuable dollars in expenses that expand your ego without really helping to advance your business. Don't give into that temptation.

Of course, the best way to hit the sweet spot of funding is to do adequate planning and forecasting to determine what your absolute funding requirements include. Your business plan should be detailed enough to forecast expenses for twelve months and to outline predictable cash flow requirements. Make sure that you explore every money-saving tool available to your new venture. Advances in communication and information technology have made it easier to establish virtual offices, for example, which can save startups thousands of dollars in facility, personnel, and travel expenses. You'll need to determine what kind of presence your business requires, but be sure to investigate every way that up-front technology investments might help you cut expenses. Employees represent the largest expense for just about any company. Even critical roles in your startup may be able to be filled through outsourcing, temporary positions, job shares, or other methods for reducing head count, hours, and expense.

Living the Innovative Life of a Frugal-Preneur

You may have figured out, from everything we've talked about up to this point in the chapter, that most startups are self-funded and underfunded. Well, that's true. And my own startup was no different. Although I had the cash to buy the equipment and supplies necessary to start my company, my investment wasn't adequate for building a business that was truly presentable on day one. My first office was in a basement next to a laundry room, so when I say the business wasn't "presentable," I mean I couldn't bring in a client for a meeting that didn't involve tripping over a clothes basket and pausing our conversation while the washer went into a noisy spin cycle. I'm not giving you a hard luck story, though; far from it. Starting a business is rarely a glamorous adventure. In fact, it's very humbling—and it should be. That humbleness drives the entrepreneur to continue to get better, to grow, and to succeed. The overriding need to "make do" is a motivator that no amount of money can buy, and one typically denied to the well-funded entrepreneur.

Mind you, being frugal and being cheap aren't the same thing. In fact, frugal-preneurs are pros at spending money—they just spend it wisely and conservatively. Frugal-preneurs don't hesitate to plop down a decent sum of money on a solution that they view as a solid investment in their business. Cheapskate-preneurs, on the other hand, waste money. They buy the cheapest up-front solution that ends up costing much more money when it breaks down, won't run efficiently, causes more problems than it solves, and has to be replaced sooner. I'm a committed frugal-preneur. In my startup, I was notorious for finding ways to limit expenditures in ways that amazed even our (outside) accountant. Let me tell you a bit about my frugal-preneur exploits.

As I've said, most of my new business's customer contact came through phone and catalog orders; we did, however, participate in trade shows and conferences. Cutting the fat out of our expenses in these events was a particular focus for me during my company's early years. Service fees rack up fast when you attend a conference, unless you find ways to do things yourself. So schlepping became one of my favorite methods of cutting corners: it meant that we had to haul all of the stuff we needed to get to and from our display table or booth, to avoid the drayage fees convention center dock workers charge to receive, hold, and move vendor materials. Finding ways to avoid drayage fees became something of a mission for me. One of my methods, for example, was to ship my booth and convention materials to the hotel where I was staying—much to the hotel staff's delight, I'm sure. I would then load the material into my economy rental car and drive the goods to the conference center.

The dock workers at the convention center never made my fee-avoidance activities easy; after all, they had to make a buck, too. And some conference centers were in halls that had union rules against vendors moving in their own stuff, assembling their booths, and so on—I guess I wasn't the first frugal-preneur they'd dealt with. But whenever I could work with (or around) the rules, I schlepped; I'm sure some others who attended those conferences still talk about the sweaty, bald exhibitor who used to struggle like a mad mule to drag his booth into its designated position.

Another way I discovered for maximizing my new company's conference attendance investment was by visiting customers in the surrounding area or, when I drove, along the way. Since my company was catalog driven for most of our years, I would map out which colleges and universities were on my route. Pulling off the highway to reach a college was part of my frugal-preneur routine on these trips. I didn't have an outside sales force, and we rarely were physically on the campus of the schools we sold to, so I could easily deliver a few hundred well-targeted catalogs—which saved on postage and the cost of obtaining mailing lists.

When I descended on a campus, I flooded every nook and cranny with catalogs. To reach every potential buyer, I scoured every hallway and building on campus for an opportunity to deliver catalogs. In the beginning, I hand-carried my catalogs, but eventually I lugged them around in a wheeled travel suitcase. Central staff and faculty mailboxes within the individual departments were rarely in public locations, so I would have to sneak in, quickly stuff the mail cubbies, and zip back out before I was noticed. On occasion I would get busted by a staffer asking what I was doing. Sometimes the staffer would help me stuff mailboxes; other times, I'd get tossed out on my rump—a small price to pay, as far as I was concerned.

Even after we moved out of our first basement office and began to grow, I continued to find ways to save money. I had developed an appreciation for the cost of office furniture while managing the remodeling of the Allstate Insurance home office and installing new Steelcase panel systems. There was no way in hell I was going to spend that type of money. I bought used furniture, as long as it was in decent shape and had plenty of usable life left in it. As a frugal-preneur, I viewed furniture as nonessential equipment to the business and, therefore, only worth minimal investment. Our furniture worked, looked good, and was comfortable for the user—even if it didn't all match. Entrepreneurs starting out with venture capital often have the nicest offices money can buy. They seem to fail to realize that their employees are sitting and working on their equity.

I understand that some businesses rely on their image as part of their marketing, positioning, and brand. I don't think I would feel very comfortable walking into a lawyer's office to find the type of office furniture I was setting up in my new company. But every business has nonessential expenses that can be rationed. Just because you have the money doesn't mean you need to spend it. I am sure newcomers within my company joked about how cheap I was, but it didn't matter—not to me, and not to my long-term employees. They got it, and they accepted—no, relished—that this was our company culture. We simply didn't retain employees who valued the style of their workspace more than the prospect of exceeding our sales goals.

As our employee count grew, so did the value I placed on establishing an attractive work environment. As fate would have it, right about this same time, Arthur Andersen LLP took a major legal hit for its auditing practices at Enron. When the huge accounting firm ceased doing business as CPAs, about 85,000 jobs evaporated—and a lot of really nice used office furniture became available. I tracked down the liquidator responsible for clearing leased office space in Chicago and bought a tractor trailer full of Steelcase workstations and chairs in great condition for $6,000. That price included breakdown and delivery to our location!

Shortly before that time, my landlord had nudged me into a larger working space, and it was a good thing. I filled the new space from floor to ceiling with furniture. To navigate, we left narrow aisles between the canyons of binder bins, work surfaces, and file cabinets. Some of our working files were in cabinets inadvertently surrounded by these stacks. Lisa was pregnant with our third child Nicholas at the time, and, comically, she was unable to turn sideways in these narrow corridors of furniture towers. It was an exciting time because it showed where we were going. I didn't get furniture for just the employees on hand; I had room for many more.

Believe me, the benefits of learning how to use your money wisely can help you grow and manage your new business well beyond the financial restrictions of the Startup phase. Every money-saving measure and wise spending decision you make extends and expands your critical entrepreneurial skills in creativity, innovation, and management. Money is all about control in so many situations, and that's particularly true in funding and running a business. The better your skills in planning for, acquiring, and managing your startup funds, the better able you'll be to focus on the idea that drove you to start your business in the first place. By maintaining a keen eye on the resources that matter most to your organization, you'll be better positioned to move your business on into a healthy Running phase. And, as I mentioned earlier, money is only one of the resources you'll acquire and manage as you launch your business. In the next chapter, we'll talk about another critical need for this phase of the entrepreneurial journey—human resources.

CHAPTER EIGHT

Bringing on Partners and Employees

As you've seen in the preceding chapters, the Startup phase of the entrepreneurial experience involves acquisition. You have to acquire the skills, knowledge, training, and information necessary to position your startup for success; you have to acquire the buy-in and support of financial backers, mentors, friends, and family members through a well-crafted business plan; and, of course, you have to acquire basic funding, along with the physical space, systems, and supplies necessary to conduct your business. Now we need to talk about one final—and very important—acquisition you'll need to take care of in order to launch your new venture: partners and other human resources. As you've seen in every preceding chapter of this book, no entrepreneur is an island. In order to ensure the success of your new business or operation, you'll need to find the right partners and employees to help you bring your entrepreneurial vision to life.

In my own Startup phase, I had a very clear idea of what partners and employees I'd need to bring on board. First, I needed a graphic designer to create the first catalog for my new company. To fill that role, I turned to a college classmate from Northern Illinois University who was currently working as a print designer. She graduated from the art program at NIU and was a classic overachiever—a workaholic, always taking on multiple projects simultaneously and then juggling them expertly toward a successful conclusion. In other words, she was a perfect candidate for my startup.

I offered the designer sweat equity in lieu of cash to get the catalog done, and told her that she could work flexible hours around her current job, just as I was doing. She didn't hesitate when I ran the project past her. She had already started an independent design firm on the side, and she looked upon my offer as an opportunity to develop my company into one of her premiere clients. In fact, I believe she always thought of me as her client, rather than her partner. Her entrepreneurial dreams were focused on her business, not mine. But that was perfectly okay with me; I had a designer, and I couldn't have asked for a better one. To get the first catalog out the door, we decided that I would create the entire catalog layout, the product mix, and pricing. I also would obtain copy and images from publishers, and then funnel that raw information to her.

Next, I contacted Betsy Horlock, a product manager who had worked with me at Educational Resources. She left the company after her second child's birth to focus on her young family, and I had recently heard that she was looking for some part-time work. Betsy knew the business, and she would be a great extra pair of hands. Since she was home during the day, she could be the home base for the company and answer phone calls while I was working at Educational Resources. I approached Betsy with the same offer I'd made to our graphic designer, and she quickly accepted. At that point, I had two partners and was ready to work on two more. That was when I hit my first personnel snag.

In chapter 7, I described my unsuccessful attempts to recruit two high-performing colleagues at Educational Resources to join me in my (still very much a secret) new company. As you saw in that chapter, those recruitment efforts failed as a result of my decision to self-fund my new venture, rather than take on debt. Where Betsy and my graphic designer were willing to work for equity, the two well-established and highly paid executives I'd hoped to bring over to my new business simply weren't willing to forego a salary for an unspecified period of time while my own business developed financial "legs." They believed my idea would work, but they needed more than a future promise in order to justify the immediate financial sacrifices necessary to join my startup.

Most startups face similar issues. Startups need great talent in order to propel their new business ahead in the marketplace. At the same time, by their very nature, few startups have the financial resources necessary to lure established talent into their fold. As you'll learn in this chapter, the power of the entrepreneur can sometimes be a persuasive recruiting tool, but it's a tool you have to use carefully when recruiting partners and key personnel. No level of whipped-up enthusiasm can substitute for skill, talent, and a commitment to succeed, and those are essential qualities in your Startup phase personnel. This chapter also includes a navigational heads-up about some other common partnering pitfalls for startups, along with solid ideas for forming strong, useful partnerships that will help guide you through the sometimes stormy weather ahead.

I'm also going to use this chapter to tell you about how I sailed on to the end of my own Startup phase. As you'll discover, I had plenty of learning opportunities during this time. I hope that by sharing them with you here, I can help you avoid problems and find real solutions as you bring on partners, employees, and other human resources necessary to get your own organization on its feet, functioning, and ready to enter a healthy and productive Running phase.

Avoiding the Four Worst Candidates for Startup Partnership

Going into business with one or more people is a great idea if your talents, experiences, resources, or knowledge bases complement each other and meet the needs of the business idea. Partners help ease the burden of running a business in terms of workload, investment, risk, and sharing the inherent mental pressures. But while partnering can be one of the best decisions you make in your business, bringing in the wrong partners can be very damaging to your startup and its chances for ongoing success.

During the course of sharing mutual entrepreneurial passions, people can get intoxicated with new ideas. As you've seen in previous chapters, entrepreneurs have that effect on people. The lure of entrepreneurialism is an attraction that can pull anyone off his or her previously chosen pathway, but what happens if participation represents a temporary detour, rather than a true commitment to stay the course?

An anxious entrepreneur searching for assistance can do a great job of selling his or her idea to anyone who will listen. But some of those people may sign up for the ride, with no real intention of ever actually getting into the car. The perils of blind enthusiasm are particularly challenging for bootstrapping entrepreneurs who don't have the funds to pay salaries and are willing to exchange equity in return for labor. Partners may come on board and ride the planning wave, then suddenly bail when it's commitment time. This can severely derail or set back the entrepreneur's launch plans.

To make the most of your own recruitment efforts, and to avoid the problems of "morning after" partnering regrets and eventual split-ups, I recommend that you take care to avoid the following four types of candidates when recruiting partners for your startup:

- **The "Other You" Partner.** You might be tempted to look for partners who mirror your own background, experience, and expectations, but don't let those similarities be the selling point. Although you and your buddy may be two peas in a pod, most likely your business doesn't need your twin. You need a partner who can do what you *can't* do and knows what you *don't* know. By partnering with people who complement rather than duplicate your skills, you're better able to spread around the workload and cover more bases. And although it's important that you and your partners are able to discuss differences and agree on plans for moving forward, you don't need someone who parrots your opinions on every issue. By bringing in partners with varying skills, backgrounds, and views, you're broadening your organization's potential for innovation and success.

- **The "F-Words" Partner (Friends and Family).** Although many startups draw upon the assistance of friends and family (as did mine), hiring them as full partners in your startup may not be the best idea—in fact, it can be a recipe for disaster. Some entrepreneurs hire people they're close to out of a sense of obligation, or because they feel more comfortable tackling a new business with the aid of those they love and trust. But remember this: you're starting a business, not an aid agency for out-of-work loved ones or a mutual support group. Friends and family may be willing to work for little or nothing, but if they don't work *out,* you'll find out just how costly that "cheap help" really can be. If you don't relish the idea of having to manage—or even dump—the people who mean the most to you, be extremely cautious about involving them as partners in your startup.

- **The "Poverty Level" Partner.** At the risk of starting a class war, I have to strongly urge you to find out as much as possible about the financial background of any potential partner, and to consider—very carefully—your willingness to bring on someone with little or no means of support other than your startup. When you partner with anyone, you're in essence agreeing to share the burden of that person's financial obligations. How long can the person you're considering last with the limited income you can offer during the early months (or even years) of your Startup phase? Could this person continue to work for you if you couldn't offer *any* income for a period of time? With the economic upheavals of the past several years, many people have had to gut their personal savings, leaving them with no safety net. When determining whom to cast your lot with in the hectic, demanding days of the Startup phase, you can't afford to overlook the potential loss of a partner due to financial burnout. Even someone with the best intentions of riding out the storm of Startup may have to bail if the money dries up. And if that person has a particularly desirable skill set, the likelihood of an early adios becomes even greater, and with it, the risk that you'll be left with significant shoes to fill. I'm not saying that you should never partner with anyone who's low on capital or other means of support, but you really do have to explore and consider this issue carefully when taking on key partners in your new venture.

- **The "Overcommitted" Partner.** You may be attracted to a partner because you see how hard she works. She seems to be involved and engaged in every activity imaginable. As I've said, my graphic designer was like that, always volunteering and keeping multiple balls in the air. You need to take care, however, not to partner with people who are willing to bite off more than they can chew. I was lucky; my partner could balance her workload by working 16-hour days, and seemed quite willing to do so. Often, however, partners who initially seem happy to brush off any concerns about the demands of powering up a new business run out of juice just when they're needed the most. If anyone you're considering taking on as a partner doesn't have a history of successful multitasking or startup experience, be sure to fully discuss and explore his or her other commitments and likely ability to see your business through its critical Startup phase. The last thing you need to hear from your partners is "Sorry, I just don't have time for this anymore," just when you most need their help.

Bear in mind that these four "worst partners ever" types are generalizations that many successful entrepreneurial partners contradict. In the end, you'll need to carefully vet and choose your own partner candidates, and you may decide that the right choices for you include someone who is very similar to you in experience and outlook, or who has no financial safety net, or who hasn't had an opportunity to prove her ability to juggle 14 different jobs without ever dropping the ball. It's okay to break my rules, as long as you fully understand why you're doing so. When you know what you're looking for in a partner, and what potential shortcomings or issues you need to be aware of, you're in a position to make the decision that's best for your new organization based on your own assessment, judgment, and needs.

For example, I had one other sweat equity partner in my own startup, and that was my wife Lisa. She agreed to be responsible for all of the administrative and accounting work in my new business. In many ways, Lisa was the accidental entrepreneur, the one partner I drafted from within the ranks of my close family relationships, who proved that there really are exceptions to my own rules. I couldn't have made a better choice. Not only was Lisa fantastic at her work in my business, but she was also an unfailing source of moral support and encouragement. Lisa was invaluable in her ability to help me get through some of the most difficult times of a very difficult period. She unfailingly encouraged me to go for it, and she never stopped being supportive of my dreams.

Here's another confession: she could have fallen into the overly committed partner problem as well. Lisa had a full-time job outside of my new business. She would most often start her work for me around 10 p.m., after our daughter was put to bed and all other household duties were done. I'm not trying to confuse you with this seemingly conflicting information about choosing strong partners. But I do want to show you the value of carefully considering the qualifications—and potential drawbacks—of anyone you're considering partnering with in your entrepreneurial enterprise. The four types I've outlined above are those that you're most likely to encounter and consider in your search for partners; don't fall into the trap of accepting partners who your research and instincts tell you won't work, but who seem too good (or too difficult) to refuse. Use careful consideration, and weigh all potential outcomes before making your choices.

Forging Successful Partnerships

The strength of your partnerships will never matter more than they will during the Startup phase of your business. In launching my new venture, which I had decided to name Technology Resource Center, Inc., or TRC, I had to wear many hats—as did my partners. A somewhat controlled chaos developed in my life as I started building the new business (in Betsy's basement) during the early morning and night, while continuing to report to work at Educational Resources by day. There were clear priorities at TRC, and getting out the catalog was first among them. I handled most tasks on my own or through Betsy and Lisa in order to avoid any extra expenses. Every part of the company was starting to come together.

Our office space, however, continued to be dicey. Betsy's townhouse basement was unfinished and lighted with just a few ceiling-mounted bulbs on pull strings. I brought in a couple of mismatched lamps and an old desk, while Betsy provided an additional desk and a few secondhand dining room chairs. About twenty-five feet away from our desks were the washer and dryer. We tried to plan outbound calls between rinse cycles, so we could hear over the roar of the machines. Still, it was great having Betsy available during the day to provide our customers with a human contact rather than voice mail. Around five a.m. each weekday morning, I would arrive at Betsy's townhouse and let myself in with the key she provided. The Horlock family would still be sleeping as I silently made my way to the basement. Can you imagine that routine in your house? Again, I had selected a great partner.

Occasionally, when Betsy wasn't available, my father-in-law, Frank Rubino, would make the drive to her townhome to answer calls. A small business owner himself, Frank understood the startup struggle. He had no idea how to answer questions being asked about the technology products we sold, but he was there to take messages. Frank's assistance was invaluable and helped to establish a level of customer service that I maintained through-out my time running the business. No voice mail—we answered the phone when our customers called.

Within months of our decision to form the company, I had already started producing the layout of the catalog and submitting pages to our graphic designer. Betsy and I were working with publishers on the side to secure co-op funds to cover the cost of the catalog. I had set aside $30,000 of my money to invest in the business, but I needed those co-op funds to make my own investment last as long as possible. Life was crazy working two jobs, but deep down inside I loved it. As the deadline for our print date approached, however, the excitement began to deteriorate into stress. I was targeting the catalog to hit the 1996 summer buying season, which was the peak buying period for higher education. The catalog would include over 100 pages, which meant acquiring and producing hundreds of high-resolution images and copy. I also had vendor relationships to establish and price points to determine. I was used to tackling these jobs with a fully trained team of eight people working in an established company with existing rela-tionships. Now, the responsibility seemed immense. Our graphic designer was stressing too, even though her entire professional life was built around deadlines. This one was going to be tough for all of us.

Communication technologies were still relatively new at that time, and we couldn't exchange the huge graphic files for our catalog digitally. In order to get things done, I had to get up at four a.m. and drive twenty-five miles to Betsy's house to do what work I could squeeze in before putting in my 8-to-5 day at Educational Resources. Then, it was back to Betsy's for more work, and off to our designer's house, twenty-two miles away, to drop off the new layouts and pick up completed drafts before making my final trek home. In other words, I had some serious windshield time.

I was stressing out, and it showed. One early morning I made a reverse commute to pick up finished pages at the designer's house for editing prior to starting my regular workday. On the way back to Educational Resources, while making a turn, I struck a two-foot-high concrete median dividing the highway. I don't know how it happened—I was either asleep or deep in thought about what needed to get done. No one was hurt, but I knew that was sheer luck. Another time, I was forced to call the paramedics to our house at midnight, because I was certain I was having a heart attack. I was reaching the breaking point.

Fortunately, our working partnership at TRC helped keep all of us going. As my partners and I coached each other through this hectic time, some outside client partnerships also stepped in to help ease the pressure. TRC was already starting to fulfill customer orders given to us by publishers who were unwilling or unable to process orders directly from schools. I had a great relationship with the one publishing representative who selected TRC for all of his direct educational orders. The deal was a windfall, and it was also a testament to the importance of forming strong alliances and outside relationships. Those early orders helped us create our first internal operational procedures for purchasing products, packaging them, and shipping them out. Best of all, these early orders were high margin and provided a much-needed revenue stream. We were growing, along with our new company—and our partnership.

Unfortunately, between the hectic pace of starting the company and being extremely frugal, I failed to get a legal agreement signed by my partners outlining our verbal agreement. Although I did go to a lawyer to draft our corporate bylaws, issue stock certificates, and handle related details, I failed to finalize the actual employee stock agreement. To this day, I don't understand how I neglected this. Sure, I knew that I needed to ask the people I'd brought on board to sign off on an agreement. And yes, I realized that I hadn't done that up-front. I always intended to do it later. I knew my partners well, and we had developed a strong, well-coordinated working team. But we still should have had a written partnership agreement. I put together a draft but never saw it through, and how I made that mistake is beyond me. And yes, as you'll learn later in this book, my oversight would come back to haunt me.

The key to forming and keeping a successful partnership is to establish methods that eliminate problems from occurring or mitigate their effects should they occur. The only secure way of doing that is by forming a solid partnership agreement up-front. Agreements can take all forms, and (obviously) you need to consult a lawyer to create a partnership agreement that works for you and your partners. But here are some general guidelines that you, as an entrepreneur, should consider:

- **Try not to give up more than 51 percent of your ownership.** If the business is built around your entrepreneurial idea, you need to be in control of the company, and this percentage of ownership will allow you to do so. Even if you and your partner are considered equals in bringing the idea to life, ask for controlling interest. If you hold just 1 percent more ownership than your partners, that majority could be critical down the road if a struggle develops to control the company's goals, mission, or vision.

- **Document in the agreement how and when you and your partners will get paid and if bonuses will be awarded.** These decisions should be based on predetermined metrics from your financial statements. For example, the agreement might state that you each will be paid once the company shows a net profit derived from the income statement, and you each will draw a salary of 10 percent of the stated profit each month. The more detailed the agreement the better, in order to eliminate ambiguity and to provide a clear, jointly created, and factual document that all of you can reference back to as necessary.

- **Purchase shares to put skin in the game.** A clear-cut way to determine ownership commitment is to put your own money into the enterprise. Partner investments may be part of the company's essential original funding or serve as a tool to leverage individual commitment. Founders can choose what value they want to assign to the company shares; then anyone joining as a partner must pay the designated share price for the agreed-upon percentage.

- **Think long term.** When your partners contribute sweat equity rather than putting down money to obtain shares, you must give especially careful consideration to the structure of your formal agreement. You don't want to give someone a percentage of your company only to see him or her work for six months, get tired and quit, and then walk away with part of your business. That's why many companies issue stock options that only become active or valuable under predetermined circumstances, such as the sale of the company. Your agreement's specific language addressing stock options should put conditions on the partner's commitment. For instance, your agreement might specify that only a portion of the options are valid after one year of service, a greater portion become valid after two years, and so on. Your agreement also could stipulate that partners will only realize a return upon the sale of the company. Again, the more detailed the agreement, the better.

- **Give everyone a way out.** People's lives change. Having the ability to buy and sell granted options makes it easier—and more lucrative—for partners to leave the business when they feel ready to go. Establishing a method, like EBITDA (earnings before interest, taxes, depreciation, and amortization), to determine the company valuation allows partners to sell their options back to the company and exit with a financial gain. Further, this measurement and method serves to incentivize partners to grow the value of the company as they see that value reflected in their share price. Finally, principal partners can purchase shares down the road by buying out other partners.

The point I'm trying to make is that partners are people, and people are unpredictable. If you are the one driving your idea with your passion, don't expect your partners to share your level of commitment.

PREPARE FOR EARLY DEPARTURES

Think long term as you assess your partners at the very beginning of your business conception. Lots of people will get caught up in the excitement of a new venture. After all, it touches upon a dream shared by many—that of owning their own business. As an entrepreneur, you'll speak of your business prospect with excitement and energy, and that excitement will hook into the imagination of those around you. You can expect that people will want to jump on board and hitch a ride, but you can't allow them to leave you with the risk while they attach themselves solely to the opportunity.

Your challenge is to motivate your employees and partners about your venture, but always stay grounded and remember that no one cares about your dream as much as you do. In the early months or years of your Startup phase, people will lose their excitement about the potential for the future your business holds. Be prepared to lose them. Do your best to build redundant systems and information, document procedures, and become intimately familiar with all aspects of your business. Plan for where you can find replacements for talent that walks out the door so you don't skip a beat or allow the momentum of your business to stall. Above all, protect your equity. Have a shareholder agreement drafted by an experienced lawyer who understands your motives and direction.

Growing with My Partners—And My Business

The IT industry was very small and tight knit, and publishers were beginning to talk about the Jeff Weber at Educational Resources and the Jeff Weber at Technology Resource Center, Inc. One day I was called to the carpet by the Human Resource Director at Educational Resources, who quickly laid out for me the (very accurate) details she had heard about my new company. How do I handle this?, I thought. My initial panic was triggered by the knowledge that I might be fired, but my gut-level fear actually was rooted in the idea of having to commit fully to TRC. I was passionate about my new business and my partners, but I really didn't want to lose the security of a steady job and paycheck. So I spun the story that "yes, this company exists, but Betsy Horlock is running it, and I'm merely her consultant." While I told myself that this wasn't completely a lie, I realized that soon I was going to have to make a decision about my fate, or someone else would.

My own all-encompassing goal at this point was to finish the catalog; I had little time or energy left to focus on the details of launching the company. In fact, after crashing the car, calling the paramedics, and nearly being fired, I was actually ready to call it quits. I was running out of the steam I would need to create the business post-catalog. I was exhausted and stressed, and didn't have anything really to show for all the hard work and time I had invested over the past several months. I decided that I would just complete the catalog, mail it, and then call it quits. I could say with confidence that I had tried to make my entrepreneurial dream a reality, but it just didn't work out. All I would be out would be a few thousand dollars and my time, but life would be back to normal. I wanted to get back to normal.

Happily, I can tell you now that my return to "normal" never happened. Eventually, the catalog layout was finished and off to the presses. At that moment, the slate of worry and fatigue was wiped clean, and all of the stress, frustration, and doubt washed away from our partnership. The catalog was a hit from day one. The phone rang, and purchase orders arrived via mail and fax. We were legitimate, on the street, and people were buying from us with confidence. Those first orders from our publishing client partners had helped us refine our logistics, and our operation was working smoothly. It was time to get focused on this company and start navigating it through the end of its Startup phase.

While my business and the strength of my partnerships was growing, the one element missing from this successful startup equation was me. I was still working two jobs, still waiting for the "perfect" time to jump in with both feet. I thought that once sales were up to my current salary, I could leave my position at Educational Resources and go full-time with TRC . . . a nice, smooth transition. My Risk Box was preventing me from taking that momentary financial step backward to invest in what was to come. The Risk Box was saying, "Successful people don't work in basements on old rickety chairs" and "Successful people sure as heck make more money than what you're bringing home from this venture." But my barrier was mental, not budgetary.

The company was alive and thriving, but it needed my full commitment to really succeed. Lisa and I spent our sixth wedding anniversary dinner discussing just how far we had come in our lives, and then the topic turned to those things I really wanted to accomplish professionally. Lisa truly is my best friend, main supporter, and constant cheerleader. Now, she was also my business partner. At that anniversary dinner, she firmly said to me, without hesitation, "Go in and quit!" That statement blasted through the walls of my Risk Box. I gave my notice the next day sending my life into a completely new and exciting direction. It seemed as if all the stress and anxiety immediately lifted when I quit and started to report to Betsy's basement full-time. The fact that I was fully committed to TRC would make all the difference in its growth.

I know now that my situation wasn't unique. Many entrepreneurial ideas never come to fruition or fail to survive past their first year as a result of moonlighting. Instead of devoting all of their time and effort to a new business, entrepreneurial moonlighters keep one foot placed comfortably in their old job. I'm not encouraging anyone to rush and quit the day job. Rather, careful observation and planning is needed to know when the time is right to strike out on your own full-time. The Risk Box will continually pull you back in as long as you keep a foot inside that wall. Only when you step all the way through will you realize your full potential and allow your business the greatest opportunity to thrive. If you find yourself trying to "offshore" the work of managing your entrepreneurial startup to others while you wait to jump in at the most opportune moment, you need to seriously consider how strongly committed you are to making your new venture a success. You can't leave the business of running your business up to others for long, at least not if you want it to survive and thrive in a tough marketplace. No matter how many good, committed partners you may have, you need to take the helm, and that will require your full-time commitment.

As we moved further along in our startup, I hired our first employee: Chris Skrzypchak, a college student from nearby Judson College in Elgin. What this kid must have thought about us when he started! But he soon became intoxicated with TRC's mission and growth. He had a visible entrepreneurial passion of his own, and he really identified with what we were doing. He became a very loyal and valuable employee who stayed with us seven years after his graduation.

TRC was outgrowing its surroundings, and it was clear to me that it was time to legitimize this baby of ours by getting some office space. In nine months we had grown to a point where cash flow was predictable enough to cover the monthly rent. One of my greatest days at TRC was moving out of my partner Betsy's basement and into our modest office space. Signing that two-year lease was a big deal for me and my partners. I was confident the business would continue to succeed. In fact, I was more concerned that the business would fail if we did not make this move. Our new location was in a retail strip mall in West Dundee with a video store and dry cleaner as our neighbors. There were no office partitions to provide privacy for the four desks we started out with. It was simply a long, rectangular space that was bare of everything except the necessities to run our business. As you saw earlier in the chapter, my skills as a frugal-preneur helped fill that space, and the next, with the furniture we needed—and could afford.

That first permanent location wouldn't last long, all thanks to the efforts of another outside partner—of sorts. Less than six months after TRC moved into its offices, my landlord asked if I would like more space. Ladi, as he liked to go by because his full Ukrainian name was difficult to pronounce, was a colorful personality and an entrepreneur in his own right who owned the entire mall. I thought his proposal was nuts. We had picked up one additional employee and didn't see space issues on the horizon. Perhaps Ladi had a greater vision for me than I did at the time; he suggested we move down four doors to a double unit that would be vacant the next month. After some deliberation, coercion, and soul searching, my partners and I agreed. We took the double unit, which lent itself to the phrase "If you build it, they will come." We quickly started adding employees to fill our expanded space.

I've heard it said that goldfish only grow to the size of their tanks, and I think the same truth applies to business. If your organization is in a confined physical space, its growth is going to be stunted, too; a large space will encourage quicker growth. Call it psychology or a self-fulfilling prophecy at work, but I believe it's true. A growing company should acquire adequate space to expand. Moving into your own dedicated space will be one of the defining moments of your own experience as an entrepreneur. Seeing your sign on the door and stepping back and looking at this business you created from scratch is an amazing experience—just one of many you will encounter as you prepare to move beyond the Startup phase of your journey.

Developing a Winning Team

Those early years were fun as we achieved phenomenal sales growth year over year. Employees were continually being added, and the office was abuzz. Customers were developing a deep loyalty to our company, thanks to its exceptional customer service and focus on their business needs and processes. Everyone who worked at TRC understood our mission, and all of us were excited to be a part of a startup.

I was always self-conscious of our appearance to new hires, as we were a business-to-business operation, located in a neighborhood retail consumer strip mall, in offices that certainly weren't lavish. This was the dot-com age, and I couldn't compete with these physical facilities and in-office perks the IT startups were using to attract and retain employees. It took a long time for me to realize that none of these things mattered to my employees—they were attracted to the entrepreneurial passion of our work. The power of that passion also helped attract another important partner to my new business—someone who would become my right-hand man, as well as an equity partner.

Sam DeSoto walked into our new office space only a few weeks after our arrival in 1997. Sam had been one of my product managers at Educational Resources. Sam had been silently observing our progress at TRC from basement to storefront. We exchanged a few emails, and he dropped in one day to see what we had going. We talked for a while about his plans and about my vision for TRC. I let him know, right up-front, that I wanted him to lead our sales team.

Thankfully, the powers of the entrepreneur had an impact on Sam. Instead of seeing a half-filled office space in a strip mall, he saw opportunity. He saw success. Sam took the position and made the commitment to ride it through to the end. Sam became my number-two person at TRC, and our skills sets and approach to forward thinking complemented each other. I could count on him to question, push, and challenge me, and that's an important function for every principal partner.

As you move from being the driving force behind a startup to being the leader of a thriving full-scale operation, you have to be very careful to avoid "yes-men" (of either sex). They don't belong in any environment, let alone an entrepreneurial one. If you see a yes-man developing among your workforce, challenge that person to change or leave the company. The last thing you need is to work with someone whose only contribution is to mimic your ideas and opinions. That type of employee or partner offers nothing to your business, and as you begin running a stable organization, you need to make sure that everyone around you brings their own talents, skills, ideas, and innovations to the table.

It's important to have people around you that push your limits, like Sam and Ladi did for me. Even though you are a leader, you don't want others on your team to continually look to you for directions about their next move. If you find that situation developing, do something to change it; otherwise, you may never leave your comfort zone. As a leader, you will have to foster an environment of feedback and commentary, and create an open forum for suggestions if you want to encourage strong thinking and decision making throughout your organization. Entrepreneurs get stale as a result of their isolation, and the stagnation of that "lonely at the top" existence encourages them to fall into a routine, rather than to continually innovate and improve the organization. Don't let all of the thinking in your business get pushed onto you; everyone on your team needs to understand that they are respected—even required—to present their own ideas and make their own decisions, in order to grow the startup into a more competent and vibrant organization.

As an entrepreneur, you will have a vision for your company that will extend far beyond its actual image during startup, and it will be your burning desire to get to that ultimate vision as fast as possible. In doing so, you will find yourself evangelizing your business to anyone who will listen. In the early days of the Startup phase, many of your partners and employees will act almost like followers of a cult-like leader, and they will be devout in their role of achieving your vision. But as you move to the end of that phase, you will need to redirect the power of your passion to take your organization to the next level.

The charisma of the entrepreneur and my belief in the future that my company could create for all of us were powerful tools that helped me harness the greatest resources for TRC and drive the company onward to become a fully operational business that could truly realize my vision. With the addition of Sam and my other new human resources, along with my expansive new office space, I left the Startup phase of my entrepreneurial experience with TRC. It had been an intense ride; from those first moments of sharing my idea with my wife and other new partners, to drawing up my first business plan and finding the human and physical resources to help me bring it to life, I had transformed my entrepreneurial idea from a dream into a reality. Now came the difficult challenge of running the business. In the next part of this book, we'll explore the hard and exciting work of the Running phase. There, I'll share more of my experiences and hard-won lessons to help prepare you for the long ride ahead, as you make your own transition from entrepreneurial upstart to seasoned business leader.

PHASE III

At this point, you have completed the two hardest stages of your entrepreneurial journey. You have established an idea that satisfies the requirements of the E-Formula and thereby allows you to activate as an entrepreneur. After making the decision to go for it, you have adequately planned and prepared to start your company. You then assessed your desire against what you valued most in your Risk Box, and jumped in with both feet to make the business a viable success. As you reach the Running phase of the entrepreneurial journey, you have done far more than most of the people who have ever dreamed of starting their own business.

The fear of committing that you experienced in the Idea phase turns into a fear of failure in the Running phase of the business. In even the most successful businesses, entrepreneurs are constantly concerned with survival. This fear may rest in the back of your mind, but you can expect it to be always present as you grow and develop your business. Don't think of that fear as immobilizing, however; instead, consider it your motivator to build and execute winning strategies for success. Now that you are fully engaged in the business and have proven its viability, your actions all must be targeted toward growth and innovation. Your efforts as an entrepreneur have paid off.

The set of rules you might have developed for the Startup phase of your business won't necessarily work in the Running phase. Your company is becoming more responsive to customer demand, rather than generating it. You have to develop processes to run the business in a consistent and predictable way. Your role as an entrepreneur in the business also needs to change; at this point, your focus has to be on scaling, innovating, and leading.

As you move through this phase of your journey, you should get used to measuring success in accomplishments rather than in dollars. Money is merely a business metric, not a true measure of success. If you do your work effectively and grow your business according to your plans, your money metric should grow in kind. If you can maintain this perspective, you will come to regard even your failures as successes, because you will learn something invaluable from each experience. The popular *Chicken Soup for the Soul* book and subsequent series was reportedly rejected 77 times before HCI Books picked up the first title and went on to sell over 100 million copies. The success was not the 100 million books sold but the fact that the authors did not give up after continual rejection and failure.

Unfortunately, as many business owners grow to become successful, they begin to lose an understanding of why their customers buy their products or services. They focus more on the revenue coming in and less on measuring their marketing efforts. They may start to remove themselves from actively soliciting customer feedback. That's a danger in the Running phase. Businesses get so focused on fulfilling demand that they simply stop listening to their customers. Startup is all about customer focus and tweaking your product or service to get it just right. And that's one startup attribute that you must never lose, no matter how long you stay in business.

Business startup spans from inception to the point of consistent customer demand and then reinvention. You actually start *running* a business once consistent demand kicks in. That is the point when your business moves from a customer-demand-generation mode of operation to a customer-demand-response mode. Danger waits for entrepreneurs who become complacent during this transition. They become reactionary instead of staying focused on customer needs, trends, and threats. When customers consistently and proactively choose your product or service, you have created a sustainable business. You are in the Running phase. Now your talent and ability must be up to the challenge of growing beyond what you have accomplished so far.

In Phase III, we'll talk about what's involved in meeting that challenge. First, we explore your role as an entrepreneur, both in building the business and in developing a culture in which your organization can continue to grow and flourish. You'll learn about the multifaceted nature of that culture and the details of its major components, including ethics and honesty, selling, and innovation and change. The final chapter in this part will discuss one of the toughest tasks that you must manage as an entrepreneurial leader—scaling your organization for growth.

CHAPTER NINE

Leading Your Business

As I've said before, lots of people dream of starting their own business so they can be "the boss"—so they can sit back, bark orders, and watch the money come in. Those people really don't want to be entrepreneurs, because most entrepreneurs are actively involved in all facets of the organization. That involvement changes, however, over time. During the Startup phase, you may have worn just about every hat in your company and pitched in whenever and wherever you could. As your business enters its Running phase, that needs to change. You now must be the visionary for your organization, which means you can't be buried in the trenches of day-to-day operations. Your priority must quickly shift to hiring staff to conduct daily operational tasks and then setting up policies, processes, and procedures to help guide their activities. Then, you can focus on setting the course for your company and guiding it toward its future.

In this chapter, we'll talk about the process of designating tasks and giving authority to others within your growing organization while still maintaining policies, procedures, and oversight to help ensure that the essential work of your new business remains on track (and above board). This chapter also offers guidance for the critical task of establishing a culture of ethics and honesty to help guard against fraudulent attacks from both inside and outside the organization. And, because most entrepreneurs started a business in order to follow their passion, we'll also look at ways you can use and develop your own interests to help drive your personal growth and that of your business. At the end of this chapter, we'll take a brief (I promise) but critical look at the situational approach to leadership and how you can use it to develop your most effective leadership style. As I've matured in the role of entrepreneurial leader, I've developed my own approach to leadership. I'll open this chapter by sharing with you some of the principles that guide my attitudes and actions as a leader.

Following the 10 Principles of Leadership

A lot of the material in this chapter deals with delegation. That's because one of the most difficult things for entrepreneurs to overcome is their need to be in charge of every aspect of the organization. But what does being "in charge" really mean? Many entrepreneurs feel it is noble and necessary to be the hard worker who puts in countless hours churning through even the most mundane business tasks in order to play the good role model for others in the organization. Other entrepreneurs continue sinking their time into everyday operational tasks because they simply aren't familiar or comfortable with their role as a leader. It's true that working a production line can give you a sense of immediate accomplishment. But by letting nonleadership chores distract you from your primary responsibilities, you might actually be stifling the potential progress of your entire organization.

As an entrepreneur, you need to put yourself in a position to observe customer needs and your own organization's strengths, weaknesses, opportunities, and threats. Your responsibility as an entrepreneurial leader is to grow your company, and that requires a broader perspective than you can gain by burying yourself in the trenches. Here are 10 core principles that I've developed and used over the years to help me delegate more effectively and maintain focus on the essential tasks of leadership.

1. Work toward making the business independent of you.

Entrepreneurs have reached an important milestone of success when they can step away from their business for prolonged periods of time and not be missed. The only way you can reach this milestone is by (1) hiring employees you can trust and (2) establishing a culture reflective of the values that you want to guide your organization. These aren't simple accomplishments. It takes well-designed hiring processes and a strong commitment to managing your own actions and decisions to build the staff and culture that will enable you to put some space between yourself and the company. But doing so is absolutely essential to your ongoing success. Creating an organization that can function independent of your constant oversight is the only way you will have the freedom to pursue ideas, innovate, and plan strategy— activities that are critical to your company's ongoing survival and success. And, it ensures that the business can continue on, even if you are for some reason unable to lead it.

2. Build controls that protect the assets of the company.

You can just about count on some internal or external source trying to defraud your business. Checks and balances around your cash and assets will help deter fraud, and they'll help you detect when someone has a hand in the cookie jar. Attacks on your company may come from outside sources such as the Internet, but most fraud develops from within. The best prevention is to remove temptation and install checks and balances into the processes surrounding your most sensitive assets: your cash and your merchandise. Pay special attention to areas such as check processing, petty cash, payroll processing, expense reimbursements, and invoicing. As most of you know, fraud grows deeper and more sophisticated as you move to the web. In the early days of TRC, we were getting weekly attempts at online fraud through our e-commerce mechanisms. Today, those attacks are hourly in most big online firms. Thinking through policies and procedures and understanding those tasks up-front will decrease opportunities for fraudulent behavior.

Remember, your people are your assets, too, and they need to be protected from temptation and undue suspicion. That's just one reason that you need proper screening for new hires and well-established physical building security measures. You also can protect your people by providing benefits, flexible work hours, and a competitive market wage. Your customers are your other important assets, and to protect their data and privacy, you need to ensure you provide a safe product and internal security measures.

3. Have a solid financial understanding of your business.

Most small and even medium-size businesses don't have a chief financial officer (CFO) on staff. Instead, they hire an accountant to produce financial statements, file taxes, and perform related obligations. In those cases, the CFO's responsibilities for managing the financial risks of the business typically fall to the entrepreneur. No matter your organizational structure, as the founder of your business, you must develop a solid understanding of its basic financial statements and the cost of goods, margins, expenses, and income. This advice may seem obvious, but a fair amount of entrepreneurs don't want to be involved in these aspects because they are too focused on the product or service that led them into the business. Financial oversight isn't a lot of fun, but it's one of those things you have to master in order to successfully lead a growing organization.

4. Hire great talent.

As we discussed in chapter 8, your people will always be your organization's greatest asset, so you should fill strategic positions with the best people you can find. The people you place in critical roles should be independent and able to grow within a rapidly changing environment. Most important, they should be able to run with your vision and effectively manage the department or division you have assigned to them. Your key personnel should challenge you and the people who report to them.

Hiring can be a lengthy, grueling process, and you might become tempted to just hire someone and be done with it. Resist that urge. You'll spend a great deal more time dealing with a bad hire than you will making a good hiring decision. And if you think financial matters are tedious and nerve-racking, wait until you have to go through the process of dumping an ineffective or inept employee. That process can be costly, disruptive, and incredibly demoralizing to those watching the revolving door. Always conduct background checks and contact references for all hires; the investment of time and money spent screening candidates will be repaid by a thoroughly vetted workforce.

5. Create a clear, market-differentiating vision for your product or service.

A great deal of your time and energy as a leader should be spent continually innovating your business around your customer. The intellectual property (IP) created by your company is its market differentiator; it determines not just what your organization is, but what your organization is *like*. Businesses that copy other businesses typically don't have sustained success. The companies they've copied quickly come up with new innovations to distinguish themselves in the marketplace. In turn, those innovations attract new customers and create new markets.

By carving out your own unique presence and reputation for ongoing innovation, you can secure your market presence, rather than temporarily taking up space in someone else's niche. Finally, the IP you develop will help establish a higher valuation when it comes to selling or financing your business. Ultimately, innovation defines the entrepreneurial enterprise; without it, you'll be left to compete on little more than price.

6. Develop an exit strategy designed to maximize the value of the business.

If you haven't already done so (when you wrote your business plan, as I recommended in chapter 6), when you enter the Running phase of your business, you need to plan for your exit. Whether your exit strategy involves a sale to employees, transfer to a family member, sale to a private equity firm or competitor, or even retirement (remember that retirement isn't typically a strong exit strategy), you have to visualize your exit plan and then position your company for that scenario. Planning an exit strategy isn't just about maximizing your payout; it's also an essential tactic for strengthening the company's position and enabling it to continue on toward its mission without you at the helm. We talk more thoroughly about the Exit phase of your business in the last part of this book, but forming and following that strategy is a core principle of strong leadership. Your ability to manage, document, and develop your business with the appropriate exit in mind will ensure a smooth transition for all *and* maximize the organization's potential valuation.

7. Manage profitably.

Understanding your financials is one thing; managing them is another. As founder, you need to have a solid understanding of how your business will make and spend money. Some entrepreneurs describe themselves as creative thinkers—idea generators with no interest in the money aspect of their business. That's a dangerous route to take. You need to know exactly how your company will generate profits: not just sales and revenues, but sustainable and growing profits. Further, you need to know how to contain and control costs.

Establishing a yearly budget for every department will be your first step. Your second will be establishing policy and procedures for how money is to be spent and how profit is to be derived. Trust me, if you don't cap or limit spending, it can quickly spiral out of control. The same is true for establishing pricing policies that don't give away the farm. Inexperienced salespeople will use price more often than not as their leverage to close a deal. Developing a strategic sales process and pricing guidelines will help protect your bottom line.

Two key areas on the operational side of the business will help you monitor profitability, and those are accounts receivable and interest expenses. Letting your accounts receivable functions slide is a cardinal mistake in managing cash flow. Entrepreneurs who put all of their energies into attracting and winning customers are often gun-shy when it comes to collecting payment from them. The fear of hurting the relationship is paramount in their minds, and it becomes easier to ignore the problem—until they find they are unable to meet payroll. The likelihood of collecting past-due amounts greatly diminishes after ninety days, and many young and growing organizations haven't dedicated manpower to the collection process.

Increasingly, companies are turning to factoring as a method to speed their cash flow and outsource collections. In factoring, a third party (the factor) purchases your outstanding invoices (a financial asset) at, say, 90 percent of their value, paying in cash, immediately. The factor then is left with the task of collecting from the invoicees (the debtors) while you move on to the next sale. The credit worthiness of your customers determines the purchase rate the factor will offer you for your invoices. For factoring to work for you, your invoices must include a factoring margin, or the factoring cost has to be built into the selling price.

Margin consideration also must be factored into interest expenses on your past-due invoices, bank fees, or credit card balance. You may be able to maintain the minimum balance on your personal credit cards, but it's stupid, if not impossible, to do so using a corporate account. Credit cards can be a great source of short-term financing, but you must pay them off in full each month to preserve profits. Using these and other techniques to track and manage interest expenses is an essential component of skillful leadership.

8. Don't copy—be copied.

Startups that have moved into the Running phase of their business life can easily get distracted by their own growth and overly influenced by competitors and larger companies with greater resources. These businesses can be tempted to stray from their original mission by constantly seeking new markets or by copying competitors. Avoid this trap. You have nothing to gain by comparing yourself to the big, established player in your industry. In fact, doing so can demotivate and deflate you, and leave you feeling inadequate and incapable of ever being able to compete. More importantly, those kinds of comparisons can tempt you to try to copy other businesses and their models. That will only deteriorate your market differentiation and thereby leave you with price as your sole customer enticement.

You won't win the marketplace by copying the big dogs who play in it. Study your competitors to see how you can become even more different from them. Look for ways to do things for your customers that the competition can't provide. Learn what customers *don't* like about your competitors, rather than dwelling on their successes.

You started your business to bring something new and different to the marketplace, and that's how you will succeed. As a new and growing organization, you can model your business around customer needs better than those large competitors who, in most cases, require customers to accept their model and way of doing business. Watch and listen to your customers, and don't be distracted by large, well-established competitors.

9. Don't starve yourself.

Many entrepreneurs pinch pennies for years in an attempt to beef up their bottom line, and paying themselves a ridiculously low salary is a common element of their austerity program. Taking a low salary may be necessary during the early days of your startup, but at some point, your need to provide for your family must overshadow your need to save money. Pay yourself the best salary you can, when you can, and set a realistic goal early in your Running phase to get to that point. Failing to do so not only robs you of money you could use now or save for the future, but it will also negatively affect the valuation of your business when you are negotiating its sale.

Why does your low salary lower the sale value of your business? Most buyers will recognize the expense gap in salary and factor that into their evaluation—negatively affecting the amount they are willing to pay. Buyers know they will have to pay someone at least a current market rate to run this business, so your organization's current profitability is artificially inflated by your lower-than-market-rate salary.

And, here's one final reason that you need to pay yourself well for the work you do: running your business is a lot more fun when you are making money!

10. Work "on" your business, not "in" it.

This phrase has been used by many, most notably by author Michael Gerber, who has written extensively on the topic of leadership in small businesses. This golden rule should be your guide to delegating the daily tasks of your business. Ideally, your time as an entrepreneurial leader should be largely engaged with observing and studying your business from every perspective and reflecting on its progress and potential for innovation and growth. You'll interrupt this process if you spend too much time on any one particular task or area by moving from studying it to *doing* the tasks involved in it. By remembering that your job, as a leader, is to innovate and grow your business, you'll be better able to resist the temptation to immerse yourself in today's mundane tasks so you can maintain your focus on the road ahead.

CEO? PRESIDENT? WHAT'S THE DIFFERENCE?

Your ability to determine your role in the Running phase and to understand your responsibilities and duties as a leader will, in part, depend on your organizational structure. The shape of that structure begins with your title. Many entrepreneurs use the titles of CEO and president interchangeably, but the two roles are symbiotic, rather than identical.

By definition, a chief executive officer is primarily responsible for strategy, including long-range planning and company direction. The president's role, on the other hand, is tactical, with a focus on operations and a responsibility for ensuring that the daily business of the company is conducted according to plan. In larger companies, the president reports to the CEO, who also acts as the interface between the board of directors and stockholders. Startups without a board of directors or shareholders don't need to name a CEO, and so the title of president is sufficient for their top leadership role.

Delegating with Authority

As you've seen, delegation is a necessary function of leadership. It's particularly important to delegate tasks that simply aren't "your thing." You have to be aware of these tasks, of course, and how they impact your business so you can monitor and manage them properly. Understanding the function, impact, and purpose of every aspect of your business is an essential step in developing policies and procedures to manage it effectively. These policies can provide clear expectations to those you assigned to carry out the tasks and, in worst-case scenarios, prevent or expose embezzlement, waste, and inefficiency.

Even after you've delegated responsibilities to others within the organization, you still need to keep them on your radar. Far too many stories of fraud originate with entrepreneurs who take little interest in their company's accounting functions. You may feel the same disinterest; after all, if you were interested in accounting, you probably would have started an accounting firm. Entrepreneurs are visionaries with passions for creating businesses rather than managing their finances. I can't name one entrepreneur among my acquaintances who spends a great deal of time in the accounting department.

But before you decide to completely check out of the accounting aspect of your organization, take a minute to consider how many times you've heard the stories or read the headlines about the long-term, trusted bookkeeper who quietly stole company funds over several years of dedicated service. Believe me, these people understand the accounting procedures of the organizations they work for. In many cases, the embezzler may have actually been the one that created them. That access, combined with the entrepreneur's lack of interest and/or knowledge of the tasks, leads to swindles that can cost the business thousands, sometimes millions, of dollars, if not bankruptcy.

So how can you avoid becoming the subject of one of these tragic embezzlement stories?

- Understand the accounting tasks within your organization.
- Respect those tasks.
- Fully understand your role and responsibility for supporting the overall organization.
- Recognize and assess any gaps in your accounting knowledge.
- Put proper accounting controls in place.

Early in the development of TRC, I feared embezzlement and worried that I wouldn't be able to keep my eyes on the bank account. It was important for me to have a fail-safe process in place to ensure that our hard-earned money stayed where it was supposed to. I had no reason for this concern in regard to any one of my employees, but I knew it was my responsibility to put a process in place that eliminated temptation. So what did I do? I did what many startups do and put my wife in charge of the bank account.

That process worked for me in the beginning, until I was able to build a solid set of checks and balances to protect my company's funds from embezzlers. Like a firewall on your computer system, you need to ensure there are solid measures limiting who can access your money. The trusted family employee *should* be sufficient, but don't forget that brothers, in-laws, and nieces have gone down as company pilferers in the past. The key is having those checks and balances I mentioned earlier. As part of those safeguards, don't assign complete control to a single individual or even to multiple individuals who are close to one another or who can develop a conspiring relationship.

Building a Culture of Ethics and Honesty

As I said earlier, you can bet that your business will be the target of fraud from some source—internal staff, vendors and suppliers, customers, online thieves, consultants, even partners or cofounders. The prevalence of embezzlement, theft, and fraud reinforces the need for the checks, balances, and financial oversight we've previously discussed. But another critical responsibility that you, as an entrepreneurial leader, must fulfill is that of incorporating ethical practices into your business plan and building a culture of ethics and honesty within your company.

You can find plenty of stories of CEOs, founders, and politicians going to jail over fraudulent business practices. I knew that I would never engage in any kind of activity that might defraud my own business, and I felt confident that I had chosen honest people for my staff and put strong practices in place designed to protect them from the temptation to engage in dishonest practices. I never anticipated, however, that temptation would present itself directly to me in the form of a familiar face.

TRC had begun to grow in size and market share when a past associate from Educational Resources called me one day asking if I would be interested in a cooperative advertising deal. I found the offer confusing, since this guy was now working with a competing reseller, but—based on our past association—I agreed to meet with him at my office to hear his proposal.

His proposition was for TRC to stuff one of his company's advertisement flyers in our daily customer shipments; in exchange his company would pay us. Instead of paying TRC cash, this guy's company would pay us in product. My ex-associate suggested that I select around $10,000 worth of computers, printers, or whatever I wanted that his company sold in exchange for this service. This kind of advertising and payment method were both common practices, but it was unheard of for one company to send out advertisements for a competitor. The deal didn't make sense—until I heard the rest of it.

My past coworker explained that I didn't have to actually put the flyers in the boxes. I could throw them in the trash as far as he was concerned. Better yet, I'd never have to see the flyers, at all. All I had to do was take $10,000 worth of his company's product, then send him an invoice for $20,000 for my bogus "advertising service." Guess who was getting the additional $10,000 worth of product? This guy was starting a business of his own on the side, and he wanted computer equipment for his own enterprise. Since he was an executive with this reseller, he could submit the paperwork without anyone ever questioning. Now I got it!

This scheme would be easy to pull off, and no one would ever find out. His company was very large, and it was doing deals like this all the time. In addition, he was the one in charge of the program. Nothing could point back to me; I could just say I put the flyers in our customer's boxes per the agreement. If this executive skimmed product off the top, it wasn't my problem. Well, I could have gone through with it and received a windfall of much-needed computer equipment. Instead, I threw him out, and told him to stay the hell away from my company. If I had been willing to compromise the honesty of my company by engaging in this kind of unethical behavior, I would have done far more damage to TRC's culture than could be offset by the acquisition of free electronics.

As my ex-associate demonstrated, even long-term trusted employees can be guilty of unethical behavior. I had seen this happen during my time at Educational Resources, when a woman in accounting was found to be writing checks to herself rather than to vendors. Poorly screened new hires were the source of another criminal act at the company, when a ring of thieves infiltrated the company's warehouse staff and began creating false customer orders, then shipping the products to acquaintances. Customers can defraud your business as well. At TRC, we lost more than $40,000 to a fraudulent customer operating out of Miami and Puerto Rico who was using quick mail shops to receive product on credit, then vanished without paying. Even though we found the guy's real name and a business he actively promoted on the Internet, I could not get the FBI to take any action. It was too overloaded with other fraud cases. I felt tempted to dole out some justice on my own, but the prospect of ending up in a Puerto Rican jail was not that enticing.

You can't safeguard against every form of fraud, but your best protection rests in the culture of honesty and ethics that you build and maintain within your organization. By dealing honestly with everyone both inside and outside your company, and by setting and following ethical standards in all of your business dealings, you close many of the ethical gaps that provide openings to those who want to defraud you. The topic of honesty and ethics may seem trite to you when you first begin your entrepreneurial journey. Most new entrepreneurs don't have time to think about it as they're developing their businesses, because during startup, fraud doesn't seem like much of a threat. When everyone in the company is struggling to bring the business to life, it's easy to ignore the potential for ethical lapses down the road. But your business plan needs to detail the steps that you will use to set up a framework of checks and balances, establish policies guiding ethical behavior, and periodically revisit your policies to ensure the health and effectiveness of your company's culture of honesty.

Following Your Passions without Getting Lost in Them

Just as you will be quick to delegate tasks that you don't enjoy, you will naturally focus most of your efforts on the aspects of your business that appeal to you. In most cases, those areas reflect the core competency of your business and serve as its primary driver of revenue, profit, and growth. Your focus on these core business functions will help you exploit every resource you offer as an entrepreneur, and it can challenge you to continually improve. Your ongoing work in these areas can provide the adrenaline that fuels your personal and organizational growth.

Everything has its costs, however, and the flipside to focusing on tasks that you like is that you can become so engrossed in them that you disregard other essential aspects of the business. Further, you might be monopolizing an area of the business that could benefit from the input and development of other key people on your staff. By shutting others out from important functions of the organization, you might be driving away talent that could support your efforts and bring in innovative ideas, feedback, and criticism. If you're holding all the knowledge for any aspect of your business in your own head, you're killing the potential for collaboration and complicating any workable plan for succession. That exclusionary approach also means that you won't ever be able to truly get away from your business, because you're the sole source of information or the central, controlling authority for some critical aspect of its operation.

I had hired good people to run every aspect of TRC and managers to oversee them, yet I would still drift back into the trenches. I developed terrible habits of reviewing daily shipments going out the door and releasing web orders that came in to our routing system. What an absolute disruption to the work flow I was. Who needs the president to jump in to see if orders were picked properly or to release web orders prior to someone's regular approval process?

During different periods of growth, I managed to acquire similar "hovering" habits in other aspects of the business. I either outgrew these addictions on my own or had them driven out of me by the forceful pushback of the assigned coworker or manager. I really give those employees credit for putting me in my place. I know why I developed those task-centric habits. I wanted to keep busy and see immediate results of my work. The Startup phase is a fast-paced, multitasking circus, and it's hard to come off of the high of that momentum. It takes a great deal of discipline for any entrepreneur to adjust his or her role in the company—and sometimes a bit of coaxing from coworkers along the way.

The bottom line is this: for all of the reasons I've laid out in this chapter, tasks are not what you, as an entrepreneur, should be working on in the Running phase of your business. You'll harm the performance of your business; you'll harm the performance of your staff and drive away talent that you desperately need; and you'll fail to become a true leader. Like a ship's captain who spends all of his time checking the engine pressure rather than guiding his vessel, you can't afford to bury yourself in the daily operational tasks of your business. You have to focus on leading change, leading innovation, and leading the organization toward its stated goals and mission.

Walking the Path of Entrepreneurial Leadership

The key to successful entrepreneurial leadership is having a passion for pursuing a specific purpose that you and your followers support and believe in. Effective, committed leadership energizes everyone in the organization and creates a catalyst for individual and organizational growth. Even people who have never shown interest or aptitude in leadership seem to naturally fill the role once they begin pursuing their entrepreneurial passion.

Given my belief in this "natural" evolution into leadership, I associate the situational theory of leadership most closely with the entrepreneurial experience. Research from Professor Victor Vroom, Professor Arthur Jago, and psychologist Fred Fiedler support this theory, which says that the best type of leadership is driven by situational variables—in other words, effective leaders actually change their leadership style in response to the situation before them.[1] Think, for example, of the entrepreneur who is faced with constant change as she builds a company from the ground up. Just as change is a constant for the organization, that leader's style must be constantly evolving as well.

Every situation presents a point of motivation for a successful leader. Yes, the leader's big-picture focus has to be on sustaining and growing the business, but the leader also has to be able to focus on dozens of smaller issues in order to achieve that larger goal. This multipart focus is part of what motivates entrepreneurial leaders.

Corporate leaders, on the other hand, are motivated largely by self-fulfillment. They want to accomplish a task or an assigned goal, but for the most part, they do it for positioning, recognition, accomplishment, influence, promotion, or some other form of self-gratification. I'm not saying that corporate leaders lack team spirit, but ultimately, their motivator is some form of individual recognition within the organization. After all, people choose to work for a particular company for their own personal reasons, and they make contributions during their career ultimately for their own personal reasons as well.

As an entrepreneur, however, your core motivation is company/mission centered. Your focus is on growth, vision attainment, and preservation. True, being the founder, you have personal motivations as well, but they are practically congruent with the company's interests. As an entrepreneurial leader, you believe that you are in control of your future, success, and failures. Corporate leaders believe someone else controls their future, and their self-preservation is tied to their employer's performance assessment. Your self-preservation is tied directly to the preservation of your company. This difference makes you a completely different leader than your corporate counterpart.

Leadership is not management. Managers administer, while leaders innovate, develop, motivate, persuade, and create. Leadership is not about giving orders; it is about influencing. The influence must be genuine, transparent, and built on trust. Followers agree to be influenced because they believe in the cause, goal, or outcome. Business leader Alan Keith said, "Leadership is ultimately about creating a way for people to contribute to making something extraordinary happen." People get excited about being a part of something extraordinary like starting and running a successful business. The leader shares a vision that people see as achievable and worthy of effort.

This is how the situation serves as the motivation. It is the focus for the entrepreneur. The entrepreneurial leader assigns a goal or reward to the situation—a goal that the followers visualize, understand, and agree to pursue. The leader's style can be charismatic or dictatorial, but the promise of accomplishment overrides everything. Entrepreneurs don't need motivation. They need to motivate. Their motivation is manifested already in their internal desire to accomplish their mission through the work of others.

Often for entrepreneurs, the situation goal is grand, and that alone is captivating, enticing, and engaging for followers. The followers understand the enormity of the goal, and they respect the leader for the risk he or she assumes while they fill a support role to make it happen. Working toward the goal is exhilarating to the followers, and their job becomes more than work; it becomes a contribution to a mission. The entrepreneur recognizes and fosters this, which is how a great leader can get followers to achieve remarkable things.

Your responsibility as an entrepreneur is to influence, direct, and keep the mission prominent and focused. You can accomplish this through effective communication, which has four components: communicating expectations, listening, delegating, and providing feedback. You also must develop the ability to filter incoming information effectively. This skill will help you discard useless and time-wasting information, and pick up on opportunities that often are missed by managers within your organizations. You must develop an ear to listen and an eye to spot growth or innovation opportunities through all forms of feedback. That way, you will be able to pick out the tiny nuggets of information that can be used to exploit a competitor's weakness or enhance an existing strength of your business. This ability to filter, process, and use incoming information is an essential skill you must develop in order to lead your organization through change and adapt your leadership style to the situation at hand.

Evolving as a Leader—And as an Entrepreneur

Leadership at TRC was like climbing stairs. Each landing was a new goal and achievement to strive toward. My job was to continually put these small goals out for the company to attain and then to recognize and reward everyone for their efforts in reaching them. This process provided my team with continual positive reinforcement for hitting targets while also moving us closer to the goal outlined in our mission statement "to be the most recognized provider of volume software licensing in the education market."

There was a time when I thought I had taken TRC as far as I could under my leadership. We hit a dry spell in terms of creativity and growth, and I considered hiring a new president to run the company while I migrated to chairman of the board. My thought was to find someone with executive experience that could introduce new concepts, processes, or expertise. I felt that someone else could do a better job in the CEO position—maybe even be better qualified to lead the company than I was. Thankfully, I changed my mind and came to realize that no one was better qualified than I was to guide my company and my team.

Feelings of isolation can happen with entrepreneurs, as it did with me, which can lead to a sense of tunnel vision. Lack of exposure to peers, mentors, board members, or forums can lead to stale views and a sense of entrapment within your own company. I got my grounding by talking to other entrepreneurs about the dry spell I seemed to be in. They helped me realize I still had much to offer and that I probably needed to shake things up a bit to revitalize the spark. By establishing new goals in all facets of the company and placing expectations on the managers of those areas, I was able to pull my leadership out of the doldrums.

During this period of self-reflection, I began to think about what it would take for my organization to obtain $100 million in sales. We were approaching $30 million at the time, and the $100 million mark didn't seem out of line. In fact, the more I thought about it, the more unacceptable the idea of not being closer to that milestone became. Now I had to shift my energy toward charting a course toward making this goal a reality. I was refocused and revitalized. I was back at the helm!

The vision I provided to my team was crystal clear. Everyone could see it, and my team members knew what I required of them in order to make it happen. I communicated rewards to individuals, but I also made sure there was a universal understanding and acknowledgment of their achievements throughout the organization. All of us were working to grow TRC to the point where it would be acquired by a company that shared our mission and would provide the capital to scale TRC even further. For their effort, every individual at TRC would receive the additional benefits and opportunities of this larger parent organization. I wanted to build careers for my employees, and this strategy promised numerous avenues for personal development that simply weren't available at TRC.

TRC employees did extraordinary things to move the company toward its goal. On several occasions, employees took it upon themselves to work all night, literally sleeping in the office to meet deadlines. What a surprise it was for me to arrive at the office around six a.m. to find employees crashed at their workstations and realize they never left from the day before. I'm not trying to give you the impression that I ran some kind of a sweatshop, or even that I condoned these all-nighters. In fact, I encouraged people to get home to their family. But we also fostered a culture in our organization that when things needed to get done, all of us at TRC would put forth extraordinary efforts in order to meet those demands. Our employees went well beyond extraordinary efforts on more than one occasion, and they established a bond and an attitude that permeated the office.

As I said, the dedication and hard work my employees exhibited reflected the overall culture of TRC. Every leadership skill and approach we've discussed in this chapter plays a role in creating a culture that furthers the interests, goals, and mission of your organization. As a leader, you—and your actions—will set forth the values that will form your organization's guiding principles and determine the success of its development. A strong organizational culture revolves around core commitments, to growth and innovation and to promoting the organization through every means possible. That means selling the organization, all the time, every time. In the next chapter of this book, we'll talk about incorporating the sales ethic into your organizational culture so that every act and idea generated within your company walls is aimed at the goal of promoting your products and services and growing your business.

CHAPTER TEN

Selling, Selling, Selling

I NEVER SET OUT TO be in sales; in fact, I deliberately avoided it. I wanted to be an entrepreneur, and I never included sales as part of that vision. It turns out that I was dead wrong. Selling and entrepreneurship are practically synonymous. From the first moment I began formulating TRC all the way through to my exit, I found that I had to sell—and that I really liked it. Selling isn't just about ringing up a product sale at the register; it's about strategy, influence, and positioning. Learning to sell effectively will draw upon (and develop) some of your greatest skills and attributes as an individual and as an entrepreneurial leader.

Everything you do as an entrepreneur, from idea to exit, involves selling skills. In the Idea phase, you had to sell your ideas to those who were willing to listen and give valid feedback. At Startup, you sold your idea and the virtues of your company to potential investors, creditors, employees, vendors—and even to family and friends. As you made your pitch, each of these people and institutions was taking stock of you in order to judge the validity of your idea and your ability to bring it to life as a viable and valuable entity. In the Running phase, you will have your greatest sales opportunities and challenges, as you work to sell yourself, your product, and your firm to an ever-expanding base of stakeholders.

In this chapter, we're going to take a close look at the fundamentals of sales—any kind of sales, in any kind of organization. I'll offer you my own "formula" for successful sales, along with some key ideas for developing a sales culture throughout your business.

Finding the Right Formula: The Sales Maxim

I've practiced sales for many years and studied various best-practice sales methodologies. As I said, I like sales, but I also understand its critical role in growing the organization. So, I wanted to learn everything I could about developing my own talent for selling and about instilling a sales-oriented culture throughout my company. Volumes have been written on the topic of selling, but in the end, I believe that I can express every key principle of sales in one simple statement. I use this statement as the launching point for training my sales teams, but I also use it as one of the guiding principles of my operation. I call it the Sales Maxim, and here it is:

Sales = Confidence = Knowledge = Customers and Product

Like the E-Formula, the Sales Maxim serves as a simple representation of the essential elements of success: in this case, success in selling. It does not matter what you sell—a product, a service, an idea, a plan—this maxim holds true. Over the years, in studying sales representatives with strong performance and those who were struggling, I've always been able to track their strengths or weaknesses back to the elements laid out in the Sales Maxim. Now, let's take a closer look at each of those elements.

Sales = Confidence

For years, business writers, classroom instructors, consultants, columnists, and managers have said that you have to be confident to succeed in sales, but what does that mean? In my book, a confident salesperson is one who can pick up the phone to make the cold calls, knock on doors, or network to establish relationships. A confident salesperson moves comfortably into uncomfortable and unpredictable situations, can discuss a variety of issues with a variety of audiences, and always is ready to answer questions and offer solutions. Above all, a confident salesperson takes chances.

No, I'm not talking about the stereotypical slick-haired salesman who talks loud, swaggers when he walks, and wears an open shirt and gold neck chain. In fact, the kind of confidence that excellent salespeople exhibit has nothing to do with attitude, fashion, or false bravado. Instead, sales confidence stems from a belief in your ability to respond to the situation at hand by offering the ideas and outcomes that meet expectations, offer solutions, and build trust. In other words, you must have confidence in your knowledge and your ability to use it. By achieving a level of superior knowledge and understanding, you can enter any sales-related situation with conviction that you will be able to address all potential outcomes. That's the kind of confidence that translates into strong sales.

Confidence = Knowledge

Knowledge instills confidence. Well-trained salespeople don't have to artificially pump up their self-confidence in order to go out and land the sale. They master their content, and then their confidence grows naturally. Knowledge-based confidence is the number-one performance accelerator for any employee; a lack of it will kill sales. The costs related to turnover and poor performance of account managers can often be traced back to knowledge gaps.

The key to creating a great salesperson is to focus on knowledge building. For some time, business analysts have recognized that knowledge building is the key to creating a great sales staff, and that's why companies invest so much in training and development. Unfortunately, lots of those businesses fail to understand the ongoing link between knowledge and successful performance; as a result, they don't manage with that link in mind. Knowledge comes through experience and education. That's why everyone within the organization must constantly be building knowledge, not just to improve their own performance, but to grow the organization. In selling your business and its products or services—both internally and externally—knowledge and the confidence it builds are your greatest tools.

Knowledge = Customer and Product

Knowledge in every form helps build confidence and skill, but when it comes to sales, customer and product knowledge is what matters (understand that when I use the term *product* in regard to the Sales Maxim, I'm speaking of any product, service, or other business offering). When a salesperson develops a broad and deep understanding of what the organization is selling and who is buying it, that individual can walk into *any* situation and sell effectively. Knowledgeable salespeople can work through any sale without breaking a sweat or compromising their personal style.

I hired many sales representatives at TRC, and subsequently, I had to let some of them go. After years of training, mentoring, and managing my sales team and the sales process, I came to realize that in most cases the sales reps who didn't work out were those who simply never developed a full command of the company's product and customers. That's when I developed the Sales Maxim and began using it to screen and train my team.

Many businesses develop detailed profiles of their customers to add to their bank of customer knowledge. One of the simplest profile models divides customers into quadrants, ranging from high-profit and low-resource requirement customers (those who deliver the most rewards to the organization for the least investment) to low-profit and high-resource commitment customers (those who deliver the least rewards but require the largest investment). As you can imagine, high-profit, low-resource customers are the most desirable for any organization. This profiling model allows managers to focus on their best customers, work to improve those in the middle, and (perhaps) jettison the worst. This model doesn't, however, do a great job of assessing the degree of influence a given customer exerts on the organization, its marketplace, or the industry.

Although every organization may have its own way of looking at customer influence, in general you can think of it as the customer's act of promoting or advocating for your business. Your customers may recommend new customers to your business, encourage vendors to partner with you, direct funding to your company, or serve as your general promotional platform. Influential customers will tend to draw more of your resources. You have to remain acutely aware of this so you can accurately determine the return on that resource investment.

Your organization's management and leadership must also command a deep knowledge of your customers in order to evaluate whether influential customers really *are* influential, or whether your organization merely perceives of them as such. It's not uncommon for an organization's management and leadership to create a false sense of influence around a given customer. That's a real problem, because those areas of the business also allocate its resources. The old "customer is always right" motto can contribute to the misperception of a customer's influence, regardless of the customer's actual position in the profiling quadrant. Customers who are low revenue and extremely demanding of resources often yield no influence in terms of attracting new customers, suppliers, partners, or funding. Still, if management has adopted a one-size-fits-all mentality, it can fear losing even the worst customer. As a result, sales teams might be directed to pull limited firm resources from the entire customer pool and improperly allocate them to the false influencer, rather than to true influencers and high-profit customers. If any customer—even a high-profile Fortune 500 firm—doesn't bring in solid, positive benefits in proportion to the resources they demand, then they probably aren't an influential customer. To know that, you have to know your customers, what resources they demand, and what benefits they produce.

Many squeaky wheels are low-volume, low-profit customers that demand high maintenance—resources that could better go to other customers. This kind of nonproductive resource drain can go on undetected and unappreciated by management for some time and may get progressively worse. As an entrepreneur, founder, and leader, you need to be aware of the makeup of your customers and their effective degree of influence, and then make sure your business allocates its resources accordingly. Failure to appropriate resources to the best and truly influential customer segments will result in profitable customers leaving your firm in an exodus you don't notice until it's too late to reverse.

Product knowledge is tightly integrated into customer knowledge and expressed concisely through the value proposition. A company must obtain intimate knowledge of why its target customer wants or needs its service. A product with fabulous features and functionality won't be purchased if customers don't believe it addresses their particular need or solves their specific problem. This seems simple enough—yet many businesses fail to conduct the necessary research to gain this insight. Instead they create a product or service based on intuition or assumption. Mastery of your product is key, but applying how that product addresses customer needs and pain is essential.

A QUICK GUIDE TO ESSENTIAL PRODUCT AND CUSTOMER KNOWLEDGE

Every business has its own, sometimes highly customized, pools of product and customer knowledge. But the following guide quickly outlines the important topics that are common to the essential "knowledge bank" for any sales or management team.

Know Your Product
- Features & Function
  - ☐ Understand what problem the product solves.
  - ☐ Understand what need the product answers.

- Comparison & Differentiation
  - ☐ Understand the product's strengths and weaknesses alone and in relation to competitors.
  - ☐ Understand the competition's strengths and how to minimize them in the eyes of the customer.
  - ☐ Understand the competition's weaknesses and how to exploit them in the eyes of the customer.

- Production & Support
  - ☐ Understand how the product is made, delivered, and supported by the company.
  - ☐ Understand how the customer is involved with the product from purchase, to delivery, to deployment, and through its life cycle.

- Position
  - ☐ Understand what opportunities your product provides the customer.
  - ☐ Understand the threats your product removes for the customer.
  - ☐ Understand why customers do and don't buy your product or service.
- Benefits
  - ☐ Understand the pain points your product resolves or may create for the customer.
  - ☐ Understand how your product helps your customer make or save money, or if it is an expense.

Know Your Customer
- Position
  - ☐ Understand the type of customer you are engaging.
  - ☐ Understand your customer's influencers and decision makers.
  - ☐ Understand what motivates the buyer.
  - ☐ Understand what their job is and how they do it.
  - ☐ Understand who the ultimate end user is.
- Function
  - ☐ Understand the purpose your customer serves to their customers.
  - ☐ Understand why your customer exists.
  - ☐ Understand the nuances of your customer's market segment.
- Utility
  - ☐ Understand why your customer would want your product.
  - ☐ Understand how your customer will use your product.
  - ☐ Understand why your customer uses competitive products.
- Structure
  - ☐ Understand your customer's decision and authorization process.
  - ☐ Understand your customer's buying procedures.
  - ☐ Understand your customer's financing.
  - ☐ Understand the closing cycle and how to influence it.

Adding It All Up

Understanding the Sales Maxim is important for you, your management teams, and your sales groups because it's an important tool for self-assessment and improvement. Struggling sales representatives aren't always able to articulate why they are failing, and the reasons may not be apparent to you, either. Understanding that most performance deficiencies can be linked to gaps in product or customer knowledge can help sales staff and management find ways to pinpoint and correct those problems. Senior account managers whose performance has flatlined can benefit from some intense study of customers and products as well. After all, even the pros need refresher courses.

Information about your product and the customer may change over time, so you and your sales and management teams need to continually monitor customer data. By keeping everyone in your organization up to date on product and customer knowledge, you will not only breed successful sales representatives, but you'll also position your product development efforts for ongoing innovation. The elements of the Sales Maxim form the basis for launching a new business as well as for maintaining an existing one. Use these elements when writing your business plan, pitching your company for funding, negotiating terms with suppliers, hiring employees, or securing a lease. By encouraging you to thoughtfully put yourself in the customer's shoes and master the role of both buyer and seller, the maxim can help you differentiate your firm and maximize its value.

Remember, just about everything you'll do as an entrepreneur involves selling, but the Sales Maxim isn't just for entrepreneurs; it was originally formulated to assist in training new account managers, and its purpose is relevant to everyone in the organization. Time and again I have seen key personnel at small and large corporations fail at the fundamentals of selling—this includes supposed top performers, too.

Effective sales training, like sports training, is centered on fundamentals. Everything else can be built off of that foundation. Too often, businesses inundate new hires into their account management teams with too much information too soon. The fundamentals of customer, product, industry, and marketplace knowledge can get lost when a new hire is drowning in a sea of information about CRM and ERP systems, internal procedures, communication tools, and methodologies. Seasoned account managers, often those with assigned and mature accounts, can become complacent in practicing their skills and fundamentals.

When a new account manager is turned over to the sales manager, there is a sense of urgency to get the recruit into the field selling. This is when one of three things happens: the new recruit does well, takes time to ramp up, or struggles. My goal in developing and using the Sales Maxim was to minimize or avoid the latter two outcomes.

New account managers typically won't tell their manager why they are not successful because they either don't understand the underlying reason or they are embarrassed, feeling pressure that "they should know this by now" based on the training they've received. Their struggle can often be pinned to their confidence to engage a customer and represent the product. Management equates this as a bad hire, believing the struggling person simply shouldn't be in sales. That may be true, but it also may be that he or she lacks confidence, because that person lacks knowledge about the company's products and customers. I am convinced more account managers can ramp up faster and be more effective when they and their management follow the Sales Maxim on a daily basis.

Selling Your Passion

A sales career is one of the greatest professions anyone can pursue in business. Successful salespeople have to draw from a wide skill set that includes comprehension, writing, speaking, listening, observing, presenting, organizing, calculating, understanding psychology, and translating body language. Harnessing these talents to a well-positioned strategy can provide great professional rewards and accomplishment.

So why is it that sales is such an underappreciated department in so many companies? It most certainly has to be one of the most important areas of any organization since it represents the closest link between the business and its customers. The sales team intimately delivers the company's mission to its customer; it fuels R&D and all other aspects of the organization. In my eyes, sales is on the top of the pyramid; all other aspects of the company, including the executive branch, exist to support the efforts of sales.

If you don't appreciate your company's sales team, its efforts can become strained and inefficient, its staff distracted and off task. A companywide mindset that fails to include an appreciation for the value of sales can ultimately help create the departmental silos that slow performance throughout the organization. Your business might be running great at 10 percent annual growth, but is it possible that it could hit 15 percent, if sales were fully appreciated and understood? I'm a great protector of sales teams, as all too often I've seen organizations unconsciously erect barriers to sales efforts and ignore the frontline reconnaissance that only sales representatives can deliver. And I don't just appreciate salespeople; I'm one of them. No matter what role I fulfill in the organization, I am always one of its most committed salespeople.

Shortly before the dot-com bubble burst, I was trying to come up with a way to sell Microsoft Select licensing. As you may recall from my recollections in an earlier chapter, I had obtained this software license authorization for my former employer, which gave it large account resellers (LAR) status and, along with it, a significant competitive advantage. Now, I needed to find a way to enable TRC to sell Select licensing.

I partnered with an existing LAR that had no focus on education, with the agreement that TRC would act as a broker to sell the Select licenses to our customers at a marked-up price. The schools would make their purchase orders out to the LAR, in care of TRC, and the LAR would fulfill the order. Aside from a variety of operational issues on the LAR's side, this worked well. Selling Select licenses created incremental revenue for TRC and helped expose us to a level of sales traditionally reserved for the biggest dealers in the country.

Since we were selling the licenses at a higher price than the LARs, we had to be able to provide more value to our customers. This necessity led TRC to innovate the way we addressed procurement, fulfillment, compliancy, and the administration of volume software licensing for our customers. We exposed all of the weaknesses and pain points associated with those four key components of software licensing that the other LARs tended to ignore. We developed value-added services and features on our website and in our sales and customer service processes, which resonated with the licensing administrator who was our customer.

As I architected TRC's new website, I incorporated these customer needs and our unique answers into a functional response system. By integrating the website into our ERP system, we could do some pretty amazing things related to enterprise software licensing. Volume software licensing was (and still is) complicated, as every publisher has a different methodology for providing volume discounts on its licenses, license maintenance, and license upgrades—not to mention the variations of licensing options like annuity, perpetual, and concurrent. All of our competitors were using a nondynamic catalog; if customers searched for Adobe Photoshop in licensing, they would get hundreds of SKUs back as search results. This made buying volume software online virtually impossible. Our competitors viewed this as the way it had to be and as the customer's problem, not theirs. They were right; it was the customer's problem. That made it my problem, too.

The system I designed at TRC categorized publisher SKUs in a hierarchical fashion that enabled users to make increasingly more granular decisions based on their own criteria. Further, the system recognized users at login and immediately showed them specific SKUs based on past purchase history, which was tied to a specific software agreement or customer type. Our system would know, for instance, that a customer was an academic Adobe

CLP, level-C customer, and we would only show this customer those applicable SKUs. Not only did this help our customers, but it improved the speed and accuracy with which our own sales team generated quotes and processed orders. TRC had not only automated the complicated volume software license process but greatly enhanced the user experience and made online volume software license purchasing a reality.

Customers wanted to buy online, but the dealer channel just wasn't making it easy for them. The problem didn't fit into the dealer's established system, which was working fine for the dealer. All of my developments were created from user feedback and by studying the common recurring errors caused by this inefficient system. I listened to the complaints from our sales team, reviewed the return reports, and spoke to our customers for the answers. Our system reduced errors by 90 percent and decreased the time to process an order by more than 70 percent. I went on to make further enhancements, constantly refining and adding new features based on the user experience.

This innovation became our competitive advantage in the marketplace; it shifted the focus away from price to instead highlight how our system could eliminate the host of headaches caused by the complicated and changing world of volume software licensing. By adding Microsoft licensing to our new web engine, we were attracting an entirely new type of customer. The large public research institutions, which we rarely did business with, were now awarding TRC their request for proposals (RFP) for volume software licensing. To our humble satisfaction, we won the University of California System's RFP for not only Microsoft, but for five other popular publishers as well. The contract resulted in a multimillion-dollar award that locked us in for two years serving all nine campus locations.

So, as I said, I'm a salesman and proud of it. In everything I do as an entrepreneur, I'm selling my passion. Entrepreneurs follow an inspiration or passion, and that passion is what persuades others to follow entrepreneurs. The passion of the entrepreneur radiates throughout the organization, touching everyone in its path, urging everyone to take ownership in the business. That kind of passion is what the entrepreneur is always selling, and it helps form the culture of the organization even as it drives it forward toward success. Selling becomes a molecular component of the organizational culture, rather than a forced activity.

When I finally had my own business up and running, I was determined that my organizational culture would also include strong components of innovation, dynamic thinking, and disruptive change. I saw this as a really cool opportunity to do something fun. The business journals were full of reports of companies that let you bring in pets, and had basketball courts, foosball tables, beanbag chairs, stocked kitchens, outdoor adventure outings, and more. I tried several different times to create a fun-filled physical environment in order to cultivate innovation, but my initiatives didn't seem to have much impact. I soon realized that just as my behavior had helped create my company's culture of ethics, honesty, and selling, the culture of innovation had to come from me as well, not from an office playground. I couldn't plan my way to an innovative culture; I just had to live it.

In the next chapter, we'll talk more about how you can develop a culture of innovation and change within your own organization. We won't be talking about stocking your conference rooms with foosball tables and espresso machines. But we will take a closer look at how you, and your performance as an entrepreneur, can form your organization's approach to innovation and determine the success of its ongoing growth and development.

CHAPTER ELEVEN

Building a Culture of Innovation

INNOVATION HAS BEEN THE DRIVING theme throughout this book, and it also will be the engine of your success as an entrepreneur. Innovation was the key element of your entrepreneurial I.D.E.A., and it provided the creative spark that enabled you to activate as an entrepreneur during the Idea phase. The Startup phase of your organization was fueled by innovative approaches to funding your business, leveraging limited resources, and establishing a footprint in the marketplace. As you redirect your efforts from the demands of startup to those of running your business, innovation will drive product and process improvement and establish your competitive advantages in the marketplace. Innovation must remain your focal point during the Running phase of your business, but you can't be the sole source of your organization's innovative ideas. Now, fostering and maintaining a culture of innovation throughout your organization becomes one of your most critical responsibilities. You have to find and leverage every possible source of innovative ideas available to you, and in most cases those sources will be your employees.

Innovation defines your business, but it also defines who you are as an entrepreneur. Steve Jobs has been quoted as saying, "Innovation distinguishes between a leader and a follower," and this statement has profound organizational significance. The workplace structure creates jobs, each of which is a series of tasks. Combined, all of these series of tasks form the organization and determine its predictable outcomes. Your challenge during the Running phase of your business is to create an environment that preserves the integrity of tasks but also encourages creative thinking and ongoing challenges to the established processes in order to achieve constant improvement. It's not enough to want innovation from your organization; you have to actively seek it out. You also have to build an environment that promotes innovation, a system that rewards innovation, and a culture that demands it.

As your organization grows, you can be confident that new sources of innovation are lying dormant throughout your company, at all levels of your workforce. If you fail to find, foster, and harness the innovative power of the people who work for you, you are dooming your business to limited success and, in all probability, failure. In this chapter, we're going to look at innovation, in all its variety and forms. You'll learn how to recognize and use each form of innovation, and how to find sources of innovation throughout your organization.

Innovation means change, and many employees can become immobilized when thrown into an environment of constant change and adaptation. Many seasoned corporate workers are used to environments where the business is running on autopilot and their job requirement is to complete tasks in a prescribed manner. Those workers tend to be back on the employment market because their organizations haven't survived. Thriving organizations require constant assessment, critique, and improvement of both people and processes. The environment of any successful business today changes rapidly, and people who want to grow with the organization must change with it. In this chapter, we'll take a close look at one of the most important innovative tasks of any entrepreneur, that of leading an organization through change (and knowing when to be led by the change around you).

Innovators can get lost in an organization that doesn't provide a structure specifically for growing innovation organically. These organizations are unwittingly resisting opportunities for success and growth. To help you avoid this stagnant state, later in this chapter I'll offer a step-by-step guide to creating an environment in which innovation can take root and grow, followed by a brief preview of the role these seeds of innovation will play in scaling your business and expanding its presence in the marketplace.

Mining Innovation in Every Form

In Phase I of this book, we talked about the two types of entrepreneurs—revolutionary and replicative. Well, we can divide innovation into two types as well, which we'll label blue-sky innovations and integrative/transformative innovations. Blue-sky innovations are revolutionary or radical in scope. Typically associated with revolutionary entrepreneurs, blue-sky innovations transform and create industries; they also extend the economy's efficiency by enabling it to produce more with the same or fewer resources.

Many blue-sky innovations are born in test tubes, the result of high technology discoveries created by scientists or inventors and supported by the research community. A few blue-sky innovations that spawned numerous businesses include fiber optics, light-emitting diodes (LED), global positioning systems (GPS), microfinancing, biofuel, flash memory, and radio-frequency identification (RFID).

The majority of innovations are the integrative/transformative type, and these are typically generated by replicative entrepreneurs. Integrative/transformative innovations meld into existing technologies, companies, processes, and products, proving that innovation doesn't have to represent a totally novel—or even a fully formed—idea. Many successful innovations are derivatives of existing products, services, or models. Businesses have successfully built their identities and reputation on integrative/transformative innovation by altering the way they address their consumers' needs; Southwest Airlines, JetBlue Airlines, Starbucks, and Google are just a few examples.

Some integrative/transformative innovations become successful after they morph into their final form, as was the case with the idea behind Federal Express. While attending Yale University in 1962, Fred Smith wrote an economics paper outlining a new concept in overnight delivery. In 1971, after serving in the Marine Corps, Smith launched Federal Express, with the intention of providing overnight delivery for the Federal Reserve System. Unfortunately, the Fed wasn't interested, so Smith had to find a new market for his innovative service. He decided to think bigger and expanded his focus to the entire business market.

Now, I'm aware that when you read about ideas taking shape in test tubes or giving birth to the overnight delivery industry, innovation can seem beyond the reach of the average entrepreneur or organization. But that's not the case. You don't have to invent the next lightbulb to be a great innovator; you just need to spark an idea that serves an undeveloped need. Innovation can be taught, and, in fact, it's a skill that all of us have within us. Humans and other animals innovate every day in order to solve problems, even if most of those innovations have relatively modest outcomes. But we aren't trained to treat innovation as a daily necessity or an ongoing goal for our businesses, and as a result, we aren't that great at recognizing and cultivating it.

Entrepreneurs and their businesses can't succeed without innovation, but many don't seem to grasp that fact. Your innovations are what will differentiate you within your marketplace, so you need them not only to spark your initial business concept but to sustain and scale your business. You created something new when you launched your company; to run it, you have to remain in a constant state of assessment, evaluation, and adjustment. You'll need to draw on every type of innovation from every source—both inside and outside your organization—in order to maintain the culture of constant improvement necessary to sustain your success.

I loved to innovate at TRC, which meant that the company was in a constant state of change. I always preached to my team our need to regularly change to grow and survive. People who worked for me either got excited about the prospect of continual change or were immobilized by it. Immobilized employees are ineffective, and that makes them a drain on resources and progress—in my organization, they had to go. The unrelenting drive to innovate and adapt makes working directly for or in an entrepreneur's company a challenge; you either fit or you don't. Even in those seemingly low-profile positions, I was always looking for ways to enhance my employees' responsibility and improve their ROI.

Many entrepreneurs find it difficult to recognize an innovator or to know how to use that resource to the firm's benefit. In the eyes of a manager, the innovator is there to do a prescribed job. Most employees have a job description, and that in and of itself can limit innovation; the job has been defined, so it must not need further refinement. This attitude isn't uncommon, even in organizations with quality programs that preach continual improvement. Innovative thinkers in these organizations have a rough time; when they bring up new ideas or suggestions, they're too often viewed by management like children suffering from attention deficit disorder, with wandering attention and an inability to stay on task. That's a sad fact, I know, for the innovative employee, but it's even sadder for the entrepreneur whose business is missing out on grassroots opportunity for innovation and growth.

To compensate for this organizational deficiency, managers typically hold off-site seminars and breakaways designed solely to spark innovation. The idea here is certainly well intentioned, and sometimes the meetings are even somewhat productive. But innovation can't be held on a shelf until it's needed; it's a timely and perishable commodity. If the organization doesn't harness innovative energy by reviewing ideas and acting upon them quickly, those ideas fade away. That's why job descriptions and management objectives all need to have innovative requirements and encouragement and prescribed performance woven throughout them. Everyone in the organization, including top executives, needs to actively encourage ongoing innovation and be receptive to creative ideas, whenever and wherever they originate.

The platform for innovation can't be relegated to an annual planning meeting—the competition won't allow it.

As obvious as the need for innovation may seem, it can easily slip out of focus for business leadership and management caught up in the daily march of customer concerns, employee matters, cash flow, production schedules, and nonstop email. As an entrepreneur, it's your responsibility to ensure that innovation stays near the top of your organization's priority list, right where it belongs. As I said earlier, innovation is your most effective tool for growing your organization. It will differentiate you from competitors, create intellectual property, establish closer customer relationships, improve efficiencies, eliminate stakeholder pain points, and enrich employee satisfaction. That means you can look to (and for) innovation as the resolution of any issue facing your organization. At TRC, I never spent time wondering how I could increase sales. Instead I worked to find ways to do things differently, to streamline processes, cut costs, speed delivery, enhance the customer experience, and so on. The innovations we devised as a result of these efforts increased our sales and expanded the market share and value of our organization.

Leveraging Your Idea Agents

If you've ever worked with epoxy, you know that it has two separate elements—a single oxygen atom and two joined carbon atoms—that when combined set off a thermal chemical reaction that results in an incredibly strong adhesive. A similar type of social chemistry can spur employee-generated innovation in a company. You can think of the single oxygen element as any employee who generates an idea; let's call that employee the Idea Agent. The combined carbon atoms will be termed the Activation Agent; these individuals are assigned their role by management. When the Idea Agent and Activation Agent come together, they can trigger an explosion of creative energy that results in innovation. Without a deliberate system for combining these agents effectively, that powerful "chemical" reaction may never take place.

Your organization may include any number of Idea Agents; I've usually found my company's Idea Agents among frontline workers and managers. Idea Agents genuinely want to do things better and improve the systems they work with. These employees are constantly generating ideas and asking challenging questions about the company's policies, procedures, customer service practices, production processes, presentations, implementation, and efficiency. Activation Agents are there to listen to the Idea Agents, filter their ideas, and then prioritize and assign actions to the ideas they've chosen to pursue. The Idea Agent formulates innovative ideas based on his or her intimate customer and product knowledge; the Activation Agent is in a position to assess and implement the innovation. To be effective, therefore, the Activation Agents in your business must have authority to cut through silos and bureaucracy. In the Running phase of your business, your role is to innovate but also to scale innovation through trained receivers—who are your Activation Agents.

What I've just described is the innovation ideal. Unfortunately, many businesses don't reflect that ideal. In fact, many organizations stifle ideas and alienate their best Idea Agents by pushing directives down and out toward them, rather than taking in their ideas and information. They train their best creative minds to work in a prescribed manner, which limits their innovative autonomy. Management does this to standardize operations and have predictable outcomes and, sometimes, because it simply doesn't trust its people or its systems. Most organizational management is unaccustomed to bottom-up creative thinking and, instead, views itself as the source of policy, procedure, and objectives. These managers are poorly trained to act as Activation Agents, which requires soliciting and receiving creative input that, in essence, challenges the orderly structure they themselves create and manage. They discourage free thinking among frontline workers because it encroaches on measured performance.

If your organization doesn't have a deliberate and well-supported process for innovation, it is doomed to suffer from this great divide between Idea Agent and Activation Agent. Your Idea Agents will begin to say, "What's the point . . . why should I bring up ideas that won't go anywhere?" Listening is your most effective tool for encouraging the innovative output of your organization's Idea Agents. That means you need to design and promote an effective process for ideas to be heard. Unfortunately, many companies have little interest in harnessing their home-grown intellectual property. Let your competitors make that mistake. In your organization, innovation should be a companywide, everyday initiative, supported by systems and fueled by experience, intuition, and instinct.

Companies that establish Activation Agents who are trained to listen to the trials and tribulations of their frontline workers tend to outperform their industry counterparts. They react quicker to their customers and are better able to design services around their specific needs. In my opinion, companies that continue to be led by their founder tend to appreciate and expect employee feedback more than others. Either consciously or unconsciously, founders understand and know how to harness the power of their coworkers' experiences. They know how to listen, assess, contribute resources, and execute on ideas. They also have the authority to make things happen quickly. In other words, as the founder of your entrepreneurial enterprise, you're in the driver's seat when it comes to promoting innovation in your organization.

The Home Depot founders, Bernie Marcus and Arthur Blank, describe their organization as an upside-down pyramid where the executives are servants of the frontline staff who are closest to the customer. Marcus and Blank respect the frontline worker as an Idea Agent who provides invaluable intelligence to the Activation Agents in management. The Home Depot has built an innovation system that listens to the front line, filters ideas, and aggressively acts on feedback.

DEMAND BAD NEWS!

The larger an organization becomes, the more difficult it can be to establish an effective innovation system. Bureaucratic corporations have many layers of filters between their Idea Agents and those who should be Activation Agents. Often those filters work hard to keep information from permeating to the top. Bureaucracies work especially hard at keeping bad news and system-challenging information from filtering to the top; the information that makes it through the filters is little more than useless data. That's what a bureaucracy does; it supports the existing order.

Good news serves as confirmation; bad news spurs correction. You need to insist on hearing the bad news in your organization so you can isolate and understand the problems behind it. Part of regular management briefings should include a list of the top bad things happening within the company. Learn to celebrate bad news. Don't find blame in it. Don't patch over it and move on. Find innovators to explore the situations behind the problems your organization faces and create solutions that will turn bad news into an asset.

Many companies recognize the need and purpose for employee-generated innovation, yet they struggle with how to make it happen within the organization. The solution is simple: create a process for innovation, build that process into your company's core systems, and reassess, revamp, and improve it regularly. To keep that process healthy and effective, you also must establish a culture in which management endorses the innovation process and is expected to develop employee innovation. Your environment must make the effort and risk of proposing innovative ideas worth it to the employee.

Remember, every employee in your organization has a Risk Box, and you have to find a way to encourage all to leave its safety and security in order to share their creative ideas. Corporate cultures are often too quick to criticize, thus strengthening the walls of the employees' Risk Box and eroding their courage to challenge. The first person an employee may speak with about an innovative idea is a manager. Managers who aren't trained to be Activation Agents might fear that, if they move forward with an innovative idea that fails, their attempt will harm their career. These managers can stall the organization's development, as the only ideas that make it through the system are safe copies of current products, processes, or services. Those aren't the ideas that move your organization forward or grow its presence in the marketplace.

For the most part, the individual employee can't accomplish innovation alone. Really game-changing innovation typically results from close, long-term collaboration. Weekend retreats, one-day workshops, or statements that the employee is "empowered to make innovation happen" aren't enough to overcome Risk Box barriers. You have to foster innovation over time, through experience and interaction with your team. To be successful, innovation must be part of your team's daily and weekly agenda. Collaboration on innovation is difficult when the organization culture doesn't welcome all participants as equals focused on a mutually beneficial purpose.

The only way to avoid failed innovations is to avoid all innovations, and that's a recipe for stagnation and irrelevance in the marketplace. As I said early in this book, do what you've always done; get what you've always gotten. It's leadership's role to make sure that managers and employees at every level within the organization know that they are expected to innovate, and that they will be supported in that process and beyond, no matter the outcome. That's how to combine the innovative elements of Idea Agents and Activation Agents and to spark explosive creative growth.

Driving Change

Possibly the most important purpose for innovation is in driving change. Change will be your constant companion throughout the entrepreneurial journey. Understanding change and its significance is vital to promoting innovation. Apple Computer is a great example of a company that leads by driving change. So many of its product innovations over the years—the floppy disk drive for PCs, graphical user interfaces, Newton, iMac, multicolored computer casings, iPod, iPhone, iMovie, iTunes, and the MacBook Air—have forced its competitors to react, while Apple scooped up market share and built ever-healthier margins.

STICKING A FORK IN THE DEVIL'S ADVOCATE

In *The Ten Faces of Innovation*, author Tom Kelley talks about the archenemy of innovation, "the devil's advocate" who jumps in and kills ideas the moment they're introduced.[1] These innovation killers seem to lurk in every organization, just waiting for the kernel of a new idea to take shape so they can spin the worst possible scenario that might result if it's allowed to see the light of day. Kelley's research has shown that when devil's advocates are allowed to take the floor, they can effectively eliminate great ideas from the organization. That's because so many people find psychological safety by hiding in the not-doing-something-new camp as opposed to searching out new and better solutions.

As an entrepreneur, you probably have been faced with devil's advocates often in your past. Entrepreneurs actively seek out people to share their ideas, because they want to discuss and refine their assumptions. But any innovative person can be discouraged and defeated by that single devil's advocate in the crowd. Innovators may talk to five different people on five different occasions and receive encouragement and validation every time. But if the sixth conversation includes a devil's advocate, that single source of discouraging blather can be enough to close the books on that idea, forever.

Why do innovators give so much power to the devil's advocate? Perhaps they're looking for a good reason to avoid launching their journey. We like having ideas, but we sometimes fear putting them into action, because we resist the level of commitment they require. I'm describing not a fear of work but a fear of losing—a reluctance to invest in something that doesn't have a guaranteed payoff. Giving into that fear denies us the many benefits we gain from pursuing our ideas—an experience that represents one of the biggest payoffs you can get from any investment.

The lesson here is that you need to stifle the devil's advocates in your organization. There's nothing to be gained by allowing anyone to shoot down new ideas before they've had a chance for discussion and development. Eliminating these fountains of negativity from your organization is a positive step toward creating an environment that fosters innovation and growth. By instilling a demand for innovation, encouraging people to test new ideas and learn from failures, and eliminating the role of devil's advocate from every level of your organization, you can help nourish the creative minds around you and build the intellectual property of your company.

Change is best when it is the result of strategy based on decisions drawn from a logical interpretation of environmental factors. Strategizing change is a skill that separates leaders from managers. Entrepreneurial leaders produce a higher proportion of strategies that become innovations for the enterprise, while managers' strategies tend to be more operational or logistically oriented within their span of control. Managers execute strategy while entrepreneurs create strategy. Both are equally important and necessary, and both define the roles each individual plays within the enterprise.

As an entrepreneur, your strategies need to be focused on driving change if you want to grow the organization rather than just keep it alive. Entrepreneurs who fail to drive change can quickly suffocate all innovation in the organization. The lack of innovation equates to fewer value adds, fewer intellectual property offerings, and fewer other elements that differentiate your organization from its competitors. Then you'll be forced to respond to change rather than lead it.

Every firm occasionally finds itself in the back seat of change that's being driven by an outside force, so you need to prepare to benefit from the ride. Change that drives you creates what I call "scramble innovation," which is a creative reaction to changes that originated with a competitor, customer, regulation, supplier, or any other stakeholder or environmental cue. Riding in the back seat of change isn't an entirely negative position; it gives you the opportunity to learn from the lead innovators' mistakes as you craft your response. And even changes that come from outside can drive your organization to perform better, cut costs, or improve efficiencies. But because reactionary change is often unplanned, it can become a drain on resources and a distraction for leadership. You don't want to be the guy looking over the driver's shoulder all the time.

Drivers of change are intentional innovators. They don't count on stumbling across the next great idea; they're out there creating it. Their innovations are planned and calculated—and sometimes destructive. To grow sales, these companies may destroy their current models or abandon key products or processes in order to adopt new and better ones. They invest time and resources in developing careful strategies around these efforts of creative destruction to be certain that, even with monumental changes, they are continuing to work toward their organizational goals and mission.

Innovating Waves of Change at TRC

As you've seen, I didn't hesitate to reshape TRC's business model in order to innovate a new and more effective path to growth and increased market share. In the preceding chapter, I told you about my successful efforts to sell Select licensing through TRC. After we had achieved success with that new market, I thought it was time for more changes at my company. I began by making a case to Microsoft to become a LAR (large account reseller), just as I had done years earlier at Educational Resources.

TRC needed to have LAR status to be a contender with the major players, but I focused my message to Microsoft on customer need, the poor service of existing LARs, and the benefits TRC's LAR status would bring to Microsoft. After nearly nine months of presentations, conferences, and interrogations, TRC gained Microsoft LAR status—to the shock and concern of our closest competitors. TRC went on to fill a tremendous gap in the market, which customers rewarded with their purchase orders. As TRC's leader, I used that success as a launching point for ongoing, systemwide changes that continued to grow and increase the value of our organization.

TRC had created a number of innovations around volume software licensing, which contributed to our LAR authorization. TRC's automated key code and serial number delivery was revolutionary, as was our online process for searching, viewing, and managing software licensing products in our catalog. We also invested considerable effort in simplifying the software licensing titles on our price list—a substantial improvement for users and a decided advantage over our competitors, whose sites simply posted the long and nearly untranslatable titles assigned by the software publishers. An end user in search of an academic market edition of Photoshop CS4 could easily find it listed as *Photoshop CS4 Windows Concurrent License* in our online catalog, as opposed to spotting it on our competitors' website under its publisher-assigned title of *ACLP3 PhotoCS4WNCONCLC*. This innovation may seem small, but it offered big benefits to our customers. Software licenses were nonreturnable; if customers made a mistake in selecting a product from a reseller's catalog, they were stuck with it unless they managed to win a lengthy appeal process. The market applauded TRC's innovative approach to product catalog listings, as did our publishers, and we benefited greatly from these industry-leading changes to our business model.

As TRC's attention became increasingly focused on volume licensing, a flurry of innovation-driven changes erupted. After we became authorized to replicate Microsoft CD media on our customers' behalf, TRC began burning media, lowering the costs of software disk sets to less than twenty dollars, which undercut our competitors' cost on the premanufactured sets. We controlled production and could deliver media faster and cheaper than anyone in the market. Microsoft had a college student and faculty purchase program under the Select licensing agreement too, which afforded drastically discounted prices on products like Microsoft Office and the Windows Operating System upgrade. TRC simplified the process for ordering and bundling these products that was unmatched in the industry. We sold a ton of these finished pieces to college bookstores, and we were the only company in the country to do it.

We launched our new website and changed our e-commerce platform by adding an electronic software download service. Again, TRC appeared to be the only LAR with this capability in the volume software license field. When the levee breaks that followed hurricane Katrina inundated Tulane University's main campus in New Orleans, the benefits of this change became evident. Tulane quickly set up a remote IT command center in Houston, with essential computer hardware in place, but all of its software disks and key codes were lost or irretrievably damaged by floodwaters. Thanks to TRC's industry-leading functionality, Tulane was able to request the software on a Saturday morning and, within minutes, download the required software products, along with the applicable license key codes. That's just one example of the power of change.

It was truly a rewarding experience to see our innovation put to use during such a critical time of need for our customer. This event helped entrench our presence within Tulane, and we used that story to tell other customers about the unique capabilities of TRC. We were no longer selling a commoditized item based solely on price. We were selling a service. Our singular focus on software brought even more success stories and new relationships with school consortiums representing numerous colleges who endorsed TRC's services.

In the dot-com era, I was blindsided by an unexpected online competitor. Even though the competition's strategies died off before it had a chance to fatally impact TRC, that experience made it perfectly clear that TRC had to drive change moving forward and that those changes had to be centered on the customer. By focusing on innovation and leading ongoing change, I was able to develop intellectual property that was difficult to replicate; innovation was the driver that scaled our future growth (I'll tell you more about this experience in chapter 12). TRC went from $3 million in sales in 1998 to $8.5 million in 2000. By 2004, the year we killed our print catalog, we were at $21 million, all fueled through our focus on volume software licensing, and our willingness to change our business model to leverage that market.

TRC's innovative approach earned numerous industry awards and peer recognition as being one of the best, if not the best, software licensing resellers in the education market. We became one of the top education-focused dealers in the United States for Microsoft, Adobe, Symantec, and several other name-brand publishers. Our foremost intent was to constantly innovative our processes and change our industry in order to better serve our customers and eliminate their pain points. Our growing success and dominant position in our industry stemmed directly from our creative culture, our innovative energy, and our ongoing commitment to leading change throughout our organization and industry.

Tearing Down Roadblocks

I've heard it said that people who are confronted by change will fight it, ignore it, or embrace it (that is, if they even recognize it). You'll notice that all of these are reactionary responses, and we've already talked about the pros and cons of reacting to, rather than leading, change. I've also discovered, however, that many organizations crash into some common roadblocks in their attempts to either follow or lead change. If you know what those roadblocks are, you're better able to sidestep or eliminate them on your own path to and through change.

Although large companies can have several competitive advantages over their smaller counterparts, their size can be an Achilles' heel when it comes to creating and implementing changes. I have found larger companies particularly prone to tripping over these roadblocks:

1. **"Helloooo. Is anybody there?"** The frontline rank and file can be a tremendous asset to a company that wants to lead change within its industry. These hands-on workers hear and see what works well and have a good idea of what needs improvement. Even though they may be among the first in the organization to see opportunities for innovation, they may fail to have a voice within the company. If their repeated alarms about the need for change go unnoticed by management and leadership, they may get fed up and choose to remain silent. If your frontline people aren't measured, incentivized, or given recognition to innovate, they won't; and then everyone loses (except your competitors).

2. **"This is the way we do things."** Let's call this a barricade of ignorance and/or arrogance. Companies can become too inwardly focused and too stubborn to change processes already in place. If these companies have processes that shut out or complicate the customer interactions, then their solution is that the customer needs to adapt and work within the company's structure, rather than the other way around. The message to the outside world is clear: "Everything is working just fine for us, and now you want us to change? Hey, this is how we do business; if you don't like it, go somewhere else!" Yes, you have to be selective and strategic in determining when and how to introduce change in your organization and its processes, but letting internal operations trump the voice of the market is a risky practice.

3. **"Help! I can't move."** While a stubborn resistance to change can be a road hazard for any organization, a dead end awaits those companies who simply aren't capable of changing. Companies can create a layered structure so complex that it immobilizes them from enacting meaningful changes. A sort of corporate paralysis sets in; they know they need to do something about the changes taking place in the marketplace and world around them, yet they can't get their arms or legs to move. Look at General Motors, with its legacy of repetitive divisions that build basically the same cars with different nameplates, year after year after year. Imagine all of the internal politics and bureaucracy required to reform that structure so GM can compete with firms like Toyota and Hyundai. It took bankruptcy to shock the company out of its structural straightjacket, but now it has a chance to evolve.

4. **"We're too big for change to affect us."** Some companies adopt the attitude that they're too big and powerful to be buffeted by the winds of change. Their leaders believe that they can dictate the pace at which the organization responds to change—and, in some cases, they can. Those cases are relatively rare, however, and even large companies run the risk of losing market share or ratcheting up unnecessary costs as they try to catch up. This roadblock has a twin that stalls those companies who feel they're too small to worry about watching for change. These "smalls" imagine that they'll do just fine, tucked away in their little niche where the larger markets never venture. Many local town pharmacies, for example, tried to hunker down during the waves of consolidation and buyouts that swept through the market during the 1980s and '90s, only to find that either a CVS or a Walgreens had popped up overnight on prime corner locations just down the street. You don't have to go with the flow of change, but you must be prepared either to be washed away or to build a better vessel for riding the waves.

That last example just goes to show that small companies are just as vulnerable to change blockades as the big guys. Small, growing firms typically are more concerned with leading and adopting internal change. They quickly outgrow original processes, people, methodologies, and technologies, and some struggle to keep up with the demand for ongoing adaptation. The roadblocks that I find most in small growing companies include the following:

1. **"No foot-dragger left behind."** It may be difficult for some employees to adapt to the changes taking place in a growing company. You may have a solid team player who's been a great employee from day one, but when the business jumps to its next level, that employee doesn't jump with you. Loyalty tugs at you to accommodate this person and work around his or her deficiencies, but think carefully before you get pulled into a bad decision. Accommodating people who don't want to grow with the organization can stunt the entire business's growth and survival. In a culture of innovation and growth, every employee understands that employees are expected to create and embrace new ideas, not curate a museum devoted to your company's first days.

2. **"Whoa—slow down there, baby!"** Due to either constrained budgets or constrained creativity, small businesses can fall into the habit of thinking small. When faced with change, they may institute multiple tiny, incremental changes that consume valuable time and resources on the long, ongoing march of innovation. If possible, small companies should take the time to fully think through the change before them, and then make one giant leap forward, rather than baby-stepping their way toward the future. The up-front cost of that leap may be greater, but the return will come swifter and, ultimately, be more cost-effective.

3. **"We've invested a lot in the status quo."** Any new business has invested a great deal in getting itself established, both in terms of raw dollars and in time spent developing specific processes, procedures, or products. Regardless, change may come knocking at your new venture and require you to adapt and morph. When your original plans and processes no longer work, take the hit and move on. Getting upset about the necessity of change or focusing on the sacrifices involved in your original investment is futile; change is a necessary part of growth. If changes become essential—or extremely beneficial—incorporate them and move on.

Growing the Innovation Garden

When we introduced wave after wave of innovation at TRC, our motivation was to differentiate ourselves in the marketplace, not to become great industry innovators. In fact, the word *innovate* wasn't really part of our vocabulary. Organically, our company developed a structured process for gathering ideas for innovation, evaluating and selecting from among those ideas, and then rapidly deploying those we'd chosen for implementation. We could scrap or reinvent operational processes as necessary, to serve the needs of each new innovation. Without knowing it, we were practicing what Ken Blanchard and colleagues in *The One Minute Entrepreneur* call "interpreneurship," where employees take ownership of new initiatives and get others to buy in.[2]

Employee-driven innovation in any established organization can only come about when a commitment to foster innovation is developed and supported at the highest levels of leadership. Like the Six Sigma process of quality business management created by Motorola, innovation processes have to be a strategy incorporated into your overall business systems. Every aspect of a business involves some sort of process, so you can't hope to succeed at innovation if you don't create and support it with some form of procedural structure.

To assist in creating a structured process for growing and implementing new ideas, I suggest planting an "Innovation Garden," a process for fostering employee-driven innovation. The Innovation Garden involves six steps; let's walk through them.

Step 1: Prepare to plant the garden.

For innovation to originate organically from all levels of the employee population, it has to become part of the company culture. Executive management can show its commitment to innovation by establishing public goals for the outcomes of employee-driven innovation. Like tilling the soil before planting, by clearly setting forth your organization's expectations for innovation, you begin to build an environment and culture where new ideas can emerge and flourish. These are some of the practices and organizationwide goals I promote in order to "till the soil" of my organization's Innovation Garden:

- Obtain great ideas from the best source of innovation—employees.
- Nurture a culture of innovation that reduces costs and increases productivity.
- Promote a genuine feeling of ownership and empowerment to innovate in all employees.
- Become competitively superior through innovation.
- Exceed customer expectations through innovation.

While these practices and principles apply to everyone in the organization, executive management has its own unique responsibilities for defining, creating, and nurturing a culture of innovation. Beyond expecting and encouraging innovation, leadership needs to take these solid, tangible steps to prepare the organization to capitalize on its innovative potential:

1. **An innovation budget.** This budget won't cover the cost of implementing an innovation, as those costs are unpredictable. Instead, it covers the costs of creating a dedicated workplace, buying materials, training Activation Agents to develop innovative ideas, and funding employee recognition efforts.

2. **Defined employee roles.** Employees will be classified as Idea Agents and/or Activation Agents, and the organization should include these roles as part of all employee job descriptions.

3. **Employee training.** Staff development needs to define innovation to the staff and explain its strategic importance in differentiating the company. Employee training should thoroughly describe the roles of Idea Agents and Activation Agents and outline the process of screening and selecting ideas for implementation so that everyone in the organization understands the innovation life cycle.

4. **Rules and procedures.** I'm not talking about setting up a tightly managed set of prescribed activities, but the organization must make very clear its "rules of engagement" in the innovative process by creating an environment of trust, blocking the devil's advocate, and removing bureaucracy from the Innovation Garden.

Ideas are highly personal, and so your organization has to emphasize encouragement and trust in the way it handles the idea generation and vetting process. Your Innovation Garden will always involve elements of risk; ideas will be debated, challenged, and sometimes rejected. To help your team avoid feelings of embarrassment during these challenges, you need to make sure that your employees understand the process all ideas will undergo. When an innovation is challenged and chosen by a process, rather than by an individual or haphazard notion, the success or failure of the innovation is shared by everyone in the organization. Making this process very clear up-front will create an environment in which innovation can flourish, without the nasty hassle of rebuke, judgment, and fear.

The magic of the Innovation Garden is that its environment is cocooned from the status quo of the business. Entrepreneurs are drawn to fertile and open environments where they can grow and enjoy the fruits of their innovations. By preparing your Innovation Garden, you're positioning your organization to attract and keep the talent it will need to continue its growth and development.

Step 2: Dedicate resources.

The Innovation Garden needs a physical space, a forum in which people can generate and hone ideas. This fixed location also serves as a permanent reminder of the organization's commitment to innovation. The location also helps give the innovation process a physical framework in which to unfold so that it doesn't overrun and disrupt other daily business processes. You also need to dedicate time for the innovation process. Idea Agents and Activation Agents should have regularly scheduled meeting times within the forum. Innovation needs to be on everyone's calendar and part of everyone's routines, so I suggest monthly meetings that do not exceed one hour. Scheduling time for innovation is vital for establishing your long-term commitment to the process.

Participants come to the innovation forum and sessions with ideas and then spend time refining them for harvest. That means you'll need to equip the innovation forum with resources such as whiteboards, flip charts, an audiovisual projector, and other aids to convey the ideas to the Activation Agents. The notes, drawings, tools, and presentation materials left in the innovation forum may help trigger or refine other ideas.

Also, dedicate mini-spaces for innovation throughout the organization. Have whiteboards posted publically in every department to serve as innovation parking lots. During the day, as employees get a great idea, they can write it (park it) on the whiteboard. Companies can create "innovation intranet" sites that bring individuals into a virtual innovation parking lot 24/7 in order to park their ideas. These spaces help infuse your entire workspace in innovation and encourage the sharing of ideas and collaborative feedback.

Step 3: Plant the seeds.

The seeds of innovation in your garden are the ideas that spring from your Idea Agents (the majority of the employees in the company). Innovative ideas will form through individual "aha" moments and group collaboration; both sources need to be encouraged and given a nourishing spot in the garden to yield the greatest results.

People will want to begin discussing their ideas immediately, whenever and wherever they strike. The innovation whiteboards and other parking lots act as placeholders and preliminary discussion centers for ideas until time can be scheduled in the innovation forum to fully discuss them. Whatever tools you use to grab and hold ideas, they must be periodically collected and moved to the innovation forum where they can be reviewed and acted upon in a scheduled and consistent manner.

Innovation doesn't always spring from random thoughts, however, so sometimes it makes sense to establish groups for exploring specific ideas or focusing their efforts on a specific topic. These assignments purposely engage more people in the innovation process and deepen the culture of innovation. The topics for focus group innovation could relate to departmental or corporate SWOTs (strengths, weaknesses, opportunities, and threats), KPIs (key performance indicators), processes, or stakeholder pain points. The innovations that grow from these group idea "seeds" may be highly structured, and therefore take a bit longer to launch, since they won't be generated from a single source. Activation agents need to take a greater role in facilitating the group through the process and keeping all on track.

Step 4: Water and weed.

Innovation is the result of an idea put into action. Essentially, your organization's Activation Agents are responsible for watering the ideas that will grow into innovation. The Activation Agents must be specially trained to facilitate innovation, but they don't necessarily have to be managers. Activation Agents need to be trained to be keen idea receptors, selective in processing ideas, sensitive in explaining the prescribed process for challenging ideas, and capable of recognizing when refinement is necessary to bring an idea into focus. The Activation Agents should have a firm understanding of company goals, customers, processes, and related stakeholders.

Part of the Activation Agent training should be focused on using the prescribed idea selection process to collaboratively weed out ideas with the Idea Agent that don't fit criteria such as likelihood of activation, scope, or funding requirements without insulting or discouraging the Idea Agent. Weeding out weak ideas provides room for the best ideas to flourish, but the Activation Agent must be certain to listen, encourage, filter, guide, and coach creative thinking in the idea selection process. Every organization must create its own process; see the sidebar to review the one we created at TRC, where both Idea and Activation Agent address the following topics.

Step 5: Harvest.

Once the innovation has passed through the scrutiny of the idea selection process, it should be prepared for presentation to the ultimate decision makers. Depending on the scope of the innovation, the decision makers can be represented at the departmental level or by an executive committee consisting of a broad representation of the company.

- Is the innovation clearly defined for the decision maker?

- Are all possible questions addressed that may be posed by the decision maker?

- Can proof of concept be tested for the innovation?

- What expectations does the Idea Agent/Activation Agent have of the decision maker in the presentation?

THE IDEA SELECTION PROCESS

1. Define the idea clearly in a brief statement.

2. Define the primary stakeholder(s).

3. Define what the innovation stemming from the idea will accomplish:
   - Save money
   - Produce greater efficiency
   - Ensure greater customer satisfaction
   - Differentiate the company
   - Add intellectual property
   - Address a stakeholder pain point

4. Define what resources the innovation will require:
   - Is there a budget for this?
   - Can a budget be created for this?
   - Does the innovation exceed the group's authority?
   - Does the innovation exceed the group's abilities?
   - Does the innovation exceed the company's abilities?

5. Calculate an ROI (based on dollars or KPI).

6. Provide a final analysis.
   - Based on the ROI, is it worth pursuing, or are other innovations more worthwhile at this time?
   - Are other innovations better suited for the same resources or ROI?
   - Is this a viable innovation, or are we forcing it?
   - Does the innovation require involvement of senior management or other stakeholders?
   - Should the idea be parked, killed, or pursued?
   - Idea Agent completes a brief survey on the experience and rates Activation Agent.

- Are all benefits of the innovation clearly detailed for the decision maker?
- Are all known costs associated with the innovation reported?

Step 6: Reward and acknowledge.

Innovation needs to be incorporated into annual appraisals and goal settings. You need to be certain that you measure, review, and reward participation as well as performance. In other words, don't just reward the successfully executed innovations; reward the failures, too—both personally and publicly. Appreciation and acknowledgement are consistently listed as the things employees want most from their superiors and peers. It ranks higher than money! It is also an area where many companies perform poorly. Creative, consistent, and reliable ways of sincerely acknowledging good work is what humans crave.

Be innovative in how you reward. You'll be surprised that cash isn't always the most effective reward. Ask your employees for ideas on how to acknowledge innovation. In fact, send them to the Innovation Garden as their first assignment to come up with an innovative response.

Promoting Ongoing Innovation for Ongoing Growth

Innovation is vital to any business, and yet, innovation typically is the least structured and empowered area of business. CEOs in large corporations can find it challenging to incubate an entrepreneurial spirit within their staff, but many of them are even less able to understand why innovation doesn't just naturally flourish within their organization. I've seen many a CEO, director, or line manager practically begging the troops to adopt an entrepreneurial spirit and innovative mindset. What these leaders fail to recognize is that they have locked their people in an environment that chokes innovative thought and prohibits innovative progress.

The larger and older a company grows, the more confining its bureaucracy can become. Although most entrepreneurs are repelled by such controls, the truth is that organizations need bureaucracies in order to operate smoothly and effectively. Executives need to understand the bureaucratic foundation of their organization, in order to leverage the entrepreneurial spirit necessary to breed innovation. As Judith Cone of the Ewing Marion Kauffman Foundation wrote in an essay titled "Entrepreneurship on Campus: Why the Real Mission Is Culture Change," "One of the greatest challenges of our society is to keep our large organizations from falling prey to bureaucratic sclerosis. We must learn to keep them entrepreneurial from within, adaptive, and creative."[3] You'll need to lead this role in the Running phase of your organization. As TRC matured, ongoing innovation was vital to our ability to grow the business. The same will be true in your entrepreneurial journey; the more mature your company becomes, the more dependent you will be on ongoing innovation to scale the business.

The lessons I learned during the Running phase of my business helped to deepen both my customer and my product knowledge, which, in turn, helped me continue to differentiate TRC from its competition. Originally, I saw TRC as being the low-price leader, the Wal-Mart of software. However, I found that going to market on price alone diminished the value we provided to our customers and made it increasingly difficult to run the business on such low margins. Over time our innovations helped maintain acceptable price points and established brand loyalty to TRC. Due to the substantial operational and IT investment our processes required, it was difficult for our competitors to catch up, so we stood alone in the advancements we brought to market. To continue to grow, however, we still needed to do more to differentiate the products we were selling.

The flagship software lines in education were Adobe and Microsoft, each of which had high-volume license programs. Since we weren't the manufacturers of these products, we couldn't tweak them to differentiate our offerings. We couldn't innovate the products, so we had to create some method for changing the marketplace.

In my search for innovation opportunities, I discovered that just about any college in the country could be associated with an independent consortium or cooperative organization that existed solely to support, lobby, or extend the purchasing power of member schools. Traditionally, academic consortia focused on things like group insurance rates, state funding, or discounts on furniture. I decided that TRC would introduce these groups to the idea of cooperative purchasing for software licensing.

Volume software licensing is constructed on the principle of the more you buy, the lower your price. By stretching the boundaries of the publishers' intentions of their volume licensing agreements, TRC could use these consortia to get individual member schools to consolidate their orders and, therefore, achieve higher discount levels. Schools would save money on licensing, and the consortium would be recognized for providing the opportunity. And TRC's business in this market channel would explode.

The innovation was successful. TRC didn't need to discount the volume tier, because we were the only ones who could offer it to the designated consortium member schools. Schools who hadn't worked with TRC in the past were anxious to participate in this program, which substantially expanded TRC's customer portfolio. Our offer was irresistible, especially in light of our many customer-focused innovations, and we were able to easily take market share. This strategic innovation became a game changer, and many of our competitors were blindsided and unable to respond. It also helped energize TRC's successful engine of ongoing innovation.

Innovation is at the core of any new business, and it remains the beating heart of the organization as it matures. A new business will change at a far greater rate than an existing one, but ongoing innovations will continue to reshape all segments of any organization as it grows. As we've seen in this chapter, a primary responsibility you hold as an entrepreneur is driving ongoing change. Your ability to maintain a culture of innovation and an environment in which it can grow will determine how well your business is able to brand itself in the marketplace, build a loyal following of customers and clients, and attract and keep the best and brightest talent.

Many entrepreneurs are like parents when they first launch their companies: highly involved in all aspects of the operation, intimately familiar with its every detail, involved in each component's conception and creation. Then, by necessity, they begin to let go. As you and your company mature, you'll need to be able to trust aspects of its growth to your partners and employees, even as you continue adapting, changing, and reinventing the business in response to environmental cues. As an entrepreneur, you have to be able to build a workforce, systems, processes, and policies that enable your organization to constantly reinvent itself in response to its changing environment. In the next chapter of this book—and the final chapter to discuss the Running phase of your entrepreneurial journey—we'll talk about ways to scale your business and its systems so your original entrepreneurial idea can grow and mature into its best possible outcome.

CHAPTER TWELVE

Scaling for Growth

ULTIMATELY, THE STORY OF HOW you started a business is not as captivating as the story about how the business took off, grew, and became successful. People who take great interest in my entrepreneurial story always ask questions aimed at uncovering deeper details about its development. What they really are asking, whether they realize it or not, is "How did it scale?" In this chapter, I'm going to answer that question, in some detail.

Scaling is how an organization grows by becoming more efficient and profitable as it generates more business. Simply put, the business is able to take on more orders or produce more product, without eating up the additional profits by adding additional resources. Scaling is at the heart of the matter and, along with leadership and innovation, it is one of the three primary responsibilities of the entrepreneur in the Running phase.

In this chapter, I'm going to give you a detailed look at the ways we scaled TRC. Every business is unique in the ways it can and must scale as it becomes a mature and fully functional venture. By sharing the details of TRC's scaling process, I'm hoping to give you a frontline account of how one organization managed its growth in order to gain profitability and enhance its valuation. First, we'll look at the importance of building scaling into your business plan, so that every aspect of your growth and innovation is managed within the umbrella of the overriding goal of scaling the business for increased profitability and market share. Next, I'll describe how TRC used scaling as a tool for growing its business *and* for honing its competitive edge. Finally, we'll explore the importance of scaling your skills as an entrepreneur as you expand your leadership focus and wield innovative strategies and tactics in order to keep pace with the demands of your maturing business.

Planning to Scale

Scaling isn't something that happens by accident. You need to carefully plan for scaling and build specific scaling milestones and metrics into your original business plan and strategy. Creating an effective plan for scaling requires vision, as you must anticipate how your entrepreneurial idea will meld into a business that grows from a freeform startup into a sophisticated collection of processes and systems. Because this process requires advanced capabilities in planning and foresight, you may not have all the answers about how to scale your business while you are in the planning stage; nevertheless, you do need to develop a general conception of the model at that point. Generically, your plan for scaling should include techniques and timetables for establishing business systems, incorporating technology, and utilizing capital.

Below are four components of TRC's original business plan that I used to scale the operation:

1. **Know the target market and establish reproducible and expanding methods to reach that market.** Initially, we focused efforts surrounding this element of our plan on TRC's lead-generation methods. We began with a direct-mail-order catalog. The more of these catalogs we mailed out, the more sales we achieved, which made for efficient scaling. Later, these methods expanded to include marketing efforts designed to hit the target in multiple ways, as we found that the frequency of our marketing efforts fueled increased customer response.

2. **Establish operational procedures to create a similar customer experience every time.** From the beginning, we knew that building customer satisfaction and loyalty would be key to scaling TRC. We created processes and dedicated people to specific tasks to ensure quality in every operational aspect of the business that touched the customer.

3. **Replicate the sales process in a predictable manner that can be forecasted.** Once we had devised a lead-generation and sales process that worked well, we had to be able to reliably reproduce it. This involved training staff, establishing procedures, managing those people and procedures, and providing the right tools. Our best tool investment was in our ERP (enterprise resource planning) and CRM (customer relationship management) system. I may be a frugal-preneur, but I invested top dollar in the best systems for our business, and the resulting productivity and

efficiency gains were enormous. Those tools helped produce sales pipeline reports allowing us to forecast sales, review closing ratios, and zero in on significant opportunities.

4. **Invest in the capacity to scale.** At TRC, we invested in hiring and training the best people for our sales positions and in giving them the best tools for succeeding in their work. We also invested in tracking the sales team's performance and using the results to determine when we needed to address problems in individual skills or in our overall training program. We established a measurable gain in revenue and profit that, after a nine-to-twelve-month training and acclimation period, a new sales representative should be able to produce. This metric enabled us to identify which sales staff were underachieving and which were going beyond expectations. As a result, we could reward successes and address shortcomings in both people and processes in order to keep our business growing and on track.

As you can see, our plans for scaling the business focused first on making investments in people, with investments in technology coming in at a close second. Expanding our office space, improving operations, and buying technology all went into the effort to scale.

TECHNOLOGY AND SCALING

Technology can be a significant tool for scaling by replacing human efforts, increasing efficiency, and decreasing time involved within systems. Think of your systems as the major arteries that run through your organization and connect its vital functions. Tasks are subsets of processes that form these larger systems. You will build this infrastructure with the resources on hand, and it will mature as budgets, experience, and technology dictate. Because all of these factors are dependent on available capital, you can expect to go through several phases of scaling as your systems evolve to become more sophisticated and your resources become greater.

Adjusting Your Strategy for Scaling

We've discussed how change is constant for the entrepreneur and that you either drive change or are forced to react to change. It is likely any business will be on either end of the change spectrum during its journey. Two significant examples of TRC reacting to and driving change helped set the stage for our ultimate success—though we really did not realize the impact until our eventual exit.

TRC was dependent on cooperative advertising to generate our marketing materials. Using manufacturer dollars was like being able to market for free. Obviously, we needed to generate sales in the manufacturer's product line in order to keep the co-op dollars flowing. When cooperative advertising started to ebb, it was a glaring sign that things were changing for TRC and the industry. We had to adjust our strategy.

Many of our competitors didn't recognize the bigger picture behind this change. The manufacturer's shift away from co-op advertising wasn't just about fewer advertising dollars being spent; dealer margins were retracting, too. More competitors were entering the higher ed market, and most relied on replicative rather than innovative business models. Every dealer was focused on selling the same brands and the same products because that was the nature of the reseller business—to fulfill rather than generate demand. Our customers knew what they wanted and simply needed a place to buy it from. In that scenario, the only differentiator became price, and the products we sold were quickly commoditized.

Manufacturers started to realize that no matter how many ad dollars they threw at their resellers, those resellers would continue to sell the manufacturers' products at pretty much the same rate they always had—except for a rare few. TRC was among that group of higher achievers because we had built our practices around customer needs and established a reliable brand. But the industry was going through a period of significant change. Since most IT manufacturers were public companies or were striving to issue an IPO or a buyout, they faced mounting pressures to grow. At the same time, the Internet was gaining stature, and manufacturers began shifting marketing dollars from legacy dealer catalogs to the Internet. Most dealers didn't have programs to attract co-op dollars to support web activity. As TRC and the industry matured and our inside sales force grew, more of our sales were being generated from customer relationships and the web than from direct mail efforts.

This industry shift sent a message to me that was loud and clear: TRC had to retool. We had to move away from catalog distribution to the web. We decided to completely stop producing a catalog by 2004, and we were the first in our industry to make this move. It was a scary decision. Our catalog had always been our lead-generation system and a central component of our business model. Further, the decision came with a human cost. The role of the product manager, which had been core to our success as a reseller, was now obsolete at TRC. Unable to reallocate the entire staff that supported catalog operations, I had to eliminate some of these positions.

These employees had done nothing wrong, and they were tremendously talented and hardworking individuals. But times had changed, and TRC needed a new skill set—fast!

This bold move was something I was driving based on my strategy and instinct. I had learned a lesson from our past: that growth and success were likely to follow proactive changes we thrust upon the market rather than reactive changes imposed by the market on us. For instance, in the early years of the dot-com era, new competitors that had never before been in our channel were emerging rapidly. Some of these competitors were selling products at or below our cost. We cried foul to our distributors and to the manufacturers for granting these players such special pricing. Their response was that there *was* no special pricing; our cut-rate competitors had the same structure as everyone else. It took a long while for us to realize that these lower-than-cost competitors weren't in business to sell technology; they were in business to sell advertising. The low prices were used just to bring people to the website. Our customers, of course, didn't care why the prices were low, and they began demanding the same price from TRC.

Scrambling to react, I had to come up with a defense—and *defense* and *react* are two words I never like to use when it comes to business strategy. This development clearly revealed that I wasn't innovating or forcing change adequately at TRC. I was reacting to change, which, as you learned in chapter 11, meant I was in a bad pole position—behind the pack.

As my understanding of the model expanded, however, I formulated a strategy to respond. First, TRC would focus on our unique strengths, which lay in our great service and product knowledge. These new web players knew nothing of the technology they were selling; they were merely posting SKUs for a price. Their customers were advertisers, not the consumers buying product from them. Second, we would ride it out. Who knew how long this would last? These companies were competing strictly on price, and that is rarely a winning strategy.

TRC's strategy, however, proved very effective. TRC scrapped its first custom-built e-commerce platform to shift to new, less expensive, and highly customizable development. That change enabled us to build an e-commerce platform around the unique needs of our niche audience, while many of our competitors built systems aligned with the rigid needs of their own internal legacy systems. Customers started turning to TRC in frustration over the unanswered phone calls, slow shipments, and poor customer service they'd experienced in their dealings with the web price-warriors. Few of our new online competitors were offering credit payment terms or a suitable return policy. By continuing to focus on what we did best and holding steady rather than copying our competition, we emerged from this threat. Indeed, we continued to have record sales, and those competitors silently disappeared in the course of a year.

TRC was a bit lucky that our reaction to the new breed of low-priced competitors became a successful strategy. The lasting success from our deliberate intention to abandon direct mail and to move from a basic accounting package to a mid-tier ERP software system that would manage and coordinate all the operational, informational, and process-oriented functions of TRC proved to be the proactive strategic win that would have a lasting impact. We invested in a system much larger than we needed, but that we fully intended to grow into. We designed our e-commerce and shopping functionality to draw directly from this new ERP system in ways that were innovative to our customers' needs—something that would take our competitors years to duplicate.

Scaling Your Finances as You Scale Your Business

As you work to grow your business bigger to gain a sense of stability and security, other factors can make it even more vulnerable, and credit is one of them. There were three primary factors that kept the credit flowing and growing for TRC: our balance sheet, my integrity, and TRC's relationship with suppliers. With no exceptions, our balance sheet had to be sound in order for our partners to continue taking our orders. I wouldn't say our balance sheet always was stellar—after all, we were in a low-margin business. But our balance sheet was always respectable. By making sure of that fact, my reputation for integrity grew, as did my supplier relationships. Keeping all three of those important measures intact isn't easy, but it's essential for your ability to scale your business successfully. The larger and faster your company grows, the trickier this balancing act becomes.

With sales exceeding $10 million and then $20 million, TRC generated a predictable flow of monthly business, but we still were on thin ice. Any interruption in our credit capacity, which was essential to fulfilling those orders, would trigger an immediate backup of orders that could result in a shutdown of our business. As an entrepreneur, you'll find that even when your suppliers are saying, "No more orders until you pay down your balance," your customers will continue to buy, thanks to your lead-generation system. When that happens, orders start to pile up, customer complaints rise due to late fulfillment, orders get cancelled, and your business enters a tumultuous time.

The bootstrap model worked for TRC because we experienced rapid and continual growth that funded the business. Monthly cash flow came strictly from our monthly net income and cash received from outstanding accounts receivable from customers. We monitored the recurring costs of phone charges, utilities, rent, and other operational expenses under a microscope. Working with the monthly cash flow we received at TRC, my wife and partner Lisa would do her juggling act, closely reviewing our outstanding accounts payable to decide what bills had to be paid. Every single month for ten years this dance went on, and Lisa was the lead.

The art of juggling accounts payable is nothing new, but Lisa's skill was truly something to marvel at. Approximately 92 percent of our customers were given credit to pay their invoices in thirty days. This was customary and a requirement in our market selling to schools. Often our invoices required approval at monthly board meetings and then were routed through the school's own operational process. That made it difficult to get an invoice paid within thirty days. The normal float would be more around thirty-five days, but some would take even longer.

What further strained our float capability was the growth TRC was experiencing. Each month larger orders were being placed with our suppliers. The average order size was rapidly growing and significantly increased once we focused on volume software licensing. The once-unusual orders of $100k, $300k, and $500k were starting to become routine, and they hampered our credit. Add to that the costs of adding new employees, the six-month ramp-up time until they were profitable, and ongoing payroll concerns, and you have a lot of balls in the air. TRC always made payroll, although Lisa can confess to several sleepless nights spent wondering how that was going to happen. However, cash flow alone couldn't continue to sustain TRC through its Running phase. Without credit, we would have shut down.

TRC's rapid growth rate required our distributors to increase their own credit lines with us. The financial guys at these outfits would pour through our financial statements using a time-tested method that would calculate ratios to determine the amount of credit they could supply based on our cash flow, outstanding accounts receivable, pending obligations, and assets. Our accounts receivable balance would stay fairly consistent, and our customer base held a very low risk of default. However, we were now coming to our distributors with larger and larger orders, some topping a million dollars. Because there was no credit limit set for us to do those types of orders, our vendors had to get creative, and I had to sell like crazy—but to them, not just to our customers.

Still, the pace of TRC's growth rapidly outstripped any new credit we obtained, and I increasingly turned to personal credit cards to supplement payment for supplier purchases. Most of our suppliers accepted credit cards and did so out of their own necessity to extend credit risk without interrupting continual customer orders. We had twelve different credit cards with varying levels of credit, all in either my name or Lisa's, and we paid all of them, in full, every month. I was adamant about not incurring finance charges as that would have lowered our profit margins. I monitored our profits like a hawk, and literally fought any internal or external influences that eroded them.

As your business grows, you, too, will need to find ways to grow your credit without eroding profits in order to continue to scale your business. At TRC, we continually worked with our distributors to increase our credit limits throughout the life of the company. I quickly learned, for example, that I could artificially increase my credit by finding more suppliers willing to provide credit—although that could only take us so far, based on the outstanding payables on our balance sheet. The trick was to continually give more business to a supplier and pay that supplier on time (or as reasonably close to on time as possible). We could source much of the same product from multiple distributors and take advantage of various credit lines in that respect. Our continued growth kept straining the process, however, as we would pay a balance in full on one day and then completely use up our credit limit again the next day. The only relief came from the seasonality of our business, which allowed our credit time to catch up during the slow months from November through February.

Gaining this kind of support from your creditors *and* customers requires that your business be built on and maintain a strong reputation for ethics and honesty and impeccable business systems and records. Requesting credit extensions from TRC's top suppliers became standard operating procedure during our peak season. Our suppliers had seen growth like ours in other resellers, and they wanted to ride those horses. Reviewing our financials, suppliers would understand our need to reinvest earnings into the business, but closely followed key metrics to monitor and ensure things were not getting too out of control. Ultimately, it came down to trust. It was everyone's job in the company to ensure we maintained a good partnership with our suppliers, and it was my job to lead by example and establish the highest levels of personal and business integrity. That's an important piece of the puzzle in growing any business. You can't be so focused on yourself and your business that you disregard or take advantage of those you partner with. Remaining outwardly humble is paramount for successfully scaling your business during these periods of outsized growth.

INDUSTRIES CREATE SOLUTIONS TO AID GROWTH

To fuel our growth and the increasing size of our transactions, TRC used a major weapon that was fairly unique to our industry. A credit vehicle called "flooring" provided a revolving line of credit on purchases made through our major distributors. Born out of financing in the automotive industry, flooring was a separate and much larger line of credit, provided through major banks, that would grant 30–45 days on purchases made at participating distributors. Whereas a distributor granted $100,000 in credit, flooring could provide $400,000. Of course, distributors gave up a portion of their margin to provide flooring as a way to reduce their exposure and credit risk. There was no cost to TRC or other participating dealers. Flooring was great for TRC, but not such an attractive business for the banks. It was extremely low margin for the banks, and we found ourselves regularly having to find a new flooring source as institutions would abandon the market in search of higher-margin opportunities. In spite of the upheaval and administrative work to establish a new flooring company, we were always able to do so, and that kept our business humming at a very low expense.

Maturing Along with Your Business

As I worked through the Running phase at TRC, I gained a fresh vision for what my company was truly meant to be, and I instituted more changes in our operation. As you've already learned, one of our first decisions to scale the business was to stop selling everything under the sun and focus on software. When I started TRC, part of the pitch was "over fifty thousand products at the lowest prices." Maintaining fifty thousand items on our website proved to be impossible and cost prohibitive. Above all, we didn't sell all fifty thousand products; we only sold a sliver of that, and that sliver was made up of software.

My next decision was to put all of our resources and focus into being the most knowledgeable source for volume software licensing in the academic market—a process you read about in the preceding chapter. It was no accident that our strength would be in software sales since that's where I got my training. As much as I wanted to grow by having customers think of TRC for all of their technology needs, our talent resided in software. My skills as a leader and visionary were growing along with my business, and so was my ability to hone and focus my attention and to guide TRC's efforts and growth. As you grow in your role as an entrepreneurial leader, you'll need to remain poised and ready to adjust your business model and processes in order to continue to scale your organization.

Successful scaling doesn't always look like expansion; in fact, refocusing can mean reshaping and even downsizing specific areas of your operation.

It's important, therefore, that you learn to make scaling decisions based on careful planning and strategizing, rather than on outward appearances or emotional ties to past practices. Eliminating our catalog and cutting back on the variety of products TRC sold felt like I was going backward. In one sense, I was reacting to the changing environment that made it increasingly difficult to keep up with the maintenance and management of fifty thousand products. But direct mail also was a less effective sales model, and TRC had to embrace the web. Based on our reliance on cash flow, rather than debt, we couldn't maintain both models.

In fact, the decisions we made to revamp TRC's business model didn't drag us backward but instead propelled our business forward. Our original business model had constrained my ability to scale TRC. Specializing in software licensing allowed us to zero in on the specific subset of customers responsible for volume licensing decisions and direct all of our marketing efforts toward those customers. Our new strategy also enabled us to retool our operational procedures and sales processes to solely reflect licensing requirements. In turn, that change enabled us to excel at sales in this core category, rather than being mediocre in some areas of our sales.

This experience taught me that you have to continually scale your skills as an entrepreneur in order to successfully scale your business. During the Startup phase of TRC, I never wanted to say no to a sale. As my business matured, so did my understanding of excellence in service. To be great at serving our customers, TRC couldn't be everything to everybody. We had to turn down some opportunities in order to focus on what we could do best. The company had matured, and so had I. But it took awhile; members of my sales team had been telling me to go this direction for some time, but I didn't want to listen to them. So, to avoid having to respond to bids or quote customers for categories that they had low chances of winning, they had started to niche themselves before I actually pulled the trigger.

As I responded to the forces that my sales force had already been dealing with, I came to clearly see something else about my business that I had never fully understood. By bootstrapping the company during its Startup phase, I was involved in the creation of virtually every process in every facet of the company. I was thrust into sales and marketing and saw firsthand what worked, what didn't, how customers responded, and what pain and priorities drove their decisions. That process taught me that, as a reseller, TRC didn't create demand. We sold our customers a product that they knew they needed and that somebody else produced. As TRC scaled during our Running phase, however, I realized that, even though selling products was what we did, it no longer was why we were in business. Now, TRC was in business to consult on volume software licensing, to develop an easier method to procure licensing, to establish a process that ensured that our customers were adhering to their legal compliancy requirements, and to provide reporting and other administrative requirements throughout the process.

Clearly, the purpose I envisioned for TRC during its Startup phase was rather different from the one that drove its success as a mature organization. My understanding of the business changed as the company changed. When I stepped into the visionary role and out of the daily activity, I was able to assimilate what I had been exposed to and learned. As you grow along with your business, the clear focus and strategy you had at the beginning can be radically altered by the experiences you gain through customer engagements and trials. Your early strategies will always shape your organization; I am confident that the success of TRC and the advancements we made would not have occurred if I had taken on more debt and been less hands-on throughout the organization during the Startup phase. But things change, and you have to constantly evolve your leadership skills and strategies in order to continue to succeed as you move deeper into your entrepreneurial journey.

Scaling Successfully, Ethically, and Honestly

Scaling your business often requires that you take calculated risks. As TRC grew, my comfort with risk had to grow as well. To supplement their increased risk exposure, suppliers would employ additional measures of collateral, which would include my own personal guarantee—a legal document stating that I would be personally responsible and bound to meet TRC's debt obligations. If I wanted TRC to continue to grow, that was the risk I had to take. By taking out personal credit cards and personal guarantees, everything Lisa and I owned was on the line. Further, some suppliers wanted TRC to have an open bank line of credit that we could draw upon to meet payments. In order to obtain that line of credit at our local bank, I had to use my house as collateral.

Through the success of my company, I had just formulated the perfect storm for personal bankruptcy should something go terribly wrong. I could lose everything. To an outsider, I might have looked like the classic entrepreneurial risk taker, betting the farm on his venture. All of that is true—but, I never lost a minute of sleep worrying about losing my house. In fact, I never gave it a thought. Was I just gutsy and fearless, risking everything I had, along with the future financial safety and security of my wife and three kids? Although I love the idea of being that kind of daring adventurist, the truth is bit less dramatic.

In reality, I was very careful. I simply managed risk, based on my knowledge of my business, my customers, and my industry. I understood how my customers paid; I knew how not to overextend myself and where I could cut back if needed to reduce expenses. I carried no debt, other than credit balances. I never paid interest fees to erode profit margins. I calculated every expense. I studied my financials to know my monthly income and expense and how to manage my cash float. I added employees and other expenses within a prescribed formula, never exceeding my benchmarks. The bottom line was that I was confident in my business and the control I had of it. External forces would not bankrupt me as I controlled the structure and level of risk. I knew if my doors had to close on any given day I could release my employees and pay all of my obligations based on my accounts receivable—which I knew I could collect. Every element of my plan revolved around the relationships I established with my creditors, my customers, my vendors, my partners, and my staff.

Business and life are about relationships. If you can't communicate well with the people you are in business with, or if you don't like working with your vendors, then get out or get someone in who can. To manage our credit, I had to constantly obtain additional credit and maintain the credit we had; that required skillful selling and a reputation for solid ethics. I had many conversations to explain to our partners our financial outlook and provide them with the certainty they needed in order to extend additional credit to TRC. I had to address these individuals with confidence, look them straight in the eye, and explain my model so that they could walk away feeling confident that they had made the right decision.

The truth is that, in nearly every aspect, growing and scaling your business successfully comes down to your reputation for trustworthiness and honesty. You can't fool people you work with over the long haul, and you certainly can't fool your customers and clients. Any deception you try to pull off, no matter how small, eventually grows into a sharp-toothed monster that will track you down and bite you at some point down the road. As the leader of the company, you have to always remember that your actions are under constant scrutiny. To maintain the kind of transparency you need to have in order to run your business effectively, you must earn the confidence of those around you and model the kind of ethical behavior you expect to receive in return.

The Running phase of the entrepreneurial business represents a significant milestone for both the business and the entrepreneur. The now sustainable business has moved from a customer-demand-generation mode of operation to a customer-demand-response mode, forming bureaucracy to enforce proven systems and processes that maximize efficiency. Herein lies the inevitable danger for the business to become complacent and reactionary to continual environmental changes.

This marks a critical juncture for the entrepreneur to understand and change his role in the company's journey. Now more than ever, the entrepreneur must convey a clear vision of where the company is going and delegate tasks to those whose efforts will ultimately result in the desired goal attainment. An entrepreneur who has found how to lead in the Running phase maintains a culture of innovation that continually learns customer intelligence and drives product changes that disrupt the market.

As the company scales its growth during the Running phase, exciting and rewarding new challenges will arise and bring more change. The entrepreneur needs to recognize at this point that he will ultimately need to leave the business he founded, for a multitude of personal and business reasons. When and why an entrepreneur moves on will vary, but it is certain he will move on—and advanced planning is the only way to ensure that both the business and the entrepreneur continue to thrive and achieve their goals.

The entrepreneur's Exit phase should represent the culmination of a strategy put in motion in the Idea phase. Although the strategy may have morphed from that early vision as the entrepreneur learns and adapts to change during the life cycle of the business, the evolving strategy for the entrepreneur and the business to exit actually creates a new phase—life after the business.

PHASE IV

LEAVING A COMPANY YOU FOUNDED is a soul-searching prospect. After all, this venture has exacted most of your energy, emotion, money, and time since you first began crafting your entrepreneurial idea. Eventually, however, you begin to consider the possibilities of moving on—maybe as a result of the constant advertisements from mergers and acquisitions brokers that have been hitting your desk, or maybe because you've been watching your competitors consolidate or, even worse, go out of business. Sometimes all it takes is a really lousy day to leave you wishing you could just pitch it and walk away. You go home, you get a good night's rest, and things look better the next day; still, you can't help but feel excited when you wonder just how much your business might be worth to the right buyer.

Of course, if you've followed the advice I've offered in this book, by the time you reach this point in your journey, you will have already planned for your exit from the business. As we discussed early in this book, your exit plan helps you target all of your subsequent decisions and goals toward achieving the endgame you most desire for your involvement with your business. This may be an opportunity to pass the business on to a family member or trusted and deserved partner. It may usher in a new role for you in the organization, as board member versus CEO. Hiring a replacement to run the daily aspects of the business may allow you to look at the business more as an investment than a job, or it may simply be time to cash out. But in almost all cases, whether planned or not, a critical part of your exit strategy will involve the process of selling your business.

If you are like most entrepreneurs, your business is the most important and valuable tangible asset you will ever own. That's why it always surprises me that so many entrepreneurs do so little to prepare for transitioning out of the business and turning that asset into cash. My experience and research seem to show that a dramatic number of private company owners fail to establish an exit plan. As Benjamin Franklin said, "By failing to prepare you are preparing to fail." Creating an exit plan early in your business planning stage is a critical factor in directing other aspects of your overall plan. A well-planned exit strategy isn't just a good idea; it's your fiduciary obligation as an entrepreneur.

Entrepreneurs who fail to gather the information and expert guidance they need for this process are negligent. By not being fully educated in the selling process, they neglect their responsibilities to their shareholders—and that's a problem, even if the entrepreneur is the sole shareholder. For all of the many factors that might prompt you to sell your business, perhaps the most compelling reason arises when your business is in a position to maximize shareholder value through a sale. To realize that goal, you'll need to fully understand the sale process. Failure to do so can cost you—and your shareholders—dearly. Either you'll spend too much in consulting, broker, legal, and other related expenses, or you'll end up leaving money on the table.

Based on 2008 census data, nearly half of US business owners are in a position to sell their company within the following ten years. Based on historic data, we can assume that a third of those will sell to an independent third-party buyer, another 30 percent will sell or transfer ownership to a family member, around 18 percent will consider employee purchase options, and the balance will most likely liquidate and close the company's doors. In other words, nearly 20 percent of these entrepreneurs are likely to close their business without realizing a profit in their exit! Selling a business is not like putting a Business for Sale sign in the window. A business should be sold because a plan to do so exists.

In Phase IV of *From Idea to Exit*, we're going to take a close look at the critical aspects of selling the business you started. We'll begin with my own version of the top ten, as we examine the ten most common signs that it's time to move on to a new journey—entrepreneurial or otherwise. Next, we'll clear a path through the sometimes dense forest of details involved in putting your business on the market, and we'll end with a chapter devoted solely to the fine art of negotiating the deal. When you reach the end of this part of the book, you'll not only have a solid foundation in the information and skills you'll need in order to successfully reach the end of your first entrepreneurial journey; you'll be well prepared to start planning your next one.

CHAPTER THIRTEEN

Knowing When It's Time to Go: An Entrepreneur's Top Ten

ADMITTING THAT IT'S TIME TO sell the business can be difficult for any entrepreneur. Every chapter of this book has outlined the gut-level longing that drives us to start an entrepreneurial venture and the many difficulties and obstacles we have to overcome to transform our compelling idea into a successful, thriving organization. So why would we want to sell it?

Be prepared to hear that question a lot when you make the decision to sell your "baby." When I first told my friends and relatives that I'd sold my business, many of them immediately assumed that something went wrong, forcing me to sell. Very few people congratulated me, even though that would have been the most appropriate reaction. I haven't funded research into the psychological reasons behind these glum—and, typically, quite incorrect—assumptions, but I suspect that they're related to the Risk Box.

Those who draw negative conclusions from "I sold my business" view entrepreneurship as a job, a source of income, and security. To them, selling the business equates with losing your job—a destabilizing, demoralizing freefall into uncertainty that upturns the tidy world contained within the Risk Box. That's not the way it is at all. Instead, selling the business is the entrepreneur's ultimate reward for years of hard effort.

So to answer the question I asked at the top of this page, there are a host of reasons why you might decide to sell your business. And, it's true, some of them are negative; think financial strains, divorce, death, differences between partners, lost contracts and agreements, family disputes, and disasters such as fire or flooding, just to name a few. These are the events most of those sad and sympathetic people imagine have driven you to the ultimate sacrifice of putting your business on the market.

The positive reasons for selling, however, are much more likely to drive your decisions. First among these is your commitment to ongoing change, which extends beyond your business practices to your own challenges as an entrepreneur and a leader. On the other hand, you might simply be ready for a lifestyle change, or you may want to use the sale to merge your business and ensure its future growth. Maybe the sale will bring you the capital you need to start a new business, or maybe it's just the most rational way to realize the profits you've been working for since you opened your doors.

For many entrepreneurs, the desire to sell their business coincides with their decision to retire. As I mentioned earlier in this book, retirement isn't a good motivator for a strong sale. Entrepreneurs who sell their business in order to retire are in a vulnerable position and, as I'll explain later in this chapter, run the risk of not fully realizing the full value of their business. As I said, there are a lot of reasons for selling your business, and it's important that you understand *your* reasons and how they fit into your current situation and your original exit strategy. I'll end this chapter by telling you about my own process of deliberation, as I came to understand that it was time for me to enter into my last phase as owner of the company I founded.

But let's begin by examining the 10 most common reasons for choosing to sell a business, drawn from the experiences of investment banker Bob Contaldo, of the mergers and acquisition firm Corporate Finance Associates.[1] Contaldo has worked closely with a number of clients over the years, helping them make decisions about selling their organizations. Taking the time to consider these ideas from all angles can help inform your decision as you weigh the pros and cons of kicking your own exit plan into action.

1. The Thrill Is Gone

No matter how well your business is progressing, at some point it may no longer fuel the passions you originally felt for it. That's okay; in fact, it's only natural. As your years with the company mount, you can develop frustrations with customers, credit, employees, regulations, and a hundred other factors. I certainly experienced that "thrill is gone" moment a few times at TRC. Struggling with shrinking margins and customers obligated by state regulation to buy on price rather than value became an increasingly disheartening prospect.

Your exasperation might be just a passing moment that a short vacation can alleviate, rather than requiring that you put your company on the market. But most entrepreneurs are accustomed to periods of exasperation or exhaustion with their business, and few would be driven to sell when they simply need to regroup and re-energize in order to tackle the issues they're facing. When no amount of rest or revitalization can shake the notion that you simply no longer enjoy running your business, you have to take a much more serious look at your emotional state and what it means for your continued participation in the organization.

If you come to the conclusion that you do need to sell the business, make sure that your emotions aren't leading your decisions or actions. Selling on emotion is dangerous—and it can be extremely costly. If you can't assess your situation with emotional balance, you run the risk of selling your company for less than its true market value. You should avoid acting on emotion in any facet of business, but you need to be particularly certain that you don't allow emotion to play a role in your decision to sell or the negotiations that follow.

2. The Marketplace Is Changing

Professor John M. Richardson, of the School of International Service at American University, Washington, DC, has been quoted as saying, "When it comes to the future, there are three kinds of people: those who let it happen, those who make it happen, and those who wonder what happened." Professor Richardson is talking about change in that quote, and, as we learned in chapter 11, successful entrepreneurs embrace and seek out change. Given all of that change, however, eventually your business and its environment may bear little resemblance to the organization you founded. Even though you drove many of those changes, the constant demands of leading *or* responding to significant change may wear you down over the years.

Changing markets can also take their toll on entrepreneurs. Those changes might include competitors, regulations, customer qualifications, labor requirements, patents, technological advancements, and supply constraints. You'll easily glide through some market changes, but others may require large investment in capital or regulatory compliance. Such changes can exceed your company's credit limitations, and they can be especially disruptive to complacent businesses that have not foreseen them coming. Failure to adapt to market changes can be costly as well. If you respond or react too slowly, you may eventually be forced to close your doors before you've had an opportunity to find a market in which to sell your company.

Entrepreneurs who are on their game are able to look to the horizon and adapt accordingly. Only complacent entrepreneurs allow their business to exist solely in the present, rather than planning for tomorrow. You can't sustain your business that way. If your marketplace has changed dramatically, and you find that you simply are no longer willing to embrace those changes, that's a strong sign that you're ready to move on.

3. Risk Has Become a Four-Letter Word

Throughout this book, we've seen that risk is almost synonymous with the term *entrepreneurism*. However, time and routine can entrench even the most ardent entrepreneur and discourage risk taking. If that happens to you, your performance as an entrepreneur and a leader can begin to slide.

The elements of your Risk Box are constant and can hold you back from getting to the next level. Most entrepreneurs are financed by personal guarantees on bank loans and lines of credit. If that's been the case with your entrepreneurial venture, taking the company to the next level may not be realistic using traditional financing vehicles, and you may not have the stomach or knowledge to obtain more elaborate methods of funding. If, as an entrepreneur, you are unwilling to work with these new methods to grow your business, or if you've simply run out of gas in juggling the cash flow against obligations, then it may be time to get out of the driver's seat.

4. A Change Would Be Good for the Family

This reason for selling can be very compelling, if you're a workaholic entrepreneur who invests all of your effort and abilities into your business at the expense of family time. Let me remind you, however, that business ownership and marriage are not mutually exclusive relationships. Businesses don't require physical and emotional nurturing, but family most certainly does. Temporary neglect may be acceptable to your family, but it can't be a long-term situation. If you don't know how to make the shift away from "all business, all the time," selling may be your best option. (Remember, though, that few successful exit strategies involve waiting until your family is ready to kick you out to begin the sales process.)

If this feels like your most important reason for selling, you should consider all of your options. There are plenty of paid services, experts, coaches, and friends who could help you balance your commitments, and I advise you to explore those alternatives before opting to sell your business.

5. There's an Unprecedented Seller's Market

Bob Contaldo considers an unprecedented seller's market as being a logical consideration for an entrepreneur contemplating a sale, but I worry that this reason is really just a bit of self-promotion for business brokers. I'm wary of the idea that we're *ever* in an unprecedented seller's or buyer's market. I suppose there are cycles when low interest rates, tax considerations, foreign interest, or other factors trigger unusual spikes in merger and acquisition activity. Conversely, M&A activity virtually ceased as credit markets went into a deep hibernation during the economic slump of 2008–2009. Anyone hoping to sell during this time undoubtedly found fewer buyers, and I'm certain that more deals fell apart and forced the postponement of many sales.

For the average entrepreneur, however, the time to sell a business is unlikely to be influenced by the "perfect storm" market scenarios business brokers like to conjure up. Again, if this reason is playing a strong role in your considerations, take an especially long and careful look at the market place and its historic evidence before you make the call.

6. An Eager Buyer Has Offered a Cash Deal

On the surface, it sounds like every business owner's dream: a buyer with deep pockets of cash who is just aching to acquire your company. That cash deal is attractive. About 80 percent or more of all businesses sold are financed in some fashion, and financing a sale increases the cost, lengthens the time to close, and poses the risk that the deal might falter due to complications with the financiers. The buyer might even be willing to pay more than your company is worth, simply because the deal (and the worth of your business) won't be subject to the scrutiny of those financing the purchase. Well, as Contaldo said in his article that outlines these ten reasons, "We can dream, can't we?"

Actually, this buyer scenario happens probably less than 1 percent of the time for small-to-medium businesses, even though it's the scenario brokers paint most vibrantly and the one that tugs most often at the emotional heartstrings of entrepreneurs. Let me assure you, though, that if you don't plan or have a vision for this type of exit strategy, you have virtually no chance of making it happen. If this is the way you want to end your connection with your business, be sure that you craft this exit strategy during the Idea phase of your entrepreneurial experience and work toward it every day thereafter. That's your best hope for hitting a bull's-eye with this long shot of a deal.

7. The Business Is Growing

Scaling for growth is one of your obligations as an entrepreneur, and in some cases, you may be too good at it. Fast growth is exciting and rewarding, but it comes at a price and has unique demands. As the business grows, you may not know how to boost it to the next level, or you may be unwilling to let it go there. If, as mentioned in the third item in this list, you're stymied as to how to properly manage risk and debt, you may be holding back your business. When that happens, the business can buckle under the strain of its own blocked momentum.

We've seen businesses that rise up fast and evaporate just as quickly when growth and cash flow can't be managed simultaneously. The discount retail fashion clothing chain Steve & Barry's, founded in 1985 by University of Pennsylvania classmates Steven Shore and Barry Prevor, grew at an envious pace between 2006 and 2008.[2] Its strategy during those years was to consume premium mall space at lease rates far below market because it would serve as a desirable retail anchor attracting smaller tenants. Sales skyrocketed as the company aggressively scaled growth by opening store after store. However, Steve & Barry's business and profits could not keep up with the company's real estate obligations. When those bargain-rate long-term lease agreements expired and were renewed at current market rates, mall owners were less eager to extend the same terms, and Steve & Barry's sales were not enough to keep its financial statements in the black. In 2008 the company liquidated, shuttering 276 stores dotted throughout 39 states.[3]

Even if cash flow is not the concern, experienced management may be. Entrepreneurs who recognize when to turn over the reins to a seasoned management staff that can run the business at this high-growth stage are truly visionary. Fast growth can take an entrepreneur by surprise and leave him wondering how to respond to keep the trajectory straight without having the wheels come off, so to speak. This is a critical point to recognize the value of a board, mentors, or even self-assessment as to whether you want to stay on in this role. Perhaps it's time to hire a president to manage the daily operations while you separate as chairman of the board to concentrate on vision.

8. The Business Is Flat

Whoops, too late. You don't want to be in a position of wanting (or having) to sell when your business has gone flat or is in decline. Just like taking a new car off the lot, the value of your business is going to be worth far less when you go to market with flat or declining revenues or earnings.

Unfortunately, many entrepreneurs do sell at this point. Often this occurs after the peak of their career, when they have less fire in their belly to continue with change and innovation. For many of the reasons we've discussed in this chapter, you may find yourself starting to let things slide, relax on oversight, or become complacent as a leader. You can expect the growth of your organization to stall as a result. Business also may get flat due to the particular industry, the geographic area, or other outside factors, but your business plan and exit strategy have to be prepared to deal with those contingencies. If you have—and follow—a well-constructed exit plan, you won't let things get to this point before deciding to sell. If you don't have that plan, you may get into a jam, and then be stuck trying to unload damaged goods.

In researching this book, I conducted a survey among my colleagues and associates as to what title resonated best with them. Interestingly, novices frequently suggested that I take *Exit* out of the title. They stated that some would-be entrepreneurs never want to exit their business, and that would turn them off from buying the book. Well, guess what? Entrepreneurs have no choice as to whether they will exit their business at some point. In fact, the ultimate reason for exiting is death, and I haven't found one entrepreneur able to prevent that change from occurring. So, if you've reached the stage where flat or failing profits are the reason that you're selling the business, you've waited too long to make a good decision—and the decision is inevitable.

9. Managing People Has Worn You Out

This reason is very similar to the first one we talked about—the thrill is gone from running your business. In fact, employees may be exactly why you've lost your entrepreneurial passion for the business. Most entrepreneurs of small- to medium-size businesses cite employee issues as one of their greatest headaches. Some of this pain may be self-inflicted; you need to maintain adequate managerial levels between you and your workforce if you want to be able to focus on the bigger issues of growing the enterprise. Remember, such boundaries enable you to work *on* the business, rather than in it—a necessity for visionary leadership.

Employee issues may be more elaborate if unions are involved or if your workforce requires things like work visas. But even handling employee-related costs such as medical insurance, profit sharing, taxes, and retirement plans is rarely draining enough to wear out a committed entrepreneur. The day-to-day management of people, however, can consume too much time, keeping you from your true interests and responsibilities as an entrepreneurial leader: innovating, scaling, and leading your company. If you've allowed yourself to remain too heavily involved in managing your human resources, you may have exhausted your enthusiasm for the business. At that point, selling may be the best option, for you and your company.

10. You Have Compelling Personal Reasons for Selling

Personal reasons for selling a business can encompass a whole array of concerns. If you find yourself in this position, you can only hope that the sale is a positive lifestyle transition. As I mentioned earlier, there may be a whole host of negative reasons as well that compel you, as an entrepreneur, to sell and "get out." If this is your major reason for selling, be sure to plan carefully for your next step so you are moving toward something new rather than running away from the past. Many successful entrepreneurs develop a compelling need to give back after they sell. They find themselves with both the time and the money to focus on more philanthropic concerns, and that's where they want to be and how they want to round out their legacy. Again, the best outcome from a sale prompted by this reason involves a positive move forward for you, your family, and your future as an entrepreneurial thinker and agent of change.

LET'S MAKE A DEAL!

Even if you don't have a compelling reason to sell your business, others may be happy to explain to you why it's in your best interest to do just that. Let me walk you through my experience with these pesky predators—I mean salespeople.

It's a mild June morning. I've just arrived at the Radisson Hotel in Rosemont, Illinois, the hotel and convention center mecca that surrounds Chicago's O'Hare International. I find my meeting room with the typical continental breakfast setup and mingle with a variety of fellow participants. The audience is made up, for the most part, of white men, young and old, dressed in a wide range of formal and informal attire. Our hosts are easy to spot: three well-dressed men who look like high-priced lawyers or Wall Street barons. The trio includes a senior-executive type in his late fifties, a similarly distinguished-looking gentleman in his fourties, and a young twenty-something apprentice. I was there in response to their advertisement's pitch to come and learn the strange and mysterious world of mergers and acquisitions—for only fifty dollars!

If you own a business, you will receive flyers from "salesmen" like these. And, if you ever give in to the urge to attend one of their "conferences," you'll hear the same story I heard on that lovely day in June. It goes like this:

"If you've ever considered selling your business, the timing is perfect—it's now! Even if you don't want to sell, you owe it to yourself to have this valuable information. Foreign companies are lining up to buy American companies—your American company—in all sectors, in all shapes and sizes, regardless of profitability. They want you, and they will pay top dollar! Because of the dollar's value, now is the best time for these foreign companies to invest in you. Act fast because this perfect storm in the M&A market will not last!"

I came to this gathering to learn about the process behind all of those glossy direct-mail flyers that I had been receiving. What I got was a thirty-minute intro that outlined a fast and simple sale for my business that would take place very soon—if I wrote the buyers a check for $20,000 to get the ball rolling. I quickly realized that these guys were sharks, some of the slickest, most well-scripted bait-and-switch artists I have ever come across. After hearing their opening spiel, I politely walked from the conference room and out to my car, shaking the last "salesman" off of my leg before closing the door. I learned one great lesson that day, and I'll pass it along to you here: avoid these "sell your business" hucksters like the plague. That one piece of advice will save you, at minimum, a wasted morning and a $50 registration fee—or it might keep you from writing that $20,000 check.

Putting Your Exit Plan Into Action

As I've said, it's rare for entrepreneurs to have an early-stage exit plan, but it's also rare for the sale of a small-to-medium-size business to go as successfully as did mine. Let me tell you how my decision to sell unfolded, to help you understand the importance of aligning your earliest entrepreneurial goals and subsequent leadership decisions with your final exit plans. As you'll see from my experience, although it will still take some soul searching and deep deliberation, your *best* decision about the *best* time to sell your business will be driven by the exit strategy you envision and work toward from the beginning of your entrepreneurial journey.

It was 2005, and TRC had been in business about ten years. With the many successful innovations we'd implemented, I could clearly see that the company was capable of $100 million in sales, and I figured it would take us seven years to get there. Now, the only question was how. The bootstrap model was working fine, but it seemed unrealistic that cash flow alone would be able to propel 20 percent year-over-year growth for seven consecutive years. That kind of growth would require that TRC expand its facility and credit vehicles. The additional staff we'd need to accomplish this goal would bring some additional strain and require upgrading some of our personnel systems. In fact, everything from our IT infrastructure to our lead-generation system would have to be upgraded in order to move TRC into this heightened growth mode.

It was clear to me that my old bootstrap business model wouldn't support this kind of growth. I needed capital, and that would require a bank loan, private equity, or a wealthy investor. An IPO wasn't the answer, because TRC simply wasn't going to be an attractive public company. My Risk Box alarm was going off; I was afraid that my desire to grow would overextend the company's resources—including all of us who worked there. So what did I want to do?

As I imagined my industry five years into the future, I saw a dramatically altered marketplace for enterprise software sales. I saw an approaching era of creative destruction in the reseller channel, bringing dramatic changes that would require significant capital to accommodate. As for TRC's innovations, I knew they would be outdated and replaced within this time, and that I would have to build some sort of service offering into my business model in order to maintain our competitive edge. Certainly I could continue to innovate, but did I want to? How would I differentiate my services from everyone else? How could I scale a services model nationally? The even bigger question was whether I wanted to even be in that business—and the answer was no. Services sparked little passion in me. TRC had grown to an impressive $30 million in sales, became one of the most respected resellers in the nation, and was at its peak. Now we were stuck.

I still had one other option for growing TRC to $100 million—an outright sale of the company. Perhaps I could sell the company to a firm that shared my vision of where TRC could grow and who had the capital and resources to make it happen. After all, that was the plan. When I first started the business, I intended to eventually sell it; I had even created a benchmark goal to sell at this very time frame. I knew the time was right. TRC was at the top of its game, showing consistent year-over-year revenue growth and a realistic capability to grow to our targeted levels.

I briefly considered merging with another large educational reseller, Journey Education Marketing (JEM), which was a comparable competitor of TRC. JEM had been in business longer than TRC and carved out an enviable position selling software to students and faculty, giving its model a consumer focus, rather than the business-to-business model at TRC. Merging our companies had significant benefits for JEM and TRC and would likely put our combined revenues very close to the $100 million mark. But, after an informal conversation with JEM's founder and president, I discovered that, although he had been entertaining similar thoughts, he wasn't ready to take action on them. I also realized that I wasn't completely comfortable with the idea of giving up control of my organization while retaining some shared responsibilities for its success.

Uncertain about how to best move forward, I stopped to reflect on three personal goals I set for myself many years earlier:

1. To start a business before the age of thirty;
2. To sell that business in ten years;
3. To sell it to a Fortune 500 company.

The first of these goals now struck me as being relatively common among entrepreneurs-in-waiting, but the others deserved more attention.

Why would I attach a time frame to sell before the company ever opened its doors? The answer is unique to the business I started and its industry. I was planning to be a technology reseller, and the one constant I could rely on in that business was that technology would always be rapidly changing—and that it would be changing my business as well. I had seen the trajectory of other tech companies during my career, and I knew that in 10 years, either my business would be established and ready to achieve its mission, or market advancements would have eclipsed our growth. In either scenario, we would be in a position to sell the company at that time. While I didn't view 10 years as an absolute deadline for that sale, I considered it a significant milestone for reviewing my progress.

Why had I determined to sell to a Fortune 500 company? My vision wasn't about building a company that sold software to schools, but about owning a niche market that a Fortune 500 would want to tap into. The education market represents over fifteen million students, and it refreshes every year. Factoring in the community college market, the demographic expands dramatically. If I met my business goals, TRC would attract a Fortune 500 company's interest.

If I was going to take on the risk and investment of starting my own business, I wanted it to count and count big. I envisioned a business that would build in value and be able to achieve a sales multiple that would provide a significant payout. This may seem contrary to everything I've said about following your heart rather than your pocketbook when starting a business, but there is no fault in creating a business you are passionate about and devising a way to make a lot of money from it as well. My entrepreneurial idea and the passion to bring it to life formulated my mission statement. The goal to sell to a Fortune 500 was a natural result of that mission.

After careful consideration, and in keeping with my original exit strategy, I decided to sell TRC outright. I was concerned about the industry outlook and investment needed to reach our seven-year target, and I was incredibly optimistic that this was the best time to realize my final goals for TRC. Now was an opportunity to maximize shareholder value. It felt right, and I had learned to listen to my gut. If TRC were to grow to $100 million, it would do so by putting the heavy lifting and risk on the acquirer.

I was achieving the goal that I had pitched to just about everyone we hired at TRC. In almost every interview I conducted, I laid out my goal to sell TRC to a Fortune 500 company. I did this purposely, to let potential employees know what I intended to do with the company. Not everyone can thrive in a company that they know is going to be sold, and I didn't want to encourage anyone to join our business without knowing, up-front, that this outcome would be in the future. In my eyes, the goal served to be motivational and a testament of our ambitions. I wanted to make that rhetoric a reality and, in doing so, live up to the promise of expanded career growth.

Yes, I realize that my situation and experience as an entrepreneur is unique—yours will be, too. But as you enter the Exit phase of your entrepreneurial venture, it's important that you have some firm and reliable milestones to help guide you through its complexities. Incubating an entrepreneurial idea takes incredible talent. Launching an entrepreneurial startup is an extremely difficult process. Running a business and scaling it into a successful, thriving enterprise takes monumental effort. You can't afford to let your attention and energies flag when you reach the end of your time with your business. You'll have multiple influences driving your decision to exit your business; it's up to you to make sure that you remain on course with the exit strategy you developed and followed throughout your entrepreneurial journey in order to arrive at the best possible conclusion for you and your business.

Making the decision to sell is just the kickoff of your exit strategy. Once that decision is made, you have to prepare yourself and your company for the selling process. That preparation is essential if you don't want the uncertainty of an upcoming transfer of ownership or leadership to interrupt your business processes and interfere with its profitability or perceived market value. In the next chapter of this book, we'll talk about just what's involved in putting your business up for sale while continuing to drive its success.

CHAPTER FOURTEEN

Putting Your Business on the Market

SELLING YOUR COMPANY IS THE ultimate strategic sale of your career; you can expect this stage of your Exit phase to demand the same kind of long hours you put in during the Startup phase of the business. Remember the elements of the Sales Maxim that you learned in chapter 10: Sales = Confidence = Knowledge = Customers and Product. You'll need to be extremely confident going into the sale of your business, and that means you must develop a masterful command of every detail of your product (in this case, your company) and customers (your potential buyers). You also need to be well grounded in an understanding of the marketplace. If you've become less directly involved with some aspects of your business over the years, you'll need to do some homework before you put it on the market.

Your next task is to tackle the hard work of preparing yourself, your staff, and your business for the sale. You may have such deep confidence in the unique strengths of your business that you think it will sell itself. It won't. Unless your business is a high-profile brand, you will need to muster all of your marketing and sales skills to attract the appropriate buyer. And that will be the case whether or not you use a broker or other representation. You also will need to call upon all of your abilities as a leader to keep your company on track while you're attempting to sell it. You'll be dealing with a wide variety of buyers and situations during the sale, and you'll have to find innovative ways to engage their interest and move them to make an offer. You can expect to feel the same sense of urgency for success that you felt during your Startup phase, and that energy will help carry you through this demanding time.

At the time I decided to put TRC on the market, the company was still winning business based on the value-added features and innovations we had developed. Even though margins were eroding in the market, we were still growing in the academic consumer segment and with consortia partnerships. Many of our direct competitors weren't faring as well. Our largest competitors had been developing their academic divisions over the years, and they were beginning to take market share. Some of the smaller academic dealers silently closed their doors, while others were acquired for pennies on the dollar. Many owners balked at selling their business at a price lower than its historic value. But the past is history; with their businesses in decline, these owners often were left scrambling to get their company back on course or to agree to a short sale in order to stem future losses.

I wasn't in this predicament. My business was healthy, and I had long ago created an exit plan that had helped me prepare for this phase. Once I made the decision to sell TRC, the preparations for that sale unfolded quickly. I had done my Entrepreneurial Exercises in advance and knew the route I wanted to take to put TRC on the market. I had already researched and chosen a respected Chicago law firm and a professional broker to handle the legal aspects of the sale. Over the next month, I worked with these firms to pull together the portfolio TRC would submit to firms that showed interest or that we had targeted as being potential buyers. At TRC, we did a bit of housekeeping to clean up the physical appearance of the office, and we began assembling the historical financial information that potential buyers would want to review. When our preparations were complete, TRC's information began appearing on the multiple listing feeds that announced to the M & A community that the company was available for purchase. I had no apprehensions about the sale, and I was anxious to see what the next steps would entail.

In this chapter, we're going to look more closely at these fundamental tasks that you, too, will undertake when you place your own business on the market. You'll learn how to position your organization as a viable, valuable package—and yourself as an entrepreneur and a leader—as you prepare to enter the marketplace. We'll also explore the essential steps for that preparation, including the task of getting your operation and its documentation in good order and hiring the right professionals to help you achieve the most successful outcome from the sale. Finally, I'll offer some tips to help you mentally prepare for the roller-coaster ride of negotiations that lie ahead.

Positioning for the Transition

A successful exit plan covers two main areas of consideration—transitioning the ownership and leadership of the organization, and maximizing the wealth that transition generates. Although transitions can take numerous forms, such as handing over control to a member of the family or selling the business to employees, in most cases, the transition involves an outright sale of the business. Wealth maximization is tied to securing for shareholders the best value for their ownership interest. These two phases of your exit strategy may not unfold at the same time, but after you have decided to sell the business, you must immediately begin making careful preparations for achieving all of the goals you've set forth in both parts of your plan.

To position your business (and yourself) for a positive transition and to maximize the wealth generated by the sale, you need to be able to answer some serious questions about your motivations and expectations for the sale. Why are you selling? What are your goals for the sale? What comes next? What will your business be without you at the helm? Let's examine some of the ways you can prepare to answer these questions clearly and without hesitation.

Explaining Why You Want to Sell

So, why do you want to sell your business? That will be the first question every potential buyer will ask, but it's also a question you need to answer for yourself. Although it may require some soul searching, you need to be very clear as to why you're selling in order to strike the best deal and to rest easy after the sale is done. Are you doing it for the nonemotional reasons? Have you considered alternatives to selling? Have you prepared yourself for the worst-case scenarios that might result from the sale? Have you determined the lowest returns you would be willing to accept from selling? Thoroughly think through your reasons, and be prepared to outline them simply and with conviction.

Granted, your personal reasons may differ from those you share with the rest of the world. That's where your selling skills come into play. You'll need to be able to spin your public reasons for selling into an engaging elevator pitch that you can recite with enthusiasm and confidence. Be prepared for potential buyers to do some digging in an attempt to unearth any undisclosed problems that might be driving you to sell your business and that could later expose them to risk or overpayment. In fact, savvy buyers will do all they can to find and leverage any weaknesses in your story in order to negotiate a lower sale price. The more completely you understand your motivations for selling, the better able you'll be to lay them out simply, logically, and persuasively to prospective buyers.

Outlining Your Expectations

When you sell your business, you aren't just handing over your office keys to a new owner. You can negotiate any of a variety of outcomes for this transition. When you're preparing to sell your business, it's important that you form a clear understanding of how you want your transition of ownership to unfold.

When your business is up for sale, your entrepreneurship may be up for sale as well. Entrepreneurs command tremendous influence, knowledge, and relationships, and a company that buys your business may require you to stay on for a period of time after the sale. If your potential buyer has that outcome in mind, you can expect to be scrutinized as closely as your company's books. Refusing to put in this time could kill the deal. The transition you ultimately negotiate may be influenced by the buyer's future plans for the business, but you need to be able to clearly and articulately outline your own transition expectations in those negotiations.

Before you place your business on the market, you also need to have a solid plan for maximizing the wealth generated by the sale (details about this process follow in the next section of this chapter). You are likely to have an idea of what your business is worth, and that figure may serve as the minimum bid you'll accept. The financial outcome of a sale can be very complicated, however, and involve any of a wide variety of methods for payment, including stocks, stock options, timed payments, earn-outs, or any variation and combination of these and other methods.

The vast majority of buyers will finance their purchase, which can involve a degree of risk for you, as the seller, and take an extended period of time to complete. Do you desire an asset sale or a stock sale? What are the tax and legal implications of the sale, and how are they unique to your type of incorporation? Your own research and the advice of your legal advisor or broker can help you answer the questions that will help you determine what kind of transaction you want (and/or will accept). In addition to outlining your expectations for transitioning ownership and wealth maximization to prospective buyers, you'll also need to incorporate them into your company's offering to the marketplace.

Minimizing Negative Blowback

Owners can be self-centered when it comes to selling their business. It's a very personal process, but one that involves far more people than you may realize. Stakeholders, friends, and family all will form their own interpretations of your reasons for selling your business, no matter what reasons you give them. But it's your job to shape perceptions about the sale among those whose opinions truly matter to your organization's profitability and health—and that group includes you, as the owner and entrepreneur. You need to plan for accomplishing this task before any talk of the proposed sale begins to circulate.

As you prepare to put your business on the market, determine how you will craft your customers' conclusions about the sale, since most will see little upside for them in the news. Your employees will have very real concerns about their job security and new management. Suppliers will fear losing you as a customer, and your competitors may take the news as a sign of weakness or an opportunity to obtain confidential information. For all of these reasons, it's best that you keep news of a potential sale confidential until you can release it in a very controlled manner.

Every company sale is unique, as are the reasons for that sale and the buyer's intentions for acquisition. There is such a wide spectrum of possibilities that offering direction and advice as to how to handle employee, customer, or vendor concerns is difficult. It is unlikely all parties will see a happy ending to the transaction. Think through the ramifications to each constituent, and plan for how and when to address them with the news, remembering never to burn bridges. These relationships may surface again further down the road when you emerge again, possibly with a new startup.

Even though you have to mentally prepare yourself for selling your business, you also have to prepare yourself for *not* selling it. You may go to market only to find there are no buyers who meet your reserve requirements. Or you may get an offer, and, for a variety of reasons, the deal may fall through. Every stalled or failed attempt to sell represents a loss in time commitment, resources, money, and energy. The adrenaline rush you experience when you think a deal is locked up can leave you feeling drained and discouraged if the deal falls through. By preparing yourself for the inevitable setbacks in the sale process, you can regroup and direct your energies back to scaling, innovating, and leading the business you thought you were going to be leaving. And, by minimizing information leaks about pending deals before the agreements are finalized, you'll avoid unnecessary speculation, emotional upheaval, and misdirected energy among your staff, your customers, and other concerned parties.

Preparing for the Sale

Thorough preparation was critical during the Idea, Startup, and Running phases of your business, and it's equally important now. To maximize the value of your business, you need to get your ducks in a row. Let's look at some of the most critical parts of that process.

Getting Your House in Order

Just like putting a house up for sale, you need to put your business house in order before you begin presenting it to potential buyers. You can't untangle a badly disorganized company overnight, so you're a step ahead if you've managed the business and its processes carefully over the years. Your first concern should be that all legal affairs are in order; don't even consider putting your business on the market before you're certain you've taken care of any outstanding legal issues. Any type of personal or business litigation hanging over your business needs to be concluded prior to a sale—and that includes divorce proceedings that might be in the works for you or your partners. The last thing you want is an ex-spouse making a claim against your business while you are at the negotiations table.

Cleaning house also includes touching up minor "bruises and blemishes," and the list of those problems can be rather lengthy. As an example, consider reviewing your accounts receivable for bad debt. Old receivables are going to be a point of contention during the negotiations for your sale, and their value will likely be taken off the overall business valuation after a buyer has made an offer. Anything over ninety days past due will be considered a write-off. To avoid losing value down this rabbit hole, you'll need to work really hard at collecting, hire an agency to collect for you, or consider selling off your old receivables.

Depending on how your business manages its inventory, you may be wise to draw down to a just-in-time level. If there are persistent or recurring customer service issues that you haven't yet resolved, particularly with high-profile customers, get them corrected *now*. Many of these issues should be day-to-day priorities for your business, but they become especially critical when you're getting your business ready to present to prospective buyers.

Reviewing Your Documentation

Another task you need to take care of before you go to market is a careful review of your business's internal documents and financial records. After making an offer, your prospective buyers will launch an incredibly thorough and involved due diligence process. Every legal contract you have, including those for copier leases and telecommunications services, will come under the microscope. Expect your buyer to review all agreements between your business and suppliers, customers, employees, partners, service providers, and landlords—even bids awarded by customers. Quick access to these records will make the process smoother. You might even benefit from taking a dry run with an expert, to identify any documentation deficiencies, so you can correct them prior to the chaos and frenzy of due diligence (in chapter 15, "Negotiating and Closing the Deal," you'll learn about my own painful due diligence process during the sale of TRC).

To make doubly certain that you have a clear idea of your company's valuation, run through multiple financial valuation models to calculate your own estimate (because these valuations play a critical role in the negotiating process, I also describe them in more detail in chapter 15). Also, work with your accountant or legal advisor to ensure that you have been following proper accounting principles, procedures, and documentation. Before you undertake any lengthy or expensive process, however, check with a professional to be certain that the results will be worthwhile. For example, don't rush out and conduct an audit if you've never done one just because you've heard that it's best to have been audited going into a sale. Audits are expensive, and yours may not be necessary, depending on the size of your organization.

Now is a good time to update and document your SWOT analysis (an analysis of your strengths, weaknesses, opportunities, and threats, which you learned about in chapter 6) and to catalog your organization's intellectual property and differentiating features. Together, these documents will serve as content for your company profile, which you'll use as a marketing tool when you go on the market. Be thorough in listing your company's IP assets: patents, trademarks, and copyrights will lead the list, but be sure to include any other nuance, procedure, process, or methodology that makes your company unique. The sale will hinge on a valuation of your financial model and your intrinsic/IP factors; the latter will give you your greatest leverage in boosting the price you can command from your buyer. Finally, don't forget to collect your own information and insights about your organization. There's a lot stored in an entrepreneur's head and that needs to get down on paper, not only for marketing purposes but for the eventual transition as well.

Hiring Professionals to Help with the Sale

In addition to your own research, gather the services and advice of a variety of experts to help you prepare to present your business and negotiate its sale, and do this well in advance of your actual offering. Without exception, you need to retain the services of an attorney with strong merger and acquisition experience, as well as those of an expert on applicable tax liabilities. You also may want to retain a broker and a professional negotiator.

Many people enlist the services of a business broker or M&A specialist to help create and execute their plan for selling the business; that's what I did. Take time and do your homework when finding the right person or company to help you through your sale, because skills sets and services vary greatly. I would highly recommend seeking advisors who have done considerable work in your industry and are familiar with your vertical so they can lend their experience to your company. This is the one factor that can really tip the scales in your favor during the process.

The planning activities outlined in this chapter should help you determine what services and talent you need to augment your own knowledge and ability. But in just about every case, you can expect to need the help of a broker in reaching the multiple listing services that will promote your business to private equity, third-party buyers, and foreign investors. Yes, there are a number of web-based services available, but to maintain credibility and attract quality buyers, I recommend that you work with a professional broker who knows how to reach M&A specialists.

Most brokers are similar to real estate agents in that they list your company in the multiple channels of active buyers. They have relationships with private equity and venture capital firms, private investors, foreign investors, and listing services. You want your broker to attract the largest possible pool of potential buyers to foster a competitive bidding environment. Many brokers will represent and assist you throughout the sales process, including the formal exchange of documentation and negotiations. They also should assist in "packaging"—putting together a traditional sell sheet and prospectus to present your business and its benefits to potential buyers. Like a real estate agent, a broker will take a percentage of the gross sale; many request an up-front retainer for their services.

If you talk to enough seasoned entrepreneurs, you'll find plenty of stories, both good and bad, about the brokers they have encountered. You'd like to think that your broker is on your side to maximize the value of your business, but that isn't necessarily so. In reality, most are focused on closing the deal in the shortest amount of time to collect their commission. I can't fault them too much, and there certainly are pros out there doing a great job. Ultimately, however, brokers are salespeople who have quotas to hit. You need to be aware of this as you manage your broker's work during your sale.

Pay particular attention to your broker's pitch and positioning. Like any good salesperson, a good broker knows all the emotional points to hit with entrepreneurial owners. Understand that your broker will be selling to *you*, too, through the process. You have to separate good advice from sales pitches and hold true to your goals and objectives. You also must remind yourself not to rely too heavily on your broker's efforts, as that person's faith in the value of your business will never match your own. It's easy during the long courting process to get tired and have the urge to push things off on your broker. Never take yourself out of the loop; stay in control of the sales process, from beginning to end.

DEVELOPING YOUR PRESENTATION

Just like any sale, you will need to develop an effective sales presentation for each potential buyer meeting, with a focus on that buyer's needs and how your company can address them. Your broker will help you compile a prospectus containing a high-level overview of your organization's financials, market niche, product and service features, and intellectual property. The broker will also put together a one-page sell sheet for initial mass release, designed to garner interest in your company among potential buyers. Your actual presentations, however, must be tailored to the specific company that has expressed interest in acquiring your firm and how the sale could help it accomplish its goals.

Playing Your Cards Wisely

I like to play Texas Hold'em poker with my neighbors. One thing I've learned from experience is that I may be holding decent cards from the initial deal, but they don't mean much until I see the "flop"—that's when the other players reveal their hands. In poker, it's easy for less-experienced players to get blinded by aces. For instance, if I get dealt an ace and then a nine, I can become so focused on that ace that I forget to decipher what type of hand my opponents may have. Inevitably, I miss an obvious flush or straight.

You might be a rookie when it comes to selling your company, but you don't have to be blinded by your "aces" when the time comes to put out the For Sale sign. Your business has some great attributes that make it unique. Those attributes are your aces, and you might be tempted to dig in your heels and demand a certain value for your company based on them. But you may be forgetting to consider what cards the buyer is holding. Your buyer may be interested in aspects of your business that you aren't considering, simply because they don't feel like aces to you. Getting locked into your perceived strengths may derail a deal or allow you to sell short other meaningful aspects of your business.

During the courting phase for TRC, I pushed the Microsoft Select large account reseller (LAR) status that we possessed as a significant and unique value add because only nineteen dealers in the country had this designation and no new dealers were being added. Much to my disappointment, several interested buyers couldn't have cared less about our LAR status. They didn't understand its significance, and even if they did, it served no purpose for them. To retain their interest, I had to get off my obsession with our LAR status and focus on aspects of TRC that held real appeal and value for my prospective buyers.

Selling your business is about creating a buzz. Your goal is to build within multiple buyers a sense of urgency about acquiring your business. During preparation, you assembled a list of potential or targeted acquirers, along with a list of selling points that are most likely to attract buyers. Now is the time to work those lists. As you match buyer candidates with your organization's selling points, don't limit your ideas to your industry. Create scenarios that outline roll-up strategies for going public; ideas for integrating technologies; the potential for synergistic cost savings; plans for potential geographic expansion; or plans for adding new segments, products, and customers. Buyers will have their own intentions and ideas to consider, but your creative thinking will help target a wider audience and potentially heighten buyer interest.

When TRC hit the market in late 2005, I was curious to see how the marketplace would react and what potential buyers we would attract. I had assembled a list of about twenty companies that I felt would make a complementary fit with TRC. The list included Best Buy, which was starting a new education-focused reseller division; Systemax, a conglomerate of resellers and an international personal computer manufacturer; Office Depot, which had a fledgling focus on education and software licensing; and ASAP Software (a company that Dell eventually acquired). Although my exit strategy targeted a Fortune 500 buyer, I didn't restrict myself to those prospects; I wanted to cast the widest net possible to bring in potential buyers. My goal was to attract several buyers at once, to trigger a bidding war.

As you begin the process of courting potential buyers, train yourself to look at your company through their lens and think of ways that your business could add value to each acquirer's organization. Always—*always*—keep the focus of your courting efforts on the buyer, not you! Although your business means many things to you, at the end of the day, you are selling a product that must answer a buyer's need. Your job is to find out what that need is and position your company as the solution.

Our first responses came from several small companies I'd never heard of, some in the IT industry, others engaged in unrelated products or services. A few of these prospects caught our interest, but their low-ball offers didn't. Even so, I found the experience of engaging with these companies and learning their motivation for buying TRC exciting. Each encounter gave me an opportunity to hone my selling skills and adapt my presentation to the unique needs of that potential buyer. I would decipher the buyer's intentions, then adapt my presentation to highlight the features that best fit the buyer. It was exhilarating.

Successful courting ends in negotiations, and that's a process that requires absolute objectivity. Everything you've done to prepare yourself and your organization for the sale will help arm you for the negotiations process. In the process of positioning your organization for the transition, you've prepared yourself and your business for a smooth transfer of leadership and a more profitable sale outcome. You know your reasons for selling, and how to best present those reasons to potential buyers, as well as your clients, customers, and staff. The process of getting your documentation in order has helped you refresh your command of the details of your operation. All of this careful preparation, teamed with the professional advisors you have hired to help you manage the sale process, will help you maximize the personal wealth you'll receive from the sale of your business.

In the next—and final—chapter of this book, we'll talk about how to successfully navigate the negotiating process. That process will be the culmination of every accomplishment you've made in the conception, startup, and operation of your entrepreneurial enterprise. The negotiating table stands at the final gate of your journey, so you can't afford to let your energy or focus waver as you approach it.

CHAPTER FIFTEEN

Negotiating and Closing the Deal

A FEW MONTHS AFTER TRC went on the market, my broker was pushing me to submit our material to CDW, a Chicago technology reseller that was one of the first to service the IT industry. CDW's founder, Michael Krazny, was an incredibly successful businessman, who had taken his company from a kitchen-table outline to a multibillion-dollar enterprise in just fourteen years. In 1998, Krazny and I had discussed the idea of CDW acquiring my business, with the goal of pushing TRC's revenue to the $100 million mark in just five years. At the time, my vision simply wasn't broad enough to grasp what Krazny was proposing, and I really wasn't ready to sell my business. Sensing my fear and uncertainty, Krazny had killed the deal and gracefully let me go.

Now that I was ready to sell, I told my broker not to send information about TRC to Krazny's company. I didn't think CDW needed TRC, and I didn't want to discuss the details of our innovations with this huge competitor. CDW was leading the industry, with $7 billion in annual sales and a regular slot on the Fortune 100 list. My plan was to partner with the number-two or -three player in the market to challenge Krazny's dominant position. But CDW was flush with cash and in the mood to buy in 2005, and it was being very vocal in the press about it. Knowing this, my broker pressed me to submit our teaser prospectus to CDW, and I reluctantly agreed. A week after our material landed on the desk of CDW's director of higher education, we were invited to the home office.

To my utter surprise, conversations went remarkably well, and I could sense a chemistry developing between our companies. We were speaking the same language and sharing the same customer pain points. Our intellectual property would overcome major obstacles that CDW could not address on its own. In the end, both CDW and TRC were anxious to move forward with a deal. It was time to take a seat at the negotiations table.

As you're about to learn, after you receive an actual offer for your business, negotiating the sale is one of the toughest jobs you'll have as an entrepreneur and a business owner. You and your buyer will discuss and investigate and weigh many different factors in determining the worth of your company, including employment agreements, perks and benefits, salary, asset exclusion, and so on. You don't have to face this task alone, and you probably shouldn't. Negotiating is an art, and I recommend that you hire the services of a professional negotiator to help you navigate the process. This may be your only chance to sell a business, and you want to make it count. Even then, however, your role remains critical throughout the process. You have to be on your toes to ensure the negotiations go well.

After you've negotiated the deal, you still have a major hurdle to overcome—the due diligence process, in which every minute detail of your organization's financial and legal dealings, holdings, and issues will come under intense scrutiny. As you learned in the previous chapter, thorough and accurate record keeping from day one in your business is your strongest tool for preparing to move through the due diligence process with minimal hassle. In this chapter, you'll learn about the painful stumbling blocks I experienced during the diligence stage of my own sale. I hope that story will encourage you to start your preparations for due diligence early, and to monitor their progress carefully through every preceding phase of your experience. As I said early in this book, you need to start planning for the sale of your business soon after you start planning to launch it.

In addition to my cautionary tales, this chapter offers some substantial tools for closing the sale of your business. Here, I'll walk you through an overview of each of the analyses you and your buyer will conduct to determine the value of your business. I've also included the most useful weapon you can have in your negotiations arsenal—the Negotiation Worksheet. By following the steps outlined in the worksheet, you don't have to worry about leaving money on the table at the end of your negotiations. This chapter also offers some sound advice about breaking the news of your sale to your staff, customers, and marketplace. I'll finish this final chapter of the book by sharing with you the personal perspective I gained as I reached the end of my first and most educational entrepreneurial journey.

Establishing Your Organization's Worth

When you begin negotiating the deal for the sale of your business, valuation takes center stage. Deriving your company's value is a two-part process, involving both a financial analysis and an intrinsic value analysis. The buyer is going to review the financial performance and condition of your company to establish a benchmark accounting evaluation of worth. The far less quantitative intrinsic value analysis comes next, with the purpose of assigning a value to assets such as brand name, patents, rights, agreements, contracts, talent, and so forth. The buyer will consider both factors and then make an offer, applying a multiple to either the calculated revenue or profitability if the buyer chooses to buy at a premium predicting higher future earnings (based on your historical financials). The buyer is inclined to make a below-market offer if such financials dictate. You probably won't be calculating these values or applying any of these methods yourself, but your sales advisors (attorney, negotiator, accountant, and so on) will; the more you know about these methods, the better able you'll be to translate and use their results in the negotiations for your company's sale. Let's dig deeper into each of these analyses.

The Financial Analysis

Understanding the value of a business, particularly a privately held business, is not as simple as you might assume; in fact, many business owners find the whole process to be a mystery. The truth is, however, that the financial evaluation is a very black-and-white process that can involve applying one or more accounting methods or tools to establish a company's value. Here, we'll explore the more common of these, including comparable worth, EBITDA, asset valuation, financial performance measures, and multipliers.

The Comparable Worth Method

The comparable worth method is a rather simplistic (often pre-acquisition) means for finding businesses comparable to your own and using their worth as a rough template for estimating your company's worth. You might use the sale price of a competitor with revenues similar to those of your organization, for example, as a comparison. This method has obvious weaknesses because it fails to take the firm's profitability into consideration. However, it can spur competitive offers or urgency when acquirers see buyer interest within a certain industry.

EBITDA (Earnings Before Interest, Taxes, Depreciation, and Amortization)

Your business will generate monthly or quarterly balance sheets, income, and cash flow statements, which you'll monitor in order to track business performance. But you also should be monitoring regular EBITDA statements for your business. EBITDA (earnings before interest, taxes, depreciation, and amortization) is ignored by many owners of privately held businesses; it's typically used as a valuation tool rather than an operational tool, and operations are the focus of the entrepreneur in the trenches. You should use EBITDA as a monthly operational tool or as a dashboard metric because it's one of your most reliable means for monitoring the profitability of your business. Your potential buyers most certainly will use EBITDA to establish the value of your business. Even if other valuation methods are introduced by you or the seller, EBITDA represents the clearest picture of overall value.

A FINANCIAL REPORT IS JUST THE BEGINNING

No savvy buyer will rely on a publicly held company's financial reports in evaluating that company's worth. The management of a publicly held company typically strives to show high earnings on the company's financial reports in order to attract people to buy its stock and, in the process, improve its price-to-earnings ratio. On the other hand, a company's management team may be working to minimize the earnings shown on the business's financial reports in order to minimize its tax burden. Financial reports really serve as a basis to ask questions about the business, its history, and its strategies to arrive at an appropriate financial valuation.

The Asset Valuation Method

The asset valuation method simply assigns a worth to the hard assets of your company. This method is used when a large portion of a firm's value is pegged to its fixed assets, but it's the least desirable method for establishing the value of the business. Think of a business that wanted to start producing steel; the founders would have a choice of building a new steel mill or buying one ready to go. When considering the value of an existing steel mill, these buyers couldn't just look at the current, depreciated value of the assets; they would have to consider the overall "cost of reproduction," which would involve constructing the same assets, only at current prices.

Buyers also must consider the true cost of replacement for assets they're considering for purchase. In addition to the costs of current prices, replacing existing assets would take a great deal of time, so buyers must calculate that delay into their valuations. These considerations are what led Significant Education, LLC, to acquire the assets of struggling Grand Canyon University in 2004, which, overnight, made Significant Education the owner of an entire college campus. The company took the college public in 2008 and established it as the sixth-largest online university in the country.

Financial Performance Measures

Financial performance measures review historical results of a business in order to predict its future performance. These are the most common and accepted methods for determining the value of a business because they help a buyer understand what the business will be worth after the closing. The most common financial performance methods include net present value (NPV), internal rate of return (IRR), discounted cash flow, and return on investment (ROI). You (and your buyer) should use all of these models when establishing an evaluation of your business. Your broker, your attorney, or other professionals assisting you in the negotiation and sales process can help you produce and apply these models.

Multipliers

Multipliers are figures used to calculate the projected future worth of a company based on its historical performance. A multiplier is a figure used to multiply accounting evaluations like EBITDA, revenue, or even earnings to generate the value one would pay today for the enterprise. The multiplier can be subjective, but it is often a balance between historical industry averages of comparable competitor sales and the net present value of money associated with the buyer's desired return on investment. A buyer might offer to purchase a software company at a price ten times the company's current EBITDA value; in that case, the buyer would use a multiplier of ten.

Since EBITDA does not take into account buyer benefits from the economies of scale, market conditions, intellectual property, internal motivation and goals of both buyer and seller, or other factors not explicit to the financial analysis, the multiplier must be great enough to increase the EBITDA adequately to account for that missing value. In your sale, your ability to negotiate will determine how large the multiplier is that will calculate the value of your business.

The Intrinsic Value Analysis

I typically refer to intrinsic-value items as intellectual property or IP. The IP of a company is what separates it from its competition, and it will be the factor that most influences the final valuation of the firm. IP can take various forms, including distribution methods, copyrights, business processes and methodology, technology, brand, and patents, in addition to the many other differentiators we've discussed in previous chapters. I've stressed the importance of focusing on innovation and developing your company's IP throughout this book, and nowhere will the value of that advice be more evident than when you come to the negotiating table. During your Startup and Running phases, your firm's IP was its strongest tool for attracting customers and differentiating your organization from its competition; in the Exit phase, that IP also pays dividends by boosting the ultimate valuation of your organization.

Several models for determining intrinsic value exist, but most apply to public equity. If you're selling a small- to medium-size private firm, you will need to use a multiplier to increase the strictly derived financial valuation of your IP in order to take into account its intrinsic value. This process becomes very subjective, which is to the benefit of the savvy seller. Of course, accountants and CFOs do not like subjectivity. In their calculations, they prefer that each number is supported by strict mathematical reasoning. That's why I created the Negotiations Worksheet. Although it does not remove all subjectivity, the worksheet can help you merge the financial and intrinsic valuations of your organization; it also establishes sound metrics to support some of the more subjective numbers involved in your analyses.

As the seller in negotiations, you really don't know what you leave on the table. But I'm confident that I may have walked away from millions when I sold TRC. That's just one of the reasons I created the Negotiations Worksheet. I offer it here as a tool for managing your own negotiation process. Before we get into the use of the worksheet, though, I'd like to share with you my costly negotiation mistake; this may seem like a hand-wringing confession, but I think it's a story that offers a valuable lesson about the pitfalls of the negotiating process.

The preliminary discussions about the sale of my company had gone well and were moving along quickly. CDW was anxious to seal the deal, and so was I. But when the offer from CDW's acquisition team was on my broker's desk, things broke down for TRC. Although I had explored the selling process on and off through the years, I was by no means an expert. I hired a broker to help me manage the sale, and I naively believed I could leave the details up to him.

Not only was I naïve; I was exhausted. As you'll learn when you sell your business, managing the Exit phase is a full-time job that you have to take on while you are still running your company. I had just resolved a lawsuit with my previous equity partner, and that process had been an emotional drain on me. (As I told you earlier in the book, I failed to use a legal agreement for these arrangements, and this was the painful outcome of that mistake.) Further, we had been on the market for a while before receiving the CDW offer, and I desperately wanted this deal to happen.

My broker told me repeatedly, "When the right offer comes around, you'll know it, and you'll want it bad." That's exactly what happened. CDW's offer was all cash, meaning there would be no financing delays, earn-out requirements, stock options, or other clauses. To make the deal seem even sweeter, CDW was located in our area, which would ease the transition process for my employees. The more I learned about the offer, the better it seemed. And that's when I made two fundamental mistakes that I'm sure cost me money.

First, I didn't closely manage my broker and others who were running my side of the transaction. You can't afford to let that happen in your dealings. Your sales advisors—your lawyer, accountant, and broker—view your exit from the business as a transaction on which they will be paid. Lawyers get paid as long as the deal is open; the broker gets paid when the deal is done. These people see many deals die at the negotiations table, and so are well versed in ways to keep that from happening. It will be easy for you, just like me, to get emotionally wrapped up in the entire sale process and then become completely reliant on your broker's experience to close the deal. You have to get your emotions under control so you can maintain a management role in the negotiations process. No one else will care as much as you do about the final outcome of your business.

CDW made the offer first in our negotiations, which was to TRC's advantage (you never want to be the first to extend an offer in the negotiation process; it establishes a benchmark for the other party). That's when I made my second, costly mistake: TRC did not counter. CDW's offer was a generous multiple of our projected EBITDA at closing, which was scheduled for June 2006. My broker said it was a good offer, and we should take it. In my gut, I knew we should counter, but I feared losing the deal, so I agreed. I allowed my "expert" broker to bypass this crucial step—one I'm sure our buyer was anticipating. We accepted the offer, scheduled a closing date, and started due diligence. There is no doubt in my mind that if we had countered with a higher price we would have fetched more for the company. I blew Negotiations 101—and I was using a broker!

Since making those costly errors, I've had the opportunity to study my experience and learn from professionals who train and conduct negotiations. That research helped me create the Negotiations Worksheet and the process for using it that I'm about to describe to you as a methodology to structure the selling process, hold emotions at bay, and strengthen the negotiating position. Let me show you how it works.

Using the Negotiations Worksheet, Step by Step

The Negotiations Worksheet, shown in figure 15.1, is a tool you, the seller, will use throughout the negotiation process to logically calculate your organization's financial and intrinsic valuation. Its purpose is to garner the highest valuation by documenting your organization's many individual intrinsic IP (intellectual property) items, assigning them their own multiplier, and using it to calculate their value. The more individual IP elements your organization can measure, the greater will be your chances of negotiating a higher overall value and identifying which of your company's features resonate most strongly with your buyer.

FINANCIAL ANALYSIS	Buyer	Buyer Multiplier	Buyer Total	Seller	Industry Multiplier	Seller Total
EBITDA						
Asset Valuation						
Net Present Value						
Discounted Cash Flow						
Comparable Worth						
INTRINSIC VALUE ANALYSIS	**Buyer**	**Multiplier Value**		**Seller**	**Multiplier Value**	
Brand & Trademarks						
Technology						
Proprietary Technology						
Intellectual Property						
Processes						
Geography						
Customers						
Certifications						
Human Capital						
Copyrights						
Additional Multiple Total				**Additional Multiple Total**		

Figure 15.1: The Negotiations Worksheet.

KNOW WHO YOU'RE DEALING WITH

To effectively negotiate you need to know who you are negotiating with, so make a point of learning the roles and titles of all those involved on the Buyer's side of the negotiations. Typically, the Buyer will delegate the financial assessment and review to a "numbers person"—the accountant, CFO, or other number-cruncher who is familiar with financial models. The Buyer will use that expert to assess your financials and formulate an initial offer. Determine the role the financial reviewer will play in setting and countering an offer, and how much influence the reviewer will wield in determining whether to move forward with the deal.

The person on the Buyer side reviewing the intrinsic value of your business often holds the greatest ownership of the acquisition and is likely the decision maker. The financial valuation will be fairly rigid and straightforward. The greatest leverage and basis for negotiation, therefore, will come from the intrinsic side and the decision maker assigned to its review. In other words, the decision maker will be most influenced by the financial evaluation, but most attracted to the intrinsic variables. This person holds the greatest influence in swaying the Buyer's overall opinion; your job as the Seller is to convince the decision maker of the intrinsic value of your business. The Negotiations Worksheet gives you some concrete data with which to do that.

1. Now, let's break down the use of this worksheet by following this step-by-step example, in which you are the Seller.

2. Prior to an offer, you, the Seller, will:

   a. Complete as many financial evaluation models as possible, list them in the Financial Analysis section of this worksheet with results posted under the "Seller" section to establish benchmarks, and determine which is the most and least favorable model to you as the Seller (see callout a, figure 15.2).

FINANCIAL ANALYSIS	Buyer	Buyer Multiplier	Buyer Total	Seller	Industry Multiplier	Seller Total
EBITDA						
Asset Valuation						
Net Present Value						
Discounted Cash Flow						
Comparable Worth						

Figure 15.2: The Financial Analysis section of the Negotiations Worksheet.

b. Research historic industry multipliers applied to the sale of similar companies in your industry. This information may be difficult to obtain; your accountant, lawyer, or broker should be able to find published industry benchmarks. Place the multiplier in the Industry Multiplier column, in the row next to the financial valuation method you have used (see callout b, figure 15.2). EBITDA (highlighted row) will likely be the Financial Analysis method your Buyer uses, and it is the default when the typical industry method is unknown.

c. Line-list all of the intellectual property items about your company in the Intrinsic Value Analysis portion of the worksheet (see callout c, figure 15.3). You will place an "X" or checkmark in the corresponding cell in the Seller column to designate that these intrinsic items were identified by you.

INTRINSIC VALUE ANALYSIS	Buyer	Multiplier Value		Seller	Multiplier Value	
Brand & Trademarks				X		
Technology				X		
Proprietary Technology				X		
Intellectual Property				X		
Processes				X		

Figure 15.3: The Intrinsic Analysis section of the Negotiations Worksheet.

2. When the Buyer makes an offer, you will:

a. Document that offer on the Buyer's portion of the worksheet;

b. Verify which financial analysis method the Buyer used to arrive at the offer and if the price reflects both financial and intrinsic valuations. Ask what multiplier, if any, the Buyer applied. You can use this information to dissect the offer to establish what premium the Buyer has placed on your company's intrinsic value. Any amount above the figure calculated using the stated financial model will represent the premium for intrinsic items and/or the multiple. It is critical to get the buyer to disclose if intrinsic items were recognized or not as this will influence your negotiations.

c. If the Buyer has included intrinsic value in determining a valuation for your company, you need to skillfully ask the Buyer to identify the items included in that valuation; then, make sure all of those items are listed in the Intrinsic Value Analysis section of the worksheet, and marked with an "X" or checkmark in the corresponding Buyer's column. At this point, the worksheet will begin to reveal some interesting information. In our scenario, illustrated in figure 15.4, the Buyer has calculated a $3.5 million EBITDA with a multiplier of 3, while the Seller's research has established a $4 million EBITDA and an industry multiplier of 4. Further, the Buyer identified seven items of relevant intrinsic value, whereas the Seller listed five. Even more relevantly, the Buyer identified five intrinsic items not included in the Seller's listing, meaning the Seller didn't recognize them as meaningful IP.

FINANCIAL ANALYSIS	Buyer	Buyer Multiplier	Buyer Total	Seller	Industry Multiplier	Seller Total
EBITDA	$3,500,000	3	$10,500,000	$4,000,000	4	$16,000,000
Asset Valuation						
Net Present Value						
Discounted Cash Flow						
Comparable Worth						
INTRINSIC VALUE ANALYSIS	Buyer	Multiplier Value		Seller	Multiplier Value	
Brand & Trademarks	X			X		
Technology	X			X		
Proprietary Technology				X		
Intellectual Property				X		
Processes				X		
Geography	X					
Customers	X					
Certifications	X					
Human Capital	X					
Copyrights	X					
	Additional Multiple Total			Additional Multiple Total		

Figure 15.4: The Negotiations Worksheet highlights discrepancies between Buyer and Seller valuations, based on multipliers and the itemization of intrinsic value.

3. As the Seller, you will now review the Buyer's offer and formulate a strategic response giving consideration to the following questions:

a. **Why does the Buyer's financial valuation not match yours, and why did the Buyer choose this valuation method?** Perhaps they were missing some data. In that case, you can provide that information to help them correct their calculation to your findings. If they've used a different method that produced a less favorable result, you will need to negotiate in order to convince them to use your favored method or to arrive at a compromise.

b. **Why does the Buyer's multiplier not match the historic industry multiplier?** Ask the Buyer to explain how they arrived at that multiplier, and be prepared to defend yours. Had their multiplier been higher than the one you'd selected, you should consider negotiating an even higher multiplier at this point. If at a minimum you wish to arrive at your multiple of 4, you may counter with 5, but this will be just one area of consideration to your counter offer.

c. **Why did the Buyer's list of IP items not match yours?** Discuss these discrepancies to fully understand why the Buyer values items you overlooked, and overlooked items that you listed. You can use that information to strengthen your position during negotiations.

d. **Why does the Buyer want your company?** You would be surprised at how often this question isn't addressed. The answer will help establish how much of a financial, versus strategic, acquisition this is for the Buyer. The more strategic the Buyer's interest, the greater the value of the intrinsic components of your organization will be. This is where you will gain knowledge of the importance of your specific IP and how to leverage it in negotiations. You may even ask the Buyer to rank the IP in order of importance (they may not agree to that request, but it's worth asking). Even if the Buyer states that his or her only interest is in revenue and profits, you have to remember that your organization's revenues and profits are derived from its intellectual property, and therefore, the value of those items must be considered in determining the overall value of your business.

e. **What pain will this acquisition eliminate for the Buyer?** The root of any acquisition is to eliminate or elevate a pain found within the Buyer's organization. The pain may be growth, profitability, geography, customer types, product diversification, talent, or IP acquisition.

f. **How will the Buyer finance the purchase?** Many acquisitions fall apart in the final hours because the buyer is unable to obtain the required financing. Thus, it is in the Seller's best interest to understand how the deal is being financed and how secure the financing is. In some cases, it may be better to take a lower all-cash offer to ensure the deal gets done.

g. **Is there anything else the Buyer would have liked to have seen about your company?** You may be surprised by their response and find that you have or can easily provide the value they seek through your own efforts.

4. Use the Buyer's answers to your questions to complete the worksheet, then use all of that information to formulate your first counter offer. The questions you've asked will enable you to gain some picture of the Buyer's interest in your company and valuation of your organization's IP. Complete the worksheet by adding separate multipliers to each line item of intrinsic value, adding a higher valuation to those items clearly identified by the Buyer as being significant and a lower value to those the Buyer shows less interest in.

5. Make a counter offer, using the Buyer's responses and other worksheet data as your justification. You have multiple negotiating options at this stage. You can:

   a. Negotiate the EBITDA calculation (see callout a, figure 15.5);

   b. Negotiate the financial analysis multiple (see callout b, figure 15.5);

   c. Negotiate on each intrinsic item listed, and request the Buyer to respond to each in their counter offer. As strategy, you could list a fractional multiplier, such as 1.07, with the intent of negotiating down to 1.5 or 1.0 (see callout c, figure 15.5).

FINANCIAL ANALYSIS	Buyer	Buyer Multiplier	Buyer Total	Seller	Industry Multiplier	Seller Total
EBITDA	$3,500,000	3	$10,500,000	$4,000,000	4	$16,000,000
Asset Valuation						
Net Present Value						
Discounted Cash Flow	**a**	**b**				
Comparable Worth						
INTRINSIC VALUE ANALYSIS	**Buyer**	**Multiplier Value**		**Seller**	**Multiplier Value**	
Brand & Trademarks	X			X	1.0	
Technology	X			X	0.50	
Proprietary Technology				X	0.01	
Intellectual Property				X	0.01	
Processes				X	0.05	
Geography	X		**c**		0.40	
Customers	X				0.30	
Certifications	X				1.04	
Human Capital	X				0.03	
Copyrights	X				0.04	
Additional Multiple Total				**Additional Multiple Total**	3.38	$29,500,000

Figure 15.5: Using fractional multipliers on the Negotiations Worksheet.

Getting the Most From the Worksheet

The intent of the worksheet is to formulate a logical and defensible response during negotiations. The worksheet also gives you a chance to broaden the field of negotiation by including multiple items over which you can negotiate, rather than limiting negotiations strictly to the financial analysis and a single, subjective, intrinsic value analysis. Having multiple negotiation items increases your opportunities for reaching a compromise, which will have the net effect of boosting the overall value. You can use the worksheet to direct your questions and, in the process, to get the Buyer to talk about why they want to make the acquisition, and what they value most about the company. With that information, you're better prepared to direct your negotiation strategy and tactics. The Buyer's responses on the worksheet create a dashboard to drive negotiations.

The more items in the Intrinsic Analysis section of the worksheet, the stronger your position. A buyer may reject a higher multiple on three line items but concede on the fourth. When multiples are used, incorporating fractions instead of whole numbers will aid the process. If the Buyer is firm on a 5 times multiple and won't go to 6, ask for 5.7 or 5.5. It may seem insignificant, but its effect can be dramatic.

Certainly all negotiations are unique, just as each company is unique. You'll have to use your best reasoning and negotiating skills to choose and apply multiples, and for arriving at a final price from your calculations. But the worksheet gives you a valuable tool in managing these negotiations, by giving you and your Buyer a tangible, itemized analysis of the value of your organization. By using the detailed analysis this worksheet provides, you'll be better able to maximize your shareholder value and the personal wealth generated from this sale.

Surviving Due Diligence

When you've negotiated the deal, the due diligence process is the last thing standing between you and your check, and it is by far the least favorable aspect of selling a business. The purpose of due diligence is to investigate all nooks and crannies of the company being acquired to uncover missing facts or information that may cause expense or legal exposure down the road for the acquiring firm. As I mentioned earlier, this is the moment when you will be thoroughly happy you followed my advice and began preparing for your sale from the very beginning of your entrepreneurial experience. Or you'll be deeply sorry that you did not. I wish I had been better prepared for what the law firm representing CDW threw at me.

When I talk about tasks an entrepreneur likes and dislikes, organizing paperwork is one that does not rank high for me. As owner, I was always signing off on various documents ranging from bids, reseller agreements, distribution agreements, and personal guarantees to creditors—all of which are legal documents. Over the years I could probably recite the legalese in these documents with my eyes closed. They all seemed to be the same boilerplate document. They were formality tasks standing in the way of a sale, a much-needed product, or a credit release to expand our purchasing. I took little care in overseeing whether these documents were filed properly—if at all. As fate would have it, the CDW law firm zeroed in on all of these items as standard practice.

Since we found little use for these records over the past 10 years, they were scattered throughout the building depending on what individual at the time was responsible for them. The serious aspect of due diligence is that the information it reveals can trigger changes to the terms of the deal, delay closing, or kill the deal altogether. We managed to provide all of the necessary documents for this area of focus, but what a mess and embarrassment to have such shoddy records! Unfortunately, the next stage of due diligence was even trickier.

A primary intrinsic selling point of TRC was our proprietary web development featuring the display, fulfillment, and administration of software licensing. I had hired a development firm to custom build an e-commerce tool that reflected my vision and chosen architecture. Over the years, we refined and perfected the software's functionality, based on our customers' feedback. TRC was the only dealer in the country with such a powerful tool for deliverables. This tool was the intellectual property that CDW wanted to acquire and scale across all segments of the company. The company knew that acquiring our system would be faster and cheaper than trying to build one on its own.

During due diligence, we had to validate that TRC owned the development and more specifically the code for the system. Up popped an unanticipated potential deal killer: TRC didn't own the code! I had confirmed with the developer, prior to this stage, that TRC did own the website and its functionality, but I hadn't even considered whether or not TRC owned the underlying code. I was about to discover that our developer, as was common in the industry, always maintained ownership of the code it developed. If it turned over code ownership to each client, it would be limiting its ability to scale its own development efforts for new clients. For instance, the shopping car the developer creates for one client may look entirely different from the one it creates for another client, but the shopping carts' underlying code may be very similar, if not identical. Giving clients ownership of underlying code would leave the developer constantly having to reinvent the wheel (or the cart, so to speak). Obviously, this would severely impact the developer's ability to efficiently scale its own business.

CDW wanted our developer to sign an agreement stating that TRC owned the code and the developer would not replicate that code for any other client. The developer wouldn't sign. My lawyers stepped in to work with the developer's lawyers, and the situation grew even worse. In fact, the relationship between TRC and our developer was deteriorating, through the clash of lawyer egos. My developer was no longer returning my calls, and I was very concerned that without this piece, CDW would walk. And, at this point, I still hadn't had any explanation as to why TRC did not own the code, and why it was such a big deal to the developer.

Fed up with everyone who had their hands in this mess, I removed my lawyer from the case and personally went to my developer's office to get to the root of the problem, face to face. Bringing in our lawyers had just driven a wedge into the issue. I had developed a relationship with our developer over several years, and I used that long-standing relationship to bridge the gap. After I received a clear explanation of the developer's concerns—and fully understood them—I explained to the developer how this impasse was detrimental to the success of the acquisition and asked how we could reach a mutual agreement between all parties. Logic prevailed, and the CDW lawyers drafted an intellectual property agreement that was acceptable to both the developer and CDW. We were back on track!

This story underscores a point I mentioned earlier. You, as the entrepreneur and founder of your business, must remain vigilant and engaged throughout the entire selling process. Our lawyer fees were starting to go through the roof on a developer agreement that should have been concluded after a series of emails. The more each side was pushed, the more entrenched each became in its position. Even though you have professionals handling the sale, you can't turn over the wheel of the ship to them. They're on board to help guide you through the difficult waters of the sale, but it's your responsibility to bring the ship into port. If you let the pros take control of the sale, you'll have a very difficult time taking back control if the deal goes off-course.

Announcing the Sale

When the due diligence process begins, you may consider telling your employees that you are negotiating the sale of your business. New faces from the buyer's office will likely be coming on site, and there will be a lot of unusual activity that may raise suspicion. You will need the help of your staff during this process, and the size of your firm will dictate the scope of your disclosure.

Be aware that once you disclose information about the sale to *anyone* on your staff, no matter how trusted, it's only a matter of time before *everyone* in the company, as well as your clients, customers, and competitors, will hear the news. You don't want the news circulating too early in the process because when your customers and vendors catch wind of it, they may have real concerns regarding the future owner. Certainly, employees will want to know if they will still have a job after a sale and who exactly is buying their company. When your competitors hear that you're selling the business, they'll know that you are either preparing to strengthen your market position or suffering from huge vulnerabilities. This is a daunting time for your position in the market.

When the information can no longer be contained, you can best maintain calm among the troops by making a well-thought-out announcement that clearly addresses as many concerns as possible and encourages your team to stay focused on its work. You may consider various extra incentives to reach goals that correspond to the closing date. Meet one-on-one if possible to hear concerns. Don't seed concerns by guessing what employees may be concerned about. Chances are you'll be very surprised at who is on board, who's on the fence, and who's checked out—and why.

Everyone at TRC was aware that the day would come when we would sell, and, according to my personal pledge, it would be for all the right reasons. Even with this preparation, I was not ready for the variety of responses from my workforce when word surfaced. The group who I thought would least support a buyout, the administrative operations group, became the most supportive. The sales team, the group I thought would be most energized, became the most disruptive and disgruntled. The acquisition was a tremendous career and earnings growth opportunity for everyone, but not all perceived it as such.

Members of the sales team felt threatened by the change and feared losing accounts they had managed for years. Our counterparts at CDW failed to fully disclose to our staff what their future would look like at CDW. Our team received only cryptic information about base pay, commission, and territory, and the lack of clear and immediate answers was not enough to entice some of them to stay on board. I lost my top three sales representatives, and productivity ground to a halt as rumors, fears, and misinformation filled the grapevine. To do it over again, I would have insisted on providing a clearer picture for my sales team and possibly allowed them to be part of the process. This can't be done with a large organization, but at 30 employees, we likely could have incorporated their feedback for the benefit of all involved.

Finally, however, we emerged from the due diligence process successfully. We closed the deal with CDW in June 2006, and by the end of the year, we had closed the TRC offices and moved to CDW's space. I agreed to stay on a minimum of two years after the closing to assist with the transition and knowledge transfer. It had been a long and emotional journey to get to this point, and now it was time for me and my family to celebrate.

Sailing On

Let's flash forward to January 2009, two and a half years after the sale of my company to CDW, when I was laid off from my management role at the company. When I looked back on the many accomplishments we enjoyed at TRC, I felt a tremendous sense of pride and appreciation. Sadly, I hadn't had the same sense of achievement over the past few years. Bureaucracy seemed to stifle the I.D.E.A. at CDW. The energy, enthusiasm, and passion I had when I first entered this building had slowly and systematically been replaced with conformity, procedure, and politics. This transformation frustrated me. I knew that my skills and talent were being sidelined, and that I could have done more to impact the company, even though it was my employer, rather than my entrepreneurial enterprise.

In reality, I was a square peg in a round hole at CDW, and my new position and reporting structure didn't utilize my talents. The initial appeal of being the Business Development Manager at CDW waned. There was little vision for the position. I made some decent accomplishments during my term, but it was always a struggle. Instead of being supported by the full resources and capabilities of the company, I found I had to swim upstream, with my comanagers and operational "support departments" acting more like competitors than facilitators.

Why had I stayed on longer than my original agreement? Blame it on the Risk Box. Although I was increasingly unsatisfied with my work, I felt anchored to the material security of the job, with its high salary and luxurious benefits. I had allowed my entrepreneurial soul to wither. Now, I was probably the only happy one out of the 190 people caught up in this layoff. As I pulled out of the parking lot for the last time, I felt a new sense of freedom. The entrepreneur within me that had been dormant for so long began to show life, and I felt purpose flowing back into me. The mirage that the Risk Box was projecting started to dissolve, and I was excited.

I also felt that, overall, I had chosen the right directions in my entrepreneurial journey. If I had waited just a period of months to take TRC to market, I would have missed the opportunity with CDW. And, just two years after the sale, the economic disaster of 2008 had brought merger and acquisition activity to a grinding halt. TRC would have been forced to face this economic storm by cash flow alone—and I'm not sure we would have made it through. People ask if I regret selling TRC, my first entrepreneurial dream. Not at all, I tell them—it was all in the plan.

I spent a good part of my time after leaving CDW to research and write this book. And it was during that process that I came to understand that entrepreneurism is a journey. Before you close this book and move on with your own life, I'd like for you to take one last moment to think about that journey with me, this time, as a voyage in which your entrepreneurial business is a ship. The market demand for your product or service is the wind that pushes the company forward, and your company's infrastructure, culture, and policies form the sail. You can't control the wind of market forces, but you can adjust your sail—your website, employee training, staffing, location, and so on—to gain the most momentum from it.

On this voyage, your business plan is your navigational map; it directs your progress, from lead generation all the way through product fulfillment. Your strategy is the ship's rudder, which keeps you pointing always in the right direction, and your management approach is the keel that keeps the ship from capsizing. You, the captain, make decisions, set a course, and establish your temporary anchor points and final destinations. You can never take your hands off the wheel or your eyes off the horizon as you command your vessel. Your well-chosen and highly trained crew takes care of the tasks that keep the ship moving, but it's your responsibility to keep it on course and sailing forward.

Pulling into the harbor at the conclusion of its voyage is the most dangerous time for any ship. You have to pay attention to every detail and scrutinize each decision you make during this delicate process. Positioning the ship properly will require all of your skills and abilities. But no captain and few ships stop after a single voyage. After you have successfully brought your first entrepreneurial experience to a close, you can expect to set sail again. You may be piloting a new ship, and your old ship may have a new captain at its helm. That doesn't matter; the old journey is over. It's time to get on with the next one.

Yes, I know that was a rather lengthy analogy, but I've put it here for a purpose. I want you to see the work that you do as an entrepreneur as a great and meaningful passage, from the moment you begin formulating your entrepreneurial idea and testing it in your E-Formula, through the hard work of launching your startup, running a successful business, and then negotiating the final sale or transfer of the company. You are in charge of transforming your idea into a reality—and, in the process, creating a thriving, successful generator of products, services, employment, and economic vitality. And yes, the journey will be scary at times; you'll hit snags, lose momentum, veer off-course, and have to get your bearings and find your way back. But, for an entrepreneur, the journey is everything. Missed opportunities, minor catastrophes, and full-blown disasters are just part of the experience, as will be the fascinating colleagues, achievements, successes, and discoveries you'll gather along the way.

I hope that this book has helped you realize that whatever fears you must face on the road—or the rough seas—ahead, they're not nearly as threatening to your entrepreneurial spirit as the thick, padded walls of your Risk

Box. In my experience, an entrepreneur's regrets after a business failure are much less bitter than the regret of never having tried to satisfy entrepreneurial desires.

I hope this book will help give you the advice and guidance you need to take that first step toward activating the entrepreneur within you. And I hope that it will offer you the same kind of ongoing encouragement and inspiration that I received from that tattered calendar page and its constant reminder that "If you do what you've always done, you'll get what you've always gotten." I'll leave you here with my own bit of simple wisdom:

Dreams come true by doing, not by wishing.

Enjoy your journey.

Epilogue

I WROTE THIS BOOK TO offer a clear and logical guide, a road map that anyone could use to move successfully through the entrepreneurial process. As I was wrapping up this edition, I found new meaning in its message. My life experiences had opened up a whole new world to me, and my own words were challenging me to, once again, travel a new pathway. Here's the story.

When TRC's sale was completed, I wanted to celebrate with my entire family, because all of them had contributed to the success of my first entrepreneurial journey. We decided to take an all-family vacation—my wife and kids, my parents, my wife's parents, my brother, the whole lot of us. I was really looking forward to showing all of them my appreciation. Then, as so often happens, change came calling; just months after closing the sale of TRC, my mother was diagnosed with a Stage IV melanoma. A few months later, my dad was diagnosed with esophageal cancer. My mom survived; my dad didn't.

As a result of these events, in the months following my departure from CDW, I was actively engaged in helping my parents deal with ongoing and ever-changing medical treatment plans, hospice, and the other healthcare necessities. In addition, I was also working on this book, since I was committed to publishing the insights I'd gained about entrepreneurism through my research and personal experiences. By the summer of 2009, I was wrapping up my first edition of the manuscript and making plans for speaking engagements, book signings, and seminars to support the book's sales. Once more, change uprooted my plans. This time, the news couldn't have been more unexpected or earthshaking: my 16-year-old daughter, Kaitlyn, was diagnosed with Ewing sarcoma.

The months ahead were given over to Kaitlyn's extremely difficult treatment regimen and eventual surgery to remove her tumor. Just as Kaitlyn was recovering, we were hit with yet another unexpected blow: my brother, my only sibling, had a brain tumor. My daughter's prognosis looks good; we're all incredibly thankful for her survival. My brother's condition, on the other hand, has no cure.

If you're thinking that this series of events seems almost surrealistic, I can only say that I agree with you. As I ricocheted from one family medical trauma to the next, this book was something of an anchor for me. I forced myself to focus on its final revisions and preparation for publication during some part of my days so that I wouldn't become overwhelmed with the ongoing struggles all of us in my family faced in managing so many medical plans and issues. And then, one day, as I was making some final notes and revisions to the text, I found myself staring at the E-Formula:

I.D.E.A. + Situation + Opportunity = Activation

I began thinking about those times when ideas and opportunities align, but situations are simply too daunting to allow the entrepreneur to move forward, as had been the case for me over the past four years. The entrepreneurial limbo I'd entered as a result of my family's health-related issues had caused me to question my abilities. Had I peaked? What could I contribute? Would I ever create again? It was almost like I'd never accomplished anything. I found myself thinking the way I had back when I was a teenager. I'd read about some fast-rising entrepreneur, and wonder: How did that guy start that company? What great idea could I pursue? Could I be an entrepreneur—again?

And then it hit me! Five years earlier, I had begun working on an idea for a cloud-based personal healthcare record (PHR) platform, which I touched on in chapter 2. Available technologies and the marketplace weren't ready at that time, however, and so I hadn't pursued my idea with much energy. Before I could adequately develop the idea, some big-name (and big-money) competitors announced their own beta-versions of applications similar to the system I'd been designing. I assumed that my heel-dragging had ended that entrepreneurial journey before it had even begun. But, the past few years hadn't been kind to those first-to-market competitors, and their products weren't widely adopted. As it turns out, I was right—neither the technology nor its essential infrastructure had been adequate at the time these PHR products were released, making them ineffective and unadoptable.

Now, however, a combination of government funding and mandates for more efficient healthcare management systems was resulting in costly infrastructure investments across the United States. That infrastructure would make the next generation of PHRs portable, and very much in demand. The concept I once tried vainly to explain to puzzled and largely disinterested people was now a frequent topic in national publications and broadcast news.

At that moment, I realized, my E-Formula was absolutely solid. The opportunity for my idea was now. My personal and professional situation and environmental factors were all positive. Financially, I was in a very comfortable position to fund a new startup. I had a clear vision for the business model I would use, and I even had outlined an incredibly successful exit plan. Everything in my E-Formula was telling me to go for it. But then I bumped into the walls of my Risk Box.

I was comfortable. Why not just find a corporate job to fill my days? I could secure a guaranteed salary, probably a pretty decent one, and company-sponsored healthcare. Or maybe I should do nothing at all—why not? Hadn't I earned a rest? As I sat there, considering the prospect of starting a new company, I could feel the clamor of negativity building around me: the effort, the cost, the risk—how could any outcome be worth that? And then, a single thought stopped the noise: this is what I am intended to do; I'm an entrepreneur, and my purpose is to create an idea, pursue my passion, and build an extraordinary company. I had seen too many examples of the sweetness and unpredictability of life to let my dreams wither and come to nothing. Now, I have a new opportunity to do something great with my life; this is no time for uncertainty and fear. I could be scared, but I wouldn't be petrified.

I had to consider another, very troubling, question: was I a hypocrite? I had just written a book exalting the entrepreneurial spirit, complete with a formula—which I had designed—for determining one's readiness for the entrepreneurial experience. My book was a gospel of entrepreneurism, extolling readers to understand how precious time and life is and how we shouldn't waste it on less meaningful endeavors. I had laid out a program for breaking free of the Risk Box and following a well-planned vision toward an extraordinary life, but I had been focusing more intently on publishing my advice than on following it. And, so, I turned to my own book for answers. And they were all there.

Today, I'm beginning a completely new journey, as I prepare to bring my idea for the PHR company to life. I've gone back to my own inner Grove, venturing down pathways that I've never traveled before, excited about the possibilities ahead of me. In order to find my way to the destination I'm seeking, I'll have to innovate, change, utilize all of my abilities, and fuel my efforts with passion and desire when I have no energy left to give. I'm not worried, though. In fact, I'm confident that I'll succeed. But above all else, I'm thankful. I once again have an incredible opportunity, and I'm on my way to discovering it. I have the map in front of me right now—and so do you.

Notes

Introduction

Phase I. The Idea

1. Kennicott, Robert (1835–1865?)—Henry M. Bannister (1844–1920) Papers, 1857–1905, Series 11/2/2, Boxes 1–2, Northwestern University Archives, Evanston, Illinois, accessed July 12, 2011, http://files.library.northwestern.edu/findingaids/kennicott_bannister.pdf.

Chapter 1. Being an Entrepreneur

1. Ewing Marion Kauffman Foundation, "Arts Entrepreneurship: How to Be a Hero," accessed June 30, 2011, http://www.kauffman.org/entrepreneurshp/arts-entrepreneurship.aspx.

2. Joseph A. Schumpeter, *Capitalism, Socialism and Democracy* (New York: Harper, 1975).

3. Frank H. Knight, *Risk, Uncertainty and Profit* (Boston: Houghton Mifflin, 1921).

4. William J. Baumol, *The Microtheory of Innovative Entrepreneurship* (Princeton, NJ: Princeton University Press, 2010).

5. Patricia B. Gray, "Do You Need School to Succeed? Classes for Would-Be Entrepreneurs Are a Hot Trend at America's Universities. But Can Risk Taking and Originality Be Learned?," *FORTUNE Small Business*, March 1, 2006.

6. Virgin, "About Virgin," accessed June 6, 2011, http://www.virgin.com/about-us.

7. Johnathan R. T. Hughes, "Arthur Cole and Entrepreneurial History" (paper presented at the annual meeting for the Business History Conference, Evanston, Illinois, March 10–12, 1983).

Chapter 2. Activating as an Entrepreneur

1. Arthur Cole, "An Approach to the Study of Entrepreneurship," in *Enterprises and Secular Change: Readings in Economic History,* ed. Frederic C. Lane and Jelle C. Riesmersman (Homewood, IL: Irwin, 1953).

Chapter 3. Mastering the Risk Box

1. Andrew W. Lo, Dmitry V. Repin, and Brett N. Steenbarger, "Fear and Greed in Financial Markets: A Clinical Study of Day-Traders," *American Economic Review: Papers and Proceedings* 95, no. 2 (2005).

2.   Eleanor Roosevelt, *You Learn by Living* (New York: Harper, 1960), 29–30.

3.   Robert W. Fairlie, *Kauffman Index of Entrepreneurial Activity: National Report 1996–2005* (Kansas City, MO: Kauffman Foundation, 2006).

4.   "An Exclusive Hour with Warren Buffett and Bill and Melinda Gates," interview by Charlie Rose, *Charlie Rose,* June 26, 2006.

5.   Jonathan Stempel, "Buffet, World's 3rd-Richest Person, Gets Pay Rise," *Reuters,* March 11, 2010, accessed June 30, 2011, http://www.reuters.com/article /2010/03/11/us-berkshire-buffett-compensation-idUSTRE62A5SH20100311.

6.   Fairlie, *Kauffman Index.*

7.   T. Boone Pickens, *The First Billion Is The Hardest—How Believing It's Still Early in the Game Can Lead to Life's Greatest Comebacks* (New York: Crown, 2008).

8.   Daniel H. Pink, *A Whole New Mind: Why Right-Brainers Will Rule the Future* (New York: The Berkley Publishing Group, 2006).

Chapter 4. Entrepreneurial Exercises

Phase II. Startup

Chapter 5. Positioning Your Startup

1.   James C. Collins, *Good to Great: Why Some Companies Make the Leap . . . and Others Don't* (New York: HarperBusiness, 2001); Fairlie, *Kauffman Index*; Jeff Grabmeier, "Restaurant Failure Rate Much Lower Than Commonly Assumed, Study Finds," *Ohio State University Research News,* September 8, 2003, accessed June 30, 2011, http://researchnews.osu.edu /archive/restfail.htm; Timothy Bates and Alfred Nucci, "An Analysis of Small Business Size and Rate of Discontinuance" (working papers 90–2, Center for Economic Studies, U.S. Census Bureau, *CES* 90–2, January 1990); U.S. Census Bureau, *The Business Dynamic Statistics,* Small Business Statistics and Failure Rates, 2009.

2.   Jane J. Kim, "Dealing With Debt That Refuses to Die," *Wall Street Journal,* September 30, 2008, accessed on June 30, 2011, http://online.wsj.com /article/SB122273650932088677.html.

3.   Abrams, Rhonda. "Focus on Success, Not Failure." *USA TODAY,* May 6, 2004. Accessed August 10, 2011. http://www.usatoday.com/money /smallbusiness/columnist/abrams/2004-05-06-success_x.htm.

4.   Mohammad Al-Zubeidi, "Higher Education and Entrepreneurship: The Relation Between College Educational Background and All Business Success in Texas" (PhD diss., University of North Texas, 2005).

5.   Jerry R. Mitchell, *Bootstrapping,* 7 (2009).

6.   Michael E. Gerber, *Awakening the Entrepreneur Within: How Ordinary People Can Create Extraordinary Companies* (New York: HarperCollins, 2008).

7.   Fulton Oursler, *The Greatest Book Ever Written: The Old Testament Story* (Garden City, NY: Doubleday, 1951).

Chapter 6. Planning for Success

Chapter 7. Mastering Money

1. Dow Jones VentureSource Report, "Venture Investors Put $26.2 Billion Into U.S. Companies in 2010, Up 11% From 2009," news release, January 24, 2010, http://www.dowjones.com/pressroom/releases/2010/01242011-10USVC-0105 .asp.

Chapter 8. Bringing on Partners and Employees

Phase III. Running

Chapter 9. Leading Your Business

1. Victor H. Vroom and Arthur G. Jago, "The Role of the Situation in Leadership," *American Psychologist* 62, no. 1 (2007): 17–24.

Chapter 10. Selling, Selling, Selling

Chapter 11. Building a Culture of Innovation

1. Tom Kelley, *The Ten Faces of Innovation: IDEO's Strategies for Beating the Devil's Advocate & Driving Creativity Throughout Your Organization* (New York: Currency/Doubleday, 2005).

2. Kenneth H. Blanchard, Don Hutson, and Ethan Willis, *The One Minute Entrepreneur: The Secret to Creating and Sustaining a Successful Business* (New York: Random House, Inc., 2008).

3. Judith Cone, "Entrepreneurship on Campus: Why the Real Mission Is Culture Change," *Kauffman Thoughtbook 2007* (Kansas City, MO: Kauffman Foundation, 2007), 78.

Chapter 12. Scaling for Growth

Phase IV. Exit

Chapter 13. Knowing When It's Time to Go: An Entrepreneur's Top 10

1. Bob Contaldo, "How Do I Know When It's Time to Sell My Company?" *Peoria Magazines.com*, July 2008, accessed June 30, 2011, http://www .peoriamagazines.com/ibi/2008/jul/how-do-i-know-when-it%E2%80%99s -time-sell-my-company.

2. Robert Berner, "Steve & Barry's Rules The Mall," *Businessweek*, April 10, 2006; Sakthi Prasad, "Steve & Barry's Faces Closure," *Wall Street Journal*, November 18, 2008.

3. Eric Wilson, "Is This the World's Cheapest Dress?," *New York Times*, May 1, 2008.

Chapter 14. Putting Your Business on the Market

Chapter 15. Negotiating and Closing the Deal

Epilogue

Selected Bibliography

Boswell, Grant, and Gary Hatch, eds. *Dialogues and Conversations*, 2nd ed. Needham Heights, MA: Simon & Schuster, 1996.

Chemers, Martin M. "Integrating Models of Leadership and Intelligence: Efficacy and Effectiveness." In *Multiple Intelligences and Leadership*, edited by Ronald E. Riggio, Susan Elaine Murphy, and Francis J. Pirozzolo, 139–160. Mahwah, NJ: Lawrence Erlbaum Associates, 2002.

Cullum, Paul. "Thomas Kinkade's 16 Guidelines for Making Stuff Suck." *Vanity Fair*, November 14, 2008. Accessed June 30, 2011. http://www.vanityfair .com/online/daily/2008/11/thomas-kincades-16-guidelines-for-making-stuff-suck.html.

Gartner, William B. "Some Suggestions for Research on Entrepreneurial Traits and Characteristics." *Entrepreneurship Theory and Practice* 14, no. 1 (1989): 27–38.

Gartner, William B. "'Who Is an Entrepreneur?' Is the Wrong Question." *American Journal of Small Business* 12 (1988): 11–32.

Gerber, Michael E. *The E-Myth Revisited: Why Most Small Businesses Don't Work and What to Do About It*. New York: HarperCollins, 2004.

Grant, A. "Entrepreneurship—The Major Academic Discipline for Business Education Curriculum for the 21st Century." In *Educating Entrepreneurs for Wealth Creation*, edited by M. G. Scott, P. Rosa, and H. Klandt, 28–37. Aldershot, UK: Ashgate, 1998.

Gray, Loren. "Understanding the Process of Innovation." *Working Knowledge*, August 5, 2002.

Hofstrand, Don. "What Is an Entrepreneur?" Iowa State University. Accessed June 30, 2011. http://www.extension.iastate.edu/agdm/wholefarm/html/c5-07.html.

Kelly, Kate. "His Job at Bear Gone, Mr. Fox Chose Suicide." *Wall Street Journal*, November 6, 2008.

Kelly, Kate. "Lost Opportunities Haunt Final Days of Bear Stearns," *Wall Street Journal*, May 27, 2008.

Kinkade, Thomas. "Thomas Kinkade: A Success: Morley Safer Interviews Artist Who's Also Master Marketer." By Morley Safer. *CBS News*, July 4, 2004.

Kroll, Luisa, ed. "The Forbes 400." *Forbes,* September 18, 2008.

Mander, Jerry. *Four Arguments for the Elimination of Television.* New York: Quill, 1978.

Mann, Catherine L. "The Globalization of Innovation and Entrepreneurship." *Kauffman Thoughtbook 2007.* Kansas City, MO: Kauffman Foundation, 2007, 195.

Mifflin, Lawrie. "Fattening up the Menu for Children's TV." *New York Times,* November 3, 1996.

New York Times Editorial Desk. "Military Censorship Lives." *New York Times,* September 21, 1994.

Public Broadcasting System. "John Gardner: Uncommon American." Accessed June 30, 2011. http://www.pbs.org/johngardner.

Rogers, Adam. "Television," *Newsweek Extra,* Winter 1997–1998.

United Nations Development Program. "Fighting Climate Change: Human Solidarity in a Divided World." *2007 Human Development Report (HDR 2007–2008),* November 27, 2007: 25.

Wadhwa, Vivek, Raj Aggarwal, Krisztina "Z" Holly, Alex Salkever, and Marion Ewing. *The Anatomy of an Entrepreneur: Family Background and Motivation.* Kansas City, MO: Kauffman Foundation, 2008.

Index

About the Author

In 1995, Jeffrey Weber founded a high-growth business focused on enterprise software licensing. His startup earned a ranking on *Inc.* magazine's list of the 500 Fastest-Growing Private Companies in the United States for two years in a row. In 2006, Jeff successfully positioned his company for sale to a Fortune 100 corporation. That experience became the impetus for *From Idea to Exit: The Entrepreneurial Journey*, which explains the entrepreneurial journey through four phases: Idea, Startup, Running, and Exit.

Today, Jeff shares his experience and strategies with many different groups—from business owners and startups to college students and new professionals. He has been an adjunct professor in entrepreneurism, serves on an advisory board at Judson University to establish an entrepreneurial program, counsels high-growth startups through the Illinois Small Business Development Center at Harper College, and volunteers for the Network for Teaching Entrepreneurship as well as for Future Founders, a program out of the Chicagoland Entrepreneurial Center. He offers strategies and advice for individuals who find themselves along the progression outlined in *From Idea to Exit*.

Books from Allworth Press

Allworth Press is an imprint of Skyhorse Publishing, Inc. Selected titles are listed below.

The Art of Digital Branding, Revised Edition
by Ian Cocoran (6 x 9, 272 pages, paperback, $19.95)

Brand Thinking and Other Noble Pursuits
by Debbie Millman (6 x 9, 320 pages, paperback, $19.95)

Career Solutions for Creative People
by Dr. Ronda Ormont (6 x 9, 320 pages, paperback, $27.50)

Corporate Creativity: Developing an Innovative Organization
by Thomas Lockwood and Thomas Walton (6 x 9, 256 pages, paperback, $24.95)

Effective Leadership for Nonprofit Organizations
by Thomas Wolf (6 x 9, 192 pages, paperback, $16.95)

Emotional Branding, Revised Edition
by Marc Gobe (6 x 9, 344 pages, paperback, $19.95)

Infectious: How to Connect Deeply and Unleash the Energetic Leader Within
by Achim Nowak (6 x 9, 256 pages, paperback, $19.95)

Intentional Leadership: 12 Lenses for Focusing Strengths, Managing Weaknesses, and Achieving Your Purpose
by Jane A. G. Kise (7 x 10, 200 pages, paperback, $19.95)

Millennial Rules: How to Sell, Serve, Surprise & Stand Out in a Digital World
by T. Scott Gross (6 x 9, 208 pages, paperback, $16.95)

Peak Business Performance Under Pressure
by Bill Driscoll (6 x 9, 224 pages, paperback, $19.95)

The Pocket Small Business Owner's Guide to Building Your Business
by Kevin Devine (5 ¼ x 8 ¼, 256 pages, paperback, $14.95)

The Pocket Small Business Owner's Guide to Business Plans
by Brian Hill and Dee Power (5 ½ x 8 ¼, 224 pages, paperback, $14.95)

The Pocket Small Business Owner's Guide to Negotiating
by Kevin Devine (5 ½ x 8 ¼, 224 pages, paperback, $14.95)

Rebuilding the Brand: How Harley-Davidson Became King of the Road
by Clyde Fessler (6 x 9, 128 pages, paperback, $14.95)

To see our complete catalog or to order online, please visit *www.allworth.com*.